# THE EUROPEAN CHALLENGE
## Europe's New Role in Latin America

M Coll

First published in Great Britain in 1982 by

**Latin America Bureau** (Research and Action) Ltd
1 Amwell Street
London EC1R 1UL

Copyright © Latin America Bureau (Research and Action) Ltd,
1982
ISBN 0 906156 14 9

Edited by Jenny Pearce
Design by Jan Brown Designs
Cover illustration by John Minnion
Typeset, printed and bound by Russell Press Ltd, Nottingham

# CONTENTS

# CONTRIBUTORS

**Simon Barrow** is a journalist with a London-based technical publisher also researching the international arms trade.

**Tilman Evers** formerly taught at the Latin America Institute of the Free University of Berlin and is presently researching the role of social democracy in Latin America.

**Wolf Grabendorff** is the head of the Latin America Section at the Stiftung Wissenschaft und Politik in Ebenhausen, West Germany.

**Rhys Jenkins** is a lecturer in Development Studies at the University of East Anglia, Norwich.

**Blanca Muniz** is a Research Student at the University of Essex.

**Philip O'Brien** is a lecturer in the Institute of Latin American Studies at the University of Glasgow.

**Alberto Orlandi** is on the Staff of the Division of International Trade and Development of the United Nations Economic Commission for Latin America (ECLA) in Santiago de Chile.

**Jacqueline Roddick** is an honorary research fellow in the Institute of Latin American Studies, University of Glasgow.

**Tino Thun** has studied law and politics and is preparing a doctoral thesis on the issue of human rights in West German foreign policy, for the Free University of Berlin. Between 1976 and 1978 he worked on the national board of the West German section of Amnesty International.

**Miguel S. Wionczek** is a Senior Research Fellow at the Colegio de Mexico, Mexico City.

# ꟼNTRODUCTION

For some years, the Latin America Bureau has been monitoring Europe's relations with Latin America. This has led to a series of publications: *Britain and Latin America: An Annual Review of British-Latin American Relations,* 1978 and 1979, and *Europe and Latin America,* 1980. Following on from this work, LAB embarked on a more systematic project to examine critically Europe's growing political and economic role in Latin America. This collection of essays is one outcome of that project.

LAB's objective in publishing this book is to stimulate a debate on the nature of European involvement in Latin America and to examine whether Europe is likely to play a more 'progressive' role in the region than that played by the United States. The book is aimed not at the decision makers of the regions, but primarily at those organizations and individuals in Europe which are concerned with poverty and underdevelopment and the struggle for social justice in Latin America.

The decision to focus on Europe's role in Latin America is a response to Europe's increasing activities in the region in the 1970s. Politically this has taken on considerable significance as a number of West European governments and the European social democrat movement have come to distance themselves from the policies of the traditional hegemonic power in the region, the United States. In the context of the present Central American crisis, this has given a powerful impetus to those fighting for national liberation and social change. The breach in the traditional alliance between Western Europe and the United States has made it more difficult for the US to intervene directly against them. Examples of the concrete support given by Western Europe to the struggle in Latin America include the recognition of the FMLN guerilla movement in El Salvador as a 'representative political force' by the French (and Mexican governments) and the decision by the French government, in January 1982, to provide Nicaragua with military equipment and training. West European aid and loans have also been important to Nicaragua in the face of continued US hostility.

Economically, Europe's role in Latin America is by no means a new phenomenon. Until 1914, Britain controlled almost half of total direct private investment in Latin America, followed by the United States, France and Germany. The United States emerged as the main investor and major trading partner in the region between the end of the First and Second World Wars. European direct private investment in Latin America began to grow again in the 1960s. From 1967 to 1976, Europe's share of direct accumulated investment in Latin America rose from 23 to 26 per cent while that of the United States dropped from 66 to 61 per cent. Europe's share of total direct investment in Brazil rose from 31 per cent in 1969 to 43 per cent in 1976 while that of the United States fell from 48 per cent to 32 per cent.

From the European point of view Latin America is by far the most important Third World recipient of new European investment, while for Latin America Europe is the most important source of new investment. European transnationals view Latin America as a major area of expansion for a number of reasons. Firstly it has a vast potential market. Its present population of 320 million is estimated to reach 600 million by the end of the century. Studies show that aside from the high income elite (5 per cent of the population enjoy a per capita income of US$3,200), an intermediate stratum of about 130 million people (40 per cent of the population) have sufficient income to make them consumers of manufactured goods. On the other hand, an estimated 150 million people (45 per cent of the population) live in extreme poverty but constitute an enormous reserve of domestic demand. Secondly, Latin America is by far the most industrialized region of the Third World. Although this process has been uneven, a number of Latin American countries are now classified as semi-industrialized and offer considerable opportunities for European transnationals both in terms of direct investment and in the export of technology and machinery. Thirdly, Latin America has abundant mineral and energy resources. The region produces 33 per cent of the world's copper, 26 per cent of its bauxite, 20 per cent of its iron, and 16 per cent of its tin. Estimates of Latin America's oil reserves are put at a minimum of 490 billion barrels and a maximum of 1,225 billion. Fourthly, Latin America has a large supply of cheap labour. A UN Economic Commission for Latin America (ECLA) study has estimated that the level of manufacturing wages in Britain, West Germany and the United States is on average 2.9, 4.6 and 7.1 times that of

6

Brazil, respectively, and 3.3, 5.4 and 8.3 times that of Mexico.

Latin America's traditional economic and political dependence on the United States and the strong resentments this has created within the region, have encouraged many to look positively toward European involvement. By enabling Latin American governments to diversify their sources of investment, many Latin Americans hope that Europe will help them gain greater economic independence from the United States. In the same way they hope that Europe's political support for social change in Latin America will help them achieve greater political freedom. This book sets out to examine these assumptions by analysing the forces behind Europe's involvement in Latin America and assessing what contribution it can be expected to make to the process of development within the region.

Jacqueline Roddick and Philip O'Brien provide an overview of Europe's economic interests and its role in Latin America. They point out that European capital has a long history in Latin America. However, they suggest that it has achieved 'less than inspiring results'. Their case study of Brazil, where European capital is particularly important, shows that its role has in practice differed very little from that of the United States. Both European and US transnationals are equally concerned to ensure a stable and secure environment for profit maximization, even if it means collaborating with repressive, military governments. Rather than giving Latin American governments greater bargaining power with respect to the United States, the practice of European firms shows how much their interests coincide with those of the US.

A similar view emerges from Rhys Jenkins' study of European transnationals in Latin America. He finds little evidence that such corporations behave any differently in Latin America than their US counterparts. In fact, it is increasingly apparent that in today's integrated world economy, the differences in the national origins of transnational corporations are less and less relevant. The important point stressed by Roddick and O'Brien is that the internationalization of capital enables it to move freely between countries and to those areas where labour is cheapest. Thus, it increases the bargaining power of capital over labour, by pitting Third World workers against First World workers in their fight for jobs.

Miguel Wionczek outlines the chequered history of the EEC's relations with Latin America. So far most of the proposals for the establishment of mutually advantageous forms of co-operation between the regions have proved stillborn. The EEC has complained of the difficulty of regional negotiations with the extremely diverse governments of Latin America, and points to the failure of these governments to develop any common policy towards the EEC. The

Latin American governments on the other hand, argue that the EEC has failed to develop a coherent Latin American policy and that its preferential treatment towards its own ex-colonies, as illustrated by the Lomé Convention, works to the detriment of other Third World countries. In addition to these problems, the thorniest issue which separates the regions at the moment concerns the protectionist tendencies which are growing within the EEC as the world economic recession deepens.

The EEC is Latin America's second most important trading partner after the United States accounting for 20 per cent of total Latin American exports in 1976. However, the relative importance of trade between the two regions has been declining. Latin America's share in Community imports fell from 11 per cent to 5.5 per cent between 1958 and 1978. There is also a notable disiquilibrim in the structure of Latin America's trade with Europe, 76.7 per cent of Latin America's exports to Europe are primary products, while 90.4 per cent of Europe's exports to Latin America are manufactured goods. The EEC is in fact the most important market for Latin America's commodity exports absorbing 28.6 per cent of the total. Latin America has been seeking ways to increase both its share in Community imports and to diversify the range of goods the Community buys from the region.

However, these efforts have been frustrated firstly by the restrictions implicit in the Common Agricultural Policy and the preferential treatment given to the signatories of the Lomé Convention, and secondly by the growing protection of Community markets against imported manufactured goods. The categories of goods most affected by this protection are textiles, leather goods, footwear, steel, transport equipment and electrical and electronic products. And it is precisely these categories of goods that have formed a significant part of Latin America's export drive in the past few years. The European argument for applying restrictions on imports relates primarily to its attempt to protect traditional industries and halt the rising tide of unemployment. It is clear that such policies represent a major blow to the export-led growth models being applied in Latin America. What is not so clear however, is how they will benefit the European economies. One consequence of developing regions being unable to export is that they will have to correspondingly reduce their imports. This in turn will reduce the demand for goods from Europe's industrialized sector. Latin America is an important purchaser of these goods from the EEC accounting for 7.2 per cent of total sales in the period 1973-75, compared with 5.6 per cent for the Lomé countries.

In an examination of the changing nature of the financial flows between Europe and Latin America, Alberto Orlandi looks at the decreasing role now being played by public bilateral and multilateral loans and grants. Latin America now receives very little official aid from Europe; between 1969 and 1975 it absorbed only 5.6 per cent of European total official development assistance (ODA). As official aid has declined, it has been replaced by loans provided in the main, by the transnational banks. As a result, Latin America's external debt rose from US$10 billion in 1965 to US$100 billion at the beginning of 1979. This inflow of foreign debt capital has helped to finance import needs and to stimulate economic growth particularly at a time when the non-oil-exporting countries of Latin America began to experience serious balance of payments problems. But the cost of this has been both a growing financial burden in terms of debt servicing as a percentage of export earnings and a deepening of Latin America's dependence on transnational banks.

There is no doubt that the question of aid and trade discrimination will remain a major difficulty to the achievement of closer relations between the EEC and Latin America. However, there has been one initiative, strongly influenced by Europeans, aimed at overcoming some of these problems in North-South relations. For Wionczek, the proposals outlined in the Brandt Report, with their stress on the mutuality of interests and interdependence between Third World and First World, show a more enlightened and encouraging response to the difficulties encountered in present EEC-Latin America relations. Unfortunately, although the proposals of the report have been widely publicized, they have not so far evoked a positive response from any government.

Other contributors to this book remain sceptical about the real purpose behind the Brandt Report, as well as sharing Wionczek's doubts that its proposals will ever be implemented. Tilman Evers places the Brandt Report within the context of the world economic crisis of the 1970s and the need for Western industrialized countries to make some concessions to Third World demands in order to retain the essence of the present world economic order. For Roddick and O'Brien also, an analysis of Brandt must be set squarely in the context of the economic crisis of the 1970s. They see the Brandt Report as a Marshall plan for the Third World, while Evers sees it in terms of an international extension of the role played by social democracy in a number of Western industrialized countries. In both senses, the Brandt Report is first and foremost an attempt to solve the present crisis in the industrialized countries and only secondly a response to Third World poverty. It is therefore a strategy for the survival of capitalism in both regions. Evers' analogy also stresses the role of the Brandt Report as an instrument of conflict management, between capital and labour, rich and poor. Roddick and O'Brien go on to point out the weakness of the report's proposals even within its own terms. They argue that achieving the goals of 'development' within present social structures and as defined by European and Latin American governments would have a negligible impact on the world's poor and underprivileged.

The findings of the Brandt Commission together with Europe's recent political initiatives in Latin America, have encouraged the view that an alliance with Europe is less dangerous for Latin America than continued dependence on the United States. According to this view, such an alliance may even offer some hope for change in the present international economic order. Wolf Grabendorff examines the shifting pattern of political alliances within the present international system and outlines the factors which currently affect the nature of the political relationship between Western Europe and Latin America.

Tilman Evers examines in detail one aspect of that political relationship, the role of European social democracy in Latin America. He focuses specifically on the case of West Germany. The various explanations which have been put forward for European social democracy's 'offensive' in Latin America since the 1976 Caracas meeting of the Socialist International are examined. Although most of these explanations contain important elements they fail to illustrate why the 'offensive' took place when it did and in the form that it did. A full explanation must include an assessment of developments in the international economy in the 1970s, the effects these developments have had upon the West German economy and the role West German social democracy plays in relation to domestic capital and labour.

The most recent economic and political developments in West German, particularly the crisis in the 'German Model' of continued economic growth, full employment and welfare state provision which has sustained West German social democracy until now, suggest that the conditions which led to the 'offensive' are coming to an end. The West German government's 'progressive' posture toward Latin America is already undergoing modifications.

An understanding of European social democracy's interest in Latin America is important both for those engaged in the struggle for change within Latin America and for those European-based organizations which support them. European social democracy is clearly concerned to maintain a pro-capitalist path of development in Latin America, a 'third way', in the words of Mitterrand in the late 1970s, 'between the regimes of Pinochet and Videla and the system of Castro'. It may well conflict with a more radical challenge to capitalism in the region based on the search for a model of development which lies outside the parameters of the present international system. However, in the struggle against US imperialism, and against oligarchic domination and military rule in Latin America, Europe does have an important role to play. Evers points the way to an analysis of these issues.

The last two articles in this book illustrate areas where Europe is clearly failing to provide any new initiatives for Latin America. Tino Thun shows that despite the rhetoric and resolutions of the European parliament, there has been no effective implementation of a European human rights policy. Where human rights considerations conflict with economic interests it is the latter which prevail. Indeed, there is an unwillingness even to relate human rights violations to the existence of a particular economic model at the international or national levels. This is due to the fact that a real change in these structures is often seen as detrimental to Europe's own economic and political interests. Thun suggests ways in which organizations concerned with the violation of human rights in Latin America might work at a European level to press for a more effective human rights policy.

The same contradictions between rhetoric and practice is seen in Simon Barrow's contribution on the European arms trade to Latin America. The existence of powerful economic interests in the European arms industry, and the supposed economic benefits that countries derive from arms exports have led European governments to sell considerable quantities of weapons to Latin American dictatorships. Western Europe is one of the major suppliers of arms to Latin America. Three European countries, Britain, France and West Germany, supplied over one half of the major weapons imported by Latin America during the 1970s. For example, from 1976 onward, the period of the most brutal violation of human rights in Argentina, Britain was a major supplier of weapons to that country (see table page 210). Only since the South Atlantic crisis erupted in April 1982 did the British government decide to draw attention to the human rights record of what had by then become an enemy government.

There are therefore many contradictions in Western Europe's apparently 'progressive' posture toward Latin America. There is little evidence that at the economic level, Europe will make either those trade or aid concessions necessary to ease the economic problems of Latin America, or any more radical structural changes in the international economy. Nor is there evidence that European capital is likely to make a more balanced contribution to Latin American development than its US counterpart. Constantine Vaitsos suggests that Europe's own interests make it unlikely that it can play a 'progressive' role in the Third World:

In the post-1960 period and especially during the 1970s, Europe has been rediscovering and intensifying its relations with countries in the South, which for decades, indeed centuries, in the past, were subjected to its colonial rule and arrogance. The nature and content of the emerging encounter is undoubtedly taking place within the framework of new multilateral political and economic conditions and within a drastically different world context. This new encounter is not simply consonant with Europe's past history. It emanates from present European needs and interests and the prospects for its economic and political survival or prosperity.

Within this framework progressive political forces which have emerged in Western Europe have shown themselves to support some important internal changes in the LDCs. Yet, in their external sector the nature of Western Europe's own interests might well militate in many important areas, against any serious contribution to economic development in the LDCs, regardless of what parties find themselves in power in Western Europe.*

It is hoped that this book will contribute to an understanding of Europe's role in Latin America and to a recognition of the limitations of that role. Europe can indeed act as a counterweight to the myopic political vision that the United States, particularly under the Reagan administration, applies to the region, which sees any struggle for social justice as the work of 'communist subversion'. However, there is no evidence as yet of any European economic initiative of significance for the poor and oppressed of Latin America. We hope this book will provide material for all those groups and individuals who are organizing, educating and lobbying in favour of the dispossessed Latin American majority.

*Jenny Pearce*
*Latin America Bureau*
*May 1982*

---

* Constantine Vaitsos, *From the Ugly American to the Ugly European: The Role of Western Europe in North-South Relations.* Mimeo, 1979.

# OVERVIEWS

# ŒUROPE AND LATIN AMERICA IN THE EIGHTIES

*Jacqueline Roddick and Philip O'Brien*

Links between Europe and Latin America, political or economic, are hardly a new phenomenon. It was the Spanish conquistadores and their Portuguese rivals who first integrated the region into the world economy. Britain subsequently lent a helping hand to the cause of Latin American independence and took the lion's share of trade with the region in consequence. In the early twentieth century, Germany, generally the loser in inter-European struggles for colonies in Africa and Asia, was quick to see the advantage of Latin American markets and established some of its first multinational subsidiaries.[1] Italian, Spanish and German workers largely formed the emerging labour movements of Argentina and Brazil, while their better off compatriots established local industries, frequently importing machinery and technical assistance from home — thus setting a pattern of industrial dependency which has endured ever since.[2]

In one fashion or another, most of these links have reflected the difference in economic and political power between countries at the centre of the world economy and those on its periphery. But competition between different national capitals has often been important for Latin American governments, giving them a marginal degree of freedom within which to assert some kind of national interest. The attempt to play off one imperial power against another justified the original decision of the Spanish colonies to cultivate London in the nineteenth century. In the twentieth, similar motives lay behind the brief Argentinian flirtation with the Axis powers, which was to prove so disadvantageous when the Allies won the Second World War and American hegemony in the region was buttressed by overt British support.

## The Dissolution of American Hegemony in Europe

The best case for a new alliance now between Europe and Latin

America lies in the break-up of the post-war European-American axis, which we have grown accustomed to call 'the West'. Whatever it may have meant in Europe, in Latin America the concept of the West has rarely been more than a camouflage for oppression. It has been invoked to justify the violent overthrow of Central American governments which dared to attack the interests of American multinationals. Worse still, perhaps, it has been used to suborn local armies into the service of foreign loyalties with American weaponry and American credits, American 'education' programmes for their officers and the propagation of doctrines which assured them that 'the Third World War has already broken out in Latin America' and the local population was their own worst enemy — beliefs which have justified the worst kind of atrocities against civilians in countries as far apart as Argentina, Colombia, and El Salvador.[3] The damage which American Manichaeism has done will take a generation or more to heal. But some weakening of the European-American axis, some sign that Europe was distancing itself from the USA within the alliance, would help.

The possibilities of such a loosening of the ties which bind the West together are probably greater today than they have ever been. The reasons, however, have nothing to do with Latin America, and everything to do with internal tensions between the alliance's transatlantic partners. Europe has been shaken by the Reagan administration's apparent willingness to contemplate a limited nuclear war on European soil, sparking a large protest movement in all those countries sheltering under the US nuclear umbrella. It has been a movement of European people rather than their governments, by and large still weighed down with a historic baggage of pro-US and pro-nuclear assumptions. But the new shift in perceptions has had an immediate impact on European policies towards Central America. All the continental European powers have been at pains to distance themselves from Reagan's attempts to label events in the region as a straightforward case of communist subversion.

The present attitudes of European governments and the general willingness of the European media to publicise the unsavoury side of American policy in El Salvador and Guatemala stand in sharp contrast to generalized European complacence when the Americans used the CIA to overthrow a government in Guatemala and sent American marines into the Dominican Republic on the same errand, a mere twenty years ago. A good many factors have contributed to this transformation, some of them marking a greater awareness on the part of Europeans that Latin America exists, some of them marking more simply a decline in the real ability of the USA to ensure stability in the region along the old lines. As *The Economist* has observed:

'Each horror picture from El Salvador, each cascade of savage-words-but-no-action from Mr Alexander Haig, feeds the coming season of anti-nuclear demonstrations in Europe and drains support from what Mr Reagan is trying to do in Poland'.[4]

The real importance of present European attitudes towards Central America lies in their ability to create tensions within the NATO alliance, tensions which seem gradually to be forcing the Reagan administration, against its will, towards negotiations with the Democratic Revolutionary Front (FDR), along lines proposed by the Mexicans and the French. But the roots of this crisis have little to do with Central America itself and everything to do with European perceptions of a risk to détente due to American warmongering which could trigger a new confrontation with the Soviet bloc, just when a crisis over Poland has been avoided. The breakdown of the Atlantic alliance over this point is the possibility which has *The Economist* worried. As the likeliest site for the next world war, Europe has discovered an overriding interest in peace between the superpowers, even at the cost of loyalty to the West.

In fact, neither the USA nor Europe wants to abandon NATO, so compromises will be made. But economic pressures are also working towards a loosening of the relationship, as a similar crisis over Poland clearly revealed. West German investment in the Soviet bloc has become an important counter-weight to its ties with the USA, which no Bonn government will lightly discard.[5] Western Europe as a whole is dependent on the outside world for a high percentage of its raw materials and fuels, and the Soviet bloc, like Latin America, is an important potential source of supply.[6]

As the world slides out of the post-war boom, other tensions are emerging. The post-war world economy was created in the shadow of the USA, whose enormous home market has dominated world trade at the same time as its giant firms have played a commanding role in world production. Europe benefitted enormously from this state of affairs during the immediate aftermath of the war, directly, in the form of Marshall aid to its shattered industries and indirectly, in the opening up of markets for its own products. But harmony depended essentially on the continued expansion of world trade, and the preservation of full employment in Europe itself.

In recent years, both of these have disappeared, leading to a sequence of conjunctural tensions between American policy-makers and their European counterparts which have all been rooted in the inability of European governments to manage their economies without having their plans torpedoed by contrary policies in Washington. The European need to manage local economies in a way which avoids the worst effects of recession, in turn reflects a certain social and political structure. Europe is the cradle of the organized working class: working class pressure has resulted in its societies making place for the organized labour movement in national politics. This is the root of European social democracy, and it must be kept in mind. European labour movements have had little need to be revolutionary, certainly in the post-war period, and they have often played a role overseas which could be described as imperialist.[7] But to their credit they have a set of achievements in defence of workers' interests within Europe, and European governments have been accustomed to take them into account.[8]

The persistence of extremely high rates of unemployment threatens this framework on the one hand. On the other, it is threatened by a crisis in profit levels, combined with high rates of inflation. As Lietaer points out,

> . . . the world-wide economic slump is decreasing total world employment . . . In this shrinking world labour market, a combination of union power and monetary upheavals has drastically reduced the competitivity of European labour since 1970, and in dollar terms, labour costs in the USA went up by 30 per cent, while in Europe they more than doubled . . .[9]

European governments must either intervene to increase the competitivity of local labour by lowering living standards — involving a right-wing revolution from above which only Britain has yet attempted — or they must find a way of preserving living standards in the face of all the adverse conditions of the world economy. The second alternative involves greater state intervention in economic affairs and a higher degree of protectionism than has been customary during the post-war period. It also requires some kind of long-term strategy for survival, given continued European dependence on world trade.

Meanwhile, European companies are easing the squeeze on their own profit levels by increasing the scope of their manufacturing interests abroad.[10] The giant firms of Europe have long operated an international strategy involving overseas manufacture. Current circumstances dictate a certain tightening of their operations, involving investment in more profitable markets such as the USA or in areas where labour is cheaper, or both.[11]

Such company strategies would undoubtedly be hampered by American and other reaction to a new European move towards greater protectionism, and they could be expected to oppose any such trend. The dissolution of US hegemony thus goes hand in hand with a dissolution of the preconditions for an easy alliance between European capital and European labour.

It is within this context of social tensions and diverging social interests that one has to understand the significance of the Brandt

## TABLE 1

### Overseas Assets of ICI in 1973

| £50 million plus | £25-50 million | £5-24 million | Under £5 million |
|---|---|---|---|
| West Germany | Argentina | France | Italy |
| Netherlands | India | Malaysia | Ireland |
| United States | | Spain | Belgium |
| South africa | | | Denmark |
| Australasia | | | Finland |
| Canada | | | Austria |
| | | | Greece* |
| | | | Brazil |
| | | | Mexico |
| | | | Peru |
| | | | Uruguay |
| | | | Trinidad* |
| | | | Bangladesh |
| | | | Indonesia |
| | | | Thailand* |

Note:   Sales-only subsidiaries have been excluded.
        *Manufacturing only.

Source:   *Michael Clapham*, 'Imperial Chemical Industries Limited: A Case
          Study' in *C. Fred Bergsten, ed.*, Towards a New World Trade
          Policy: The Maidenhead Papers, *D.C. Heath, Lexington, Mass.,
          1975, p.113.*

Report. The Brandt Report very ably draws on the *European* sense of
a prevailing social crisis:

If reduced to a simple denominator, this Report deals with peace. War is often
thought of in terms of military conflict, or even annihilation. But there is
growing awareness that an equal danger might be chaos — as a result of mass
hunger, economic disaster, environmental catastrophes, and terrorism. So we
should not think only of reducing the traditional threats to peace, but also of
the need for a change from chaos to order.[12]

Its solution is effectively a Marshall Plan for the Third World, based
on the same premisses on which the USA based its own Marshall Plan
three decades ago: massive transfers of funds to establish Third World
industries and build infrastructures, free access for both sides to each
others' markets, and freedom of operation for foreign companies
within the Third World, just as Europe opened its doors to US
multinationals. The attraction of such a programme is that it promises

19

## TABLE 2

### The Global Spread of Continental Europe's Manufacturing Giants, 1900-1970

Number of manufacturing subsidiaries formed and acquired by the 85 largest continental European enterprises (sales of manufactured goods exceeding US$400 million in 1970).

| | Region of subsidiary location | | | | |
| --- | --- | --- | --- | --- | --- |
| | Developed Europe & North America | European Periphery* | Latin America | Asia & Africa | Total |
| Prior to 1914 | 122 | 37 | 2 | 6 | 167 |
| 1914-1919 | 36 | 11 | 3 | 1 | 51 |
| 1920-1929 | 162 | 49 | 15 | 23 | 249 |
| 1930-1938 | 69 | 18 | 16 | 9 | 112 |
| 1939-1945 | 25 | 10 | 4 | 5 | 44 |
| 1946-1952 | 62 | 14 | 30 | 23 | 129 |
| 1953-1955 | 60 | 16 | 23 | 18 | 117 |
| 1956-1958 | 69 | 9 | 27 | 26 | 131 |
| 1959-1961 | 128 | 14 | 30 | 60 | 232 |
| 1962-1964 | 120 | 34 | 30 | 45 | 229 |
| 1965-1967 | 346 | 39 | 76 | 71 | 532 |
| 1968-1970 | 659 | 86 | 130 | 51 | 1030 |

*includes Greece, Portugal, Spain, Turkey, Israel, and Eastern Europe prior to 1945.

Source: L.G. Franko, The European multinationals, p.106.

---

to heal the opening breach between capital and labour, by constructing a new boom in world trade based on their joint ability to meet the needs of the world's poor.

As soon as the Report becomes more detailed, however, the prospectus begins to run into difficulties. The Third World is to take over manufacture of traditional consumer goods, while Europe specializes in high technology industry. But high technology industry is increasingly capital-intensive, requiring larger and larger investments for fewer and fewer jobs. Even if it were not, its historical record as a mass employer is not one to inspire renewed confidence in Europe's social truce. The electronics and microelectronics industries have a long history of hostility to trade unions, and a well-established preference for cheap, vulnerable female labour. They have also been pioneers in the field of export platforms, the first to reduce labour costs by setting up assembly operations in the Third World where female labour was even cheaper.[13] Something of the industry's stan-

## TABLE 3
### The Growth of German Multinationals in Brazil, 1961-75

*I: Number of subsidiaries*
*II: Employment in those subsidiaries for which information was available (number in brackets)*

| Sector | 1961 I | 1961 II | | 1966 I | 1966 II | | 1971 I | 1971 II | | 1975 I | 1975 II | |
|---|---|---|---|---|---|---|---|---|---|---|---|---|
| *Manufacturing* | | | | | | | | | | | | |
| Vehicles | 8 | 14,015 | (3) | 9 | 21,356 | (5) | 11 | 43,286 | (9) | 13 | 63,071 | (13) |
| Electrical engineering | 11 | 2,720 | (3) | 12 | 3,920 | (4) | 19 | 20,523 | (13) | 25 | 31,819 | (22) |
| Chemicals | 35 | 4,478 | (14) | 39 | 5,890 | (18) | 45 | 15,345 | (32) | 58 | 25,574 | (46) |
| Metal Industry | 16 | 7,013 | (6) | 17 | 8,554 | (7) | 20 | 12,980 | (11) | 30 | 23,850 | (33) |
| Mechanical engineering | 38 | 1,262 | (9) | 49 | 2,698 | (18) | 55 | 8,865 | (29) | 74 | 17,478 | (48) |
| Precision engineering and optics | 13 | 800 | (7) | 16 | 1,811 | (9) | 18 | 3,126 | (13) | 23 | 6,070 | (17) |
| Steel, glass and ceramics | 1 | — | | 1 | — | | 1 | 308 | (1) | 1 | 314 | (1) |
| Energy and mining | 1 | — | | 1 | — | | 3 | 1229 | (3) | 3 | 2,784 | (3) |
| Other | 9 | — | | 1 | 162 | (1) | 14 | 3,534 | (7) | 16 | 6,659 | (11) |

Source: *F. Froebel, J. Heinrichs and O. Kreye The New International Division of Labour, p.28.*

dard of social conscience can be gathered from its presence in Central America, an area with a long history of the bloody suppression of popular protest in any form.[14]

## The Brandt Report and European Regional Economic Interests

The Brandt Report is also unrealistic in its perceptions of the Third World, as veterans of the search for Third World development have been quick to point out. Drawing on the bad conscience which European social democrats — quite rightly — feel in the face of mass starvation, it ignores the hard economic fact that social needs have to be transformed into market demands if they are to have a perceptible impact on world trade.[15] Existing economic and social structures in the Third World stand in the way of any simple transfer of aid to the poorest of the poor. So too does the entire logic of Western technology, which has universally favoured the interests of those with wealth, power and education as against those of the poor and illiterate — a tendency clearly visible in its most characteristic products, the car and the computer. Aid from the developed countries has to be administered by those already in control of Third World governments, the very sectors of the Third World population with enough wealth of their own to ensure that existing market forces satisfy their needs.

In the past, these sectors have been the principal source of pressure towards the development of 'imitative capitalism', as Raul Prebisch has aptly labelled it: first importing Western consumer goods and then the equipment necessary to manufacture a Western life-style locally.[16] The result has been a system with a built-in tendency to work towards the disadvantage of the rural poor, making access to cars, tractors, chemical fertilizers, irrigation networks and electricity grids, often through the medium of distant bureaucrats, a precondition for economic success. Coming to the cities, the poor have found few 'trickle down' effects in this economic model to compensate for its persistent tendency to encourage 'trickle up'. Modern factories making goods for the relatively well off have had very little need to employ the poor on a massive scale, given the labour-saving propensities of Western manufacturing technology — while its parallel tendency to break down craft skills and reduce all workers to the level of easily-trained operatives, has hindered the development of effective trade unions, placing workers in the iniquitous position of competing for scarce jobs with a large surplus population outside. Prebisch built the first-ever version of a theory of unequal exchange in part around the ability of Northern trade unions to force employers to distribute profits down the social scale, thus keeping the gains from trade in Europe and North America and swelling their mass markets for low- and high-priced consumer goods. Meanwhile, employers in the Third World were under no such pressures, thanks to their own position in a labour surplus economy and were thus free to use their profits either to cut the prices of exported goods, or simply to send them to banks in London and New York. In either case, the centres of the world economy gained at the expense of the periphery.[17]

This is not to say that progressive Third World regimes which really do have the interests of the poor at heart, do not need all the changes in the framework of international trade which the Brandt Report promises: guaranteed commodity prices for their exports, easier access to Western markets, increased flows of financial resources and imported trucks and buses (though one hopes they do not need the sophisticated electronic anti-subversive devices which are one of the present specialities of the electronic industry). It is to say that such measures will only have a real impact on the problems of world poverty in conjunction with certain kinds of Southern governments, and not with others. Progressive regimes will be those with a large chip on their shoulder where the natural operation of market forces is concerned, and a great resistance to any proposition that they might give freedom of the house to foreign firms. Experience has shown, again and again, that the natural operation of market forces in a Third World dominated by the West, does nothing to serve the interests of workers, peasants, the poor, the illiterate and the dispossessed. Rather it tends to reinforce the position of the Southern rich, in a tacit or open alliance with Western capital and, more often than not, with the giant firms themselves.

The future of this alliance is another story altogether. It has its own tensions, as the history of OPEC has reminded us. Aramco may be on hand to repair the royal household's cars in Saudi Arabia, but it cannot do much about the persistent tendency for the price of Western manufactured goods to rise more than the price of Saudi Arabia's oil exports.[18] Furthermore, as the experience of the newly industrializing countries has shown, the developmental patterns of imported capitalism lean towards the creation of new forms of debt bondage on a national scale, at least for those Third World countries not blessed with oil. The alleviation of tensions such as these has been the real subject of the North-South debate throughout which the cause of the Southern poor has been pressed into service to justify what are often essentially the interests of the Southern rich.

European social democracy cannot do very much to help the cause of the Third World's poor simply by pressing for a change in the existing rules governing international trade, still less if freedom for multinationals to operate is built into the new rules, as the Brandt

Report suggests. As Prebisch has said, problems of fundamental social change will have to be resolved by the countries of the South themselves. Meanwhile, changes in the framework of international trade will provide rain for the just and the unjust alike. But the effects of raining on the unjust bear some careful examination, not only because of their possible implications for poor people in Latin America, but also because the process has its implications as well for European workers — who are also beginning to find reasons to distrust the free operation of market forces.

For instance, a year before the Brandt Report itself was published, some of its proposals were anticipated by a European economist proposing a new strategic alliance between Europe, Latin America, and European multinationals. Some concessions were to be made to Latin American interests in the form of guaranteed commodity prices, giving Europe access to a stable flow of raw materials, together with a negotiated solution to the increasingly heavy burden of international debt carried by countries like Brazil, on the grounds that any default by Brazil would have more costly consequences for the developed countries than there could possibly be gain to Brazil itself. A new deal between local governments and European multinationals completed the picture, with the good behaviour of European multinationals, guaranteed by their supposedly more progressive record in sharing proprietary rights with local capital, transferring control over imported technology, and using less labour-intensive production processes.[19]

The problem with such scenarios is essentially that European capital has already had a long history in Latin America, with less than inspiring results. Only the accidental intervention of a World War kept it from mounting a strong challenge to American hegemony in the region in the 1940's, at least in manufacturing. Even so, the European interest is presently holding its own nicely: in Brazil, for instance, one could argue that it has begun to edge American interests out of first position (see Table 7).

In spite of Europe's insatiable demand for raw materials, this existing regional role has had only a marginal bearing on the extraction of minerals and fuels. It may therefore be true that where Latin America is concerned, European capital and European governments could best serve their own interests by guaranteeing their supplies through artificially stabilized commodity prices. Traditionally, European operations in this field have tended to be linked to the countries of the European periphery, Southern and Eastern Europe and the Middle East, or else to colonial possessions in Africa (see Table 4). Typical examples would include Rio Tinto Zinc, with its operations in Spain and Africa, and the involvement of French and British oil in-

TABLE 4

**Extractive operations of Continental European firms, including Royal Dutch Shell, by number of subsidiaries, 1900-1971**

| | Total | Europe | Middle East and Africa | North America | South America | Other |
|---|---|---|---|---|---|---|
| *Iron ore and coal* | | | | | | |
| Prior to 1914 | 18 | 11 | 3 | — | — | 4 |
| 1914-1945 | 29 | 17 | 6 | — | 5 | 1 |
| 1946-1971 | 46 | 15 | 12 | 8 | 8 | — |
| Unknown | 10 | 5 | — | 3 | 2 | — |
| *Non-ferrous metals* | | | | | | |
| Prior to 1914 | 7 | 4 | 1 | — | 1 | 1 |
| 1914-1945 | 14 | 8 | 4 | 1 | 1 | — |
| 1946-1971 | 32 | 5 | 20 | 4 | 2 | 1 |
| Unknown | 1 | 1 | — | — | — | — |
| *Oil and gas* | | | | | | |
| Prior to 1914 | 21 | 5 | 1 | 3 | 6 | 6 |
| 1914-1945 | 23 | 3 | 8 | 4 | 6 | 2 |
| 1946-1971 | 64 | 8 | 35 | 14 | 4 | 3 |

Source: *Lawrence G. Franko, The European Multinationals, p.47.*

terests in the Middle East. This picture may be changing slowly, as French, British and Dutch companies extend their Latin American activities,[20] but it still remains true that American firms such as the giant Rockefeller empire have dominated foreign activities in this field.

European interests have played a much greater role in manufacturing, the field in which Lietaer supposes that European intervention might make a difference first in the supply and then in the local production of manufactured goods. West Germany was already supplying 20 per cent or more of the imports of Brazil, Chile, Guatemala and El Salvador in 1935,[21] and the step towards manufacturing in a major market like Brazil was not a big one. Ties were close in part because of the presence of European immigrants acting as local entrepreneurs and the existing role played by European banks.[22] Coats Paton began operations in Brazil in 1906. A French chemical firm, one of the forefathers of today's Rhône Poulenc, set up operations in Brazil in 1921 and was quickly followed by the Luxembourg steel firm ARBED, the German chemical and pharmaceutical company I.G. Farben, and Nestlé, the Swiss food manufacturer.[23] In sectors such as chemicals and pharmaceuticals, the carve-up of world trade among international giants reserved a special place in Latin America for European interests, reflected to this day in the spread of German chemical and pharmaceutical subsidiaries throughout the continent.[24]

Cartelization simultaneously muddied the waters of any purely national or even continental European interest in these operations, with the possible exception of German firms suffering from Nazi nationalist pressures. The British company ICI, with interests in Chile, Peru, Brazil and Argentina in the 1930s, then found it convenient to set up firms on a joint ownership basis with the American chemicals giant Du Pont (Duperial of Argentina and Brazil) and the Belgian multinational Solvay et Cie, in Argentina.

So far as Latin America is concerned, European capital is therefore an integral part of a pattern of economic development established over the past fifty years. For a variety of reasons, the best illustration of what this pattern means for the Latin American poor and Europe's own working classes, is probably the case of Brazil.

## Brazil: A Case in Point?

Brazil has the largest land mass and the largest population in Latin America. ICI's company history mentions the belief in the 1930s that it was the country of the future. Certainly its armed forces have long harboured ambitions of playing a geopolitical role of their own, a role towards which they took a giant step recently by buying a nuclear powered electricity generator from West Germany which produces plutonium as a by-product thus giving them a future capacity to manufacture nuclear weapons.

Today, Brazil is one of two NICs — newly industrializing countries — in Latin America, hardly considered part of the Third World at all. But it has severe problems of poverty, of which perhaps the worst is concentrated in its northeast, away from the industrial centres. In 1972, 40 per cent of the *urban* labour force in the nine states in the region earned less than half the prevailing legal minimum wage, i.e. US$34 a month or less; while for more than half a million families, this meagre sum represented their entire income. Altogether, some 50 per cent of the area's urban families were attempting to survive on less than US$68 a month, and this at the apogee of the Brazilian economic miracle. Rural conditions were worse.[25]

Brazil's history as an industrializing nation goes back to the Great Depression, which abruptly cut off supplies of manufactured imports and encouraged the government of the day to make a deliberate effort to foster local production of consumer goods. High tariff walls were set up to protect local industry against foreign competition, and the government took effective control of the receipts from foreign trade.

As we have seen, European firms already figured among the local producers. The new protectionist policies gave both European and American multinationals an even more convincing rationale for establishing local subsidiaries in Brazil. 'Development' initially took the form of light manufacturing industry controlled by the private sector, coupled with a government programme of state investment in capital goods sectors, such as steel, and the extraction of Brazil's natural resources, such as oil. After the early 1950s, however, there was a shift in the direction of government economic policy, not altogether unrelated to the desire of the Brazilian military to maintain good relations with their American allies. Public initiatives such as those which had led to the creation of Petrobrás, the state oil company, were played down, and a deliberate effort was made to encourage private investment, particularly the inflow of foreign private capital. The 1950s were years of rapid economic growth, especially in the field of consumer durables, such as cars. By 1964, a third of Brazil's industrial production was accounted for by foreign-owned firms.[26]

For many reasons, this strategy of development had begun to falter by the early 1960s, leading to high rates of inflation, a burgeoning foreign debt, and greater social instability. The market for the kinds of goods now providing the axis of economic development was limited by the prevailing pattern of income distribution. Consumer durable industries, largely dependent on the local upper and upper middle classes, soon mopped up existing demand for cars and refrigerators, and then resorted to strategies of product elaboration and differentiation for smaller and smaller real returns. 'Development' was concentrated in the southeast around Rio de Janeiro and Sao Paulo. Here the prevailing political system, an authoritarian form of populist democracy, had begun to encounter problems of worker unrest. Even more disturbing to those with an interest in stability, was growing evidence that the control of rural elites over the poor in the countryside had begun to crack with the emergence of peasants' leagues demanding agrarian reform.[27] The incumbent administration of President Joao Goulart took a turn towards the left, in the direction of a reassertion of state control over the economy, limiting the scope of foreign capital by subjecting their activities to closer control, and making some concessions to workers' and peasants' demands. The outcome, in 1964, was the first of Latin America's new generation of military regimes, the model for subsequent developments in Argentina, Uruguay and Chile.

Foreign involvement in Brazilian industry at the time represented a patchwork of national colours. Drawing on a contemporary US State Department document, René Dreifuss presents the following picture, sector by sector. In the field of mining and energy extraction, US capital was the dominant foreign interest, representing about 65 per cent of total foreign-controlled assets, but British and Italian interests were also present. Steel and metal fabrication was dominated by Belgian and Japanese firms. Transport equipment was still dominated by US interests, but German and British investment was also important. French interests were the crucial foreign force in the field of glass and cement manufacture, with US interests in second place, followed by the Swiss. Britain dominated foreign investment in food manufacturing, with American and Argentinian capital its principal rivals, and together with the French, provided the leading foreign firms in the textile industry. The USA still accounted for 40 per cent of foreign assets in the field of chemicals, plastics and pharmaceuticals, but it had rivals among the French, the Germans, and the Swiss.[28]

We now know that all these multinationals played an important role in organizing and financing the 1964 coup.[29] The immediate trigger may have been a certain perception of social and political instability, though it has to be said that they and their associates campaigned very hard to highlight the impression of instability and chaos in the minds of the public and the armed forces, through such entrepreneurial organizations as IBAD and IPES, which the multinationals helped finance.[30] The longer term problems which sparked the coup had probably more to do with the strategic importance of Brazil to the companies' own global strategies, as the largest home market in Latin America. A shift in the pattern of development deliberately designed to favour lower-income groups, coupled with more careful local control over their activities, would have undermined the purpose of existing investments. They also felt that their interests were not adequately represented in the existing political system. One of the reports triggering their involvement in anti-government plots, for instance, pointed out that under the existing system of representative government, the 'productive' centre of the economy around Sao Paulo would be likely to receive only 10 per cent of the seats in Congress, even though it contributed 40 per cent to Brazil's GNP. The benefits of a democratic system were working against the interests of imported capitalism, and in favour of the interests of rural oligarchs, and perhaps ultimately also those of the rural and urban poor of peripheral areas such as the northeast.[31]

The principal role in organizing the 1964 coup fell to Brazilian associates of the Rockefeller empire, long deeply involved in strategic plans for the economies of Latin America.[32] The most famous of Rockefeller's proteges in Brazil was perhaps a local economist, Roberto Campos, subsequently to take charge of the Brazilian economy in the wake of the coup. But European companies were also involved, seeing apparently little difference between their own interests and those of the Rockefeller empire. Campos had ties with Mercedes-Benz,[33] Royal Dutch-Shell was a contributor to IBAD,[34] and the President of the crucial local organization of IPES in Sao Paulo, Joao Leopoldo Batista Figueiredo, boasted a set of ties with European firms which almost constitutes a continental tour.

**TABLE 5**

**The European Connections of IPES in Sao Paulo**
**Business interests of Joao Leopoldo Batista Figueiredo**

| Multinational | Country/ Origin | Local Subsidiary |
|---|---|---|
| Booth Steamship Co. | UK | Booth Steamship Co., Liverpool L. Figueiredo Navigacao |
| Osram (Siemens, AEG and AUER) | Germany | Allegemeine Ellektrizitäts Gesellschaft Maua S/A |
| Bayer | Germany | Ind. Química Electrocloro Copamo |
| Pirelli | Italy | Comp. Indústrial Brasileira |
| Martini et Rossi | Italy | Martini et Rossi |
| Solvay et Cie | Belgium | Eletroteno Indústrias Plásticas S/A |
| Ciba-Geigy | Switzerland | Ciba-Geigy Química S/A |
| Schweizerische Aluminium A.G. | Switzerland | AISA (Alumínio Indústria S/A) |
| Scania-Saab | Sweden | Scania-Saab do Brasil |

Source: *Dreifuss, p.523 (Appendix B).*

The immediate agents of the 1964 coup were however the military, in close association with the USA. In Brazil in 1964, the role of this alliance in safeguarding the economy for private foreign capital was paramount, and quite open. Since 1952, a treaty between the two countries had set out the terms upon which Brazil would be allowed to industrialize, committing the country to encourage

. . . the elimination of barriers, and (to) the creation of incentives for a constant increase of the participation of the private firm in the development of *foreign* countries' resources

and

. . . to *discourage*, as far as possible . . . the practice or practices of monopoly and cartel which prevail in certain countries . . .[35]

thus ruling out any extension of state involvement into privately-controlled sectors of the economy, any further restrictions on the activities of foreign capital and even attempts by the state to create the preconditions in which its own economic goals could be realized by local private capital.[36]

For the Brazilian military, this treaty was the fruit of a long history of close contacts with the American forces dating back to the Italian front in World War II. American officers helped set up the national military academy, the Escola Superior da Guerra, which paid close attention not only to professional military matters but also to broader questions of national development, which might have a bearing on Brazil's future status as a world power, within the framework of Western security. The commitment to freedom for foreign private investment was a cornerstone of their economic philosophy. The idea that the Brazilian military had to have an economic philosophy and an economic strategy was, in turn, a means of fostering contacts with the same set of economists and businessmen who were already well integrated into the local Rockefeller think-tanks, such as Campos himself.[37]

In 1964, the head of the US delegation to the US-Brazil Mixed Military Commission made a speech to the Escola superior da Guerra reminding the Brazilian military of their commitments. The principal threat to Brazil, he said, was not invasion but indirect aggression and communist subversion, and the prime aim of the Military Assistance Pact between Brazil and the US was to

. . . ensure the existence of native military forces and paramilitary forces sufficient to combat communist subversion, espionage, *insubordination*, and other threats to internal security.[38]

It was not then necessary to resort to the invention of Cuban gun-runners or massed ranks of imported North Korean soldiers to justify a military coup.

The 1964 pact between sections of the Brazilian entrepreneurial elite, locally operating multinationals and the military themselves, is a nasty piece of work altogether. It is hard not to caricature it. What must be realized, however, is that each group was serving its own real interests and the kind of future in which these interests would be protected. The Brazilian military were securing a future for Brazil in which their military strength would be buttressed by access to the most modern technology, in alliance with the greatest power in the world. The Brazilian entrepreneurial elite was similarly looking towards a prosperous future, building on its existing close ties with the most efficient firms in the world. The multinationals were strengthening their position in Latin America's largest market, 'the country of the future'. The events of 1964 testify to an effective and very real political alliance, not to any simple manipulation of local puppets by foreign powers.

But what were the results? The essential problem facing a Third World economy using an imitative capitalist style of development is the restricted size of the local market for Western-style goods — the very problem on which the Brandt Report lays its principal stress. In Brazil, this problem was solved by concentrating national income in the hands of the sectors most likely to buy consumer durables, at the expense of the mass of the population. It was achieved by the adoption of a developmental model which *deliberately* favoured 'trickle up' processes, as opposed to one which only lives spontaneously off their dynamic effects. Strikes were banned. The effect of the new government policies on real wages is shown in Table 6. Another significant result of the new programme was worsening figures for infant mortality in Brazil's major industrial cities, Sao Paulo and Minas Gerais.[39] Meanwhile, the Brazilian military pioneered techniques of torture as a means of preserving internal security, which they were subsequently to teach other regional armed forces in Uruguay, Chile and Argentina.

Is the price which the Brazilian people as a whole have had to pay for the 1964 coup, simply the by-product of a process of industrialization from which they will later reap all the benefits? No: it is the cost of pursuing a particular economic strategy, which seems likely in the long run to maintain the *status quo*, with wages consistently rising less than productivity. The new regime presided over a shift in Brazil's productive structure away from industries producing cheap consumer goods for the masses and towards the kinds of consumer durables and other products which constitute the core of Western-style development.[40] Poor people may buy radios and even refrigerators at the cost of restricting still further their already-restricted intake of food, or cutting down on clothes and shoes, as a way of purchasing some respect in this consumerist civilization,[41] but such consumer patterns hardly constitute a real gain to popular welfare and in some senses — including increasing centralization of control over the mass media — they may actually make the process of social change more difficult.

The new regime also deepened Brazil's dependence on foreign trade for inputs to this sophisticated apparatus and its tendency to acquire an ever-increasing burden of foreign debt was evident even before the rise in oil prices.[42] In 1964, the Brazilian government chose to pay the cost of an open economy by aggressively expanding its exports, both in primary products and in manufactured goods. The social costs of expanding export crops has been manifest in an increasing concentration of property holdings in the countryside, together with a virtual

## TABLE 6

### Real Wages In Brazil[a]

1960 = 100

| | Wage Index, 18 Unions | Minimum Wage City of Rio de Janeiro |
|---|---|---|
| 1957 | 98[b] | 114 |
| 1958 | 103[c] | 99 |
| 1959 | 94[d] | 113 |
| 1960 | 100 | 100 |
| 1961 | 105 | 115 |
| 1962 | 105 | 96 |
| 1963 | 107 | 89 |
| 1964 | 103 | 89 |
| 1965 | 98 | 82 |
| 1966 | 92 | 76 |
| 1967 | 89 | 73 |
| 1968 | 92 | 74 |
| 1969 | 94 | 71 |
| 1970 | 95 | 70 |
| 1971 | 98 | 69 |
| 1972 | 102 | 71 |
| 1973 | 98 | 68 |
| 1974 | 107[d] | 69 |

a. deflated by the Rio de Janeiro cost of living index. b. based on 8 unions. c. based on 10 unions. d. based on 15 unions.

Source: *Jose Serra*, op.cit., *p.106.*

---

two-fold increase in the numbers of workers dependent upon seasonal labour, and a decline in the production of staple food crops.[43] Where manufactured exports are concerned, the government's strategy depends upon a combination of subsidies and cheap labour to maintain low prices for the world market. Any major success on the part of Brazil's reviving trade union movement would threaten this programme, either by raising the cost of exported goods or by tempting the country's multinational partners to move production elsewhere — perhaps back to Argentina, whose historically strong trade union movement with a better record in defending its share of the national income, may have contributed to encouraging the multinationals shift to Brazil twenty years ago. Meanwhile, Brazil's debt and the possible threat of default has attracted the attentions of the IMF, which in 1981 succeeded in forcing Brazil's Minister of the Economy to renew the squeeze on popular consumption. However, as Table 3 illustrates, European investment in Brazil has boomed as a result of the developmental processes set in train by the 1964 coup. Foreign companies continue to dominate the strategic sectors of Brazil's industrial structure, in a way which parallels quite closely the experience of the region's other NIC, Mexico. As Table 7 illustrates, it continues to be very much *their* pattern of development. But the growing share of European and other foreign capital in this process has shifted the weight of American hegemony. Brazil's manufacturing sector, at least, is no longer dominated by American capital. This development no doubt favours the pretensions of the Brazilian military to become an independent global power.[44]

## TABLE 7

### Brazil and Mexico

The Stake of US and Other Foreign Multinational Corporations as a percentage of Assets of the 300 Largest Manufacturing Firms, Selected Industries

|  | Total Foreign Share | | US MNC Share | | Other Foreign Share | |
|---|---|---|---|---|---|---|
|  | Brazil | Mexico | Brazil | Mexico | Brazil | Mexico |
| Total manufacturing | 50 | 52 | 16 | 36 | 34 | 16 |
| Rubber | 100 | 100 | 100 | 100 | — | — |
| Transport Equipment | 84 | 79 | 37 | 70 | 47 | 9 |
| Electrical Machines | 78 | 60 | 22 | 35 | 56 | 25 |
| Non-electric Machines | 74 | 95 | 34 | 36 | 40 | 58 |
| Chemicals | 69 | 68 | 34 | 54 | 35 | 14 |
| Textiles | 44 | 5 | 6 | 0 | 38 | 5 |
| Food | 32 | 26 | 2 | 20 | 30 | 6 |

Source: *Gary Gereffi and Peter Evans, 'Transnational Corporations, Dependent Development, and State Policy in the Semi-Periphery', Latin America Research Review, XVI, 3, 1981, p.41.*
*Data taken from R. Newfarmer and W. Mueller,* Multinational Corporations in Brazil and Mexico: A Report to the US Senate Subcommittee on Multinational Corporations.

Multinationals in Brazil are co-operating with the Brazilian government in its new drive for exports and so benefiting from the government's willingness to commit resources to this programme, which, in the case of manufactured goods, amount to 55 per cent of the value of export sales.[45] In some cases, notably the local car industry, the determination of the Brazilian government to improve the country's export performance has coincided nicely with pressures on the multinationals themselves to standardize and cheapen car parts on a world basis, internationalizing the process of production in order to retain global profits in the face of a slump in demand and rising production costs.[46] Such pressures have been magnified by the decline in demand for cars within Brazil itself. As the local market is exhausted and deflationary policies become dominant, European companies are perhaps not in the vanguard of these developments to the same extent as their American counterparts. General Motors is already making engines destined for West Germany in Brazil.[47] However, the pressures on European car firms are very similar, and the volume of their exports to both European and other Third World markets is growing. Volkswagen do Brasil hopes to raise its export earnings from US$450 million in 1981 to US$600 million in 1982 and Fiat shipped 50,000 cars from its new Minas Gerais plant back to Italian markets in 1980.[48]

Brazil is not a mere export platform, with foreign capital using cheap local labour to complete the less sophisticated parts of an assembly process which begins in the developed countries and returns there to be sold. The typical example of this kind of development in Latin America has probably been the Mexican border industries, close as they are to the USA; while Froebel, Heinrichs, and Kreye have shown that European capital tends to prefer sites in Eastern Europe or Asia.[49] But the pressures of the existing development pattern are tending to force Brazil in this direction, just as it is also being forced to replace local food crops with soya for export abroad. For international firms, such developments are not a problem. This is the pattern of efficient global production strategies in the future, favoured as it has been by developments in transport and the technology of communications and centralized control. For the Brazilian people as a whole, who have to work harder to export more on behalf of a productive structure which was never geared to serving their needs, the picture is rather different. So it is too for Brazilian and European labour alike, who are now being forced into competition with one another in a way which is inimical to the standards of living of both of them, and which represents a weakening of the ability of trade unions everywhere to force a downward distribution of the profits which workers produce.

## The Real Task of European Social Democracy

Brazil is not the worst example of the effects of imitative capitalism on Latin America. Worse, probably, has been the impact on the other Southern Cone countries, Chile, Argentina, and Uruguay, where industrial structures created painfully over a period of fifty years are now slowly being dismantled in the face of a new logic of international development which seems increasingly determined to concentrate industrial production in one or two regional powers. In these countries, local capital is more obviously in control, and the ties between it and the giant powers of the world economy are hidden behind the mysteries of the world's banks. The revolutions excluding workers from power look like the free choice of national elites, even when they are not, and the bi-partisan and tri-partisan character of the underlying alliance is less easy to detect.

Worse still, obviously, is the bloody history of contemporary Central America. Nonetheless, precisely because it is not typical and does give us a chance to observe the values of European multinationals in action, the history of Brazil is a parable which should be engraved on every European socialist's heart. It shows the essential community of interests behind American hegemony in the region, and the interests of European firms. The Pentagon's mad pursuit of communists may have become an embarrassment in Europe, where the risks of nuclear war which it seems to entail are beginning to be a major preoccupation of the population at large. But in the Third World, the firm guarantee that American power could provide and that the interests of foreign private capital would always be respected, will be sadly missed and will have to be replaced with something else.

The history of Brazil also reveals the illusory character of the Brandt Report's plea for a world-wide reduction in spending on armaments. Spending on armaments is obviously counter to the interests of the world's population as a whole. When it is not pure waste, it can be a real factor in preserving existing social injustices and the powerlessness of the poor. But looked at in the context of an alliance with the ruling elites of the Third World, spending on armaments and the world-wide arms trade which it supports are of critical importance. They serve to shore up unpopular governments friendly to the interests of the West. They provide the crucial sweetener which commits the local military apparatus anxious for glory and envious of the possibilities of status on a world scale, to a long-term relationship with the countries and firms which control this kind of technology. It is not only the pursuit of employment in Germany which encourages the West German government to take dangerous risks with world peace to satisfy the Brazilian military's desire for access to nuclear power.

But what the case of Brazil reveals most clearly of all is the fact that an alliance between Europe, the existing governments of the region and European multinationals is neither in the interests of the region's poor, nor in the interests of European workers. As currently constructed, it is likely to be inimical to both. The internationalization of production has given private capital a new freedom to play off workers in one country against workers in another, in the greater interest of retaining for itself more of the profits from production and investing them in the sectors which seem most profitable on a worldwide scale. In the short term, this process is undermining the historic ability of European labour to force a compromise on local capital and the concession of higher living standards. In the longer term, it is undermining the kind of social structures capable of ensuring a distribution of the social surplus, on a world-wide basis — the kind of structures which were once important in raising the standard of living of workers and the population at large in Argentina and which forced a local elite to pay more than lip service to questions of social justice in Chile.

Workers in Latin America and in Europe both have an interest in wresting control over their productive structures from international capital, which increasingly is free to choose the national state which it would prefer to have represent it, from among a plurality of suitors. This is a relatively new phenomenon, whose importance in Europe itself has only been obvious in the past decade, like the disillusionment with American defence strategies which lies behind the renewed strength of the continental campaign for nuclear disarmament. As a pattern, it replaces older ones in which European capital and European labour could indeed gain some common advantage out of the siting of manufacturing in Europe on the basis of imported raw materials, with production being exported to the rest of the world. In many ways the Brandt Report represents an attempt to reassert that older pattern in new ways. But developments in the world economy have made such answers outmoded. European capital is no longer limited by its own geographical ties.

The real task of European social democracy in the 1980s is to reassert some limitations, in conjunction with workers and the poor in the Third World.

### Footnotes

1. Such as the German subsidiary of Metallgesellschaft established in Mexico before World War I.
2. See Henry Kirsch, *Industrial Development in a Traditional Society*, University of Florida Press, Miami, 1977, or Gustavo Polit, 'The Industrialists of Argentina',

in J. Petras and M. Zeitlin, eds., *Latin America, Reform or Revolution?*, Fawcett, New York, 1968.

3. The best single source on this theme is undoubtedly a document prepared for the Latin American church by Father Jose Comblin, *Dos Ensayos Sobre La Doctrina de La Seguridad Nacional*, Vicaria de Solidaridad, Santiago, 1979.

4. 27 March 1982, p.11.

5. See 'The German Danger', *The Economist*, 30 January 1980.

6. Europe imports 90 per cent of its copper, tin, nickel, chromium, manganese, tungsten and phosphate rock, 75 per cent of its lead, 60 per cent of its zinc, 50 per cent of its bauxite, and 37 per cent of its iron ore. See Bernard Lietaer, *Europe + Latin America + the multinationals*, ECSIM/Gower, Farnborough, 1979, p.104. Poland was a source of coal and copper for West Germany, while the USSR itself is a potential source of gas (one of the points of tension during the Polish crisis). Mineral products and oil account for 55 per cent of the EEC's imports from the USSR.

7. See Don Thompson and Rodney Larson, *Where were you, brother?*, War on Want, London, 1978.

8. This phenomenon is known as corporatism, and it has fascinated American academics, whose own national traditions are much more anti-union. See H. Wilensky, *The New Corporatism, Centralization and the Welfare State*, Sage Publications, London and Beverly Hills, 1976; and Suzanne Berger *et al*, eds., *Organizing interests in Western Europe: pluralism, corporatism, and the transformation of politics*, Cambridge University Press, 1981. A British author making similar points is Keith Middlemass, *Politics in Industrial Society*, Andre Deutsch, London, 1979.

9. Lietaer, *op.cit.*, p.105.

10. See the pathbreaking study of West German capital abroad by Froebel, Heinrichs and Kreye, *The New International Division of Labour*, Cambridge University Press, 1980.

11. Investment in the USA sometimes satisfies both conditions (see Froebel, Heinrichs and Kreye, p.259) and Volkswagen is currently basing its global strategies on such developments, according to *The Economist*. Other industries, such as the W. German textile firms of which Fröebel, Heinrichs and Kreye made a special study, seem to be transferring production essentially to Eastern Europe and Southeast Asia: involving a loss of about 10 per cent of employment in this sector in the 1970s.

12. *North-South: A Programme For Survival*, Pan Books, London, 1980, p.13.

13. Froebel, Heinrichs and Kreye cite the following report by *Business International* in 1970 (p.326):

    . . . One company that is finding Brazil a profitable export base is Burroughs, which is manufacturing made-in-Brazil products for the US and other world markets . . . The electronic components from Burroughs Brazil are all shipped back to the US, where they are integrated into the memory cores of Burroughs' computer hardware. Air cargo is used both ways, but lower labour costs and quality work in Brazil have made the transportation and training expenses worthwhile . . . A number of factors lured Burroughs to Brazil for its electronic venture — in addition to its successful office machinery venture (there). Land in the Sao Paulo suburbs was reasonably priced and real labour productivity is high. *Labour, even in Sao Paulo, is inexpensive by world standards.* Burroughs had also found in its office machinery venture that workers are easily trained, and *Brazilian women* are particularly responsive to training requiring manual dexterity . . .'' (Italics added.)

14. Thus Jenny Pearce cites a Burroughs subsidiary in Guatemala and another elec-

tronics firm in Haiti, in *Under the Eagle: US Intervention in Central America and the Caribbean,* Latin America Bureau, London, 1981. These investments seem to be part of the American 'sunbelt' pattern, their owners having a strong affinity for extreme right wing ideas and, *inter alia,* for the global philosophy of Ronald Reagan. A 1975 UNCTAD study found El Salvador to be the most important export platform in Latin America for the electronics industry, through Texas Instruments, which employed 1,800 workers. Cited in Froebel, Heinrichs and Kreye.

15. The point has been forcefully made by Amartya Sen, *Poverty and famines,* Oxford University Press, 1982. For a detailed critique of the Brandt Report, see Dudley Seers, 'North-South: Muddling morality and mutuality', and others in *Third World Quarterly,* II, 4, October 1980.

16. 'Imitation does not Work', *South,* 4, 15 January-February 1981.

17. *South, op.cit.* Prebisch coupled this idea with his better known theory that terms of trade for primary products exported by the South showed a secular tendency to decline, long before Emmanuel produced a more elaborate version of the idea. See J. Love, 'Raul Prebisch and the Origins of the Doctrine of Unequal Exchange', *Latin American Research Review,* XV, 3, 1980.

18. These problems are of course closely connected with the West's own struggle with inflation and the oligopolistic powers of its principal producers.

19. Bernard Lietaer, *Europe + Latin America + the multinationals, op.cit.*

20. British oil interests played an historic role in developing oil production in Trinidad and Venezuela. Besides these fields, Royal Dutch Shell is currently exploring for oil in Argentina and for other minerals in Brazil. Elf Acquitaine is producing oil in Guatemala and searching for it in Brazil and Colombia: it also owns holdings in Nicaragua. Historically, British interests also played an important role in the development of Chilean nitrates, only to be displaced by Americans in the 1920s.

21. L.G. Franko, *The European Multinationals,* Harper & Row, London, 1976, p.107.

22. See Kirsch, *op.cit.,* and Warren Dean, *The Industrialization of Sao Paulo,* University of Texas Press, Austin, 1969, p.55.

23. Franko, *op.cit.,* p.106.

24. Froebel, Heinrichs and Kreye, *op cit.,* give the following picture for West German investment in 1961-1976: p.202, 216.

|  | All German sub-sidiaries | Chemicals |
|---|---|---|
| Brazil | 267 | 61 |
| Argentina | 52 | 14 |
| Mexico | 63 | 27 |
| Colombia | 15 | 10 |
| Chile | 13 | 9 |
| Venezuela | 12 | 4 |
| Peru | 11 | 8 |
| Uruguay | 10 | 4 |
| Guatemala | 7 | 6 |
| El Salvador | 4 | 3 |
| Puerto Rico | 3 | 1 |
| Dominican Republic | 2 | 1 |
| Nicaragua | 2 | 1 |
| Bolivia | 1 | 1 |
| Trinidad & Tobago | 1 | — |
| Netherlands Antilles | 1 | — |

25. See Simon Mitchell, ed., *The Logic of Poverty: The Case of the Brazilian North East*, Routledge and Kegan Paul, London, 1981, p.6. In 1978 in Sao Paulo, the centre of Brazil's industrial development, 24 per cent of the population with a money income of some kind were earning less than the minimum legal wage, then worth a mere US$19 a month and 17.5 per cent of the population over 10 were illiterate, in both cases a slight increase over 1977 figures. *Latin American Reports: Brazil*, 4 July 1980.

26. The recent economic history of Brazil has become an academic industry in its own right. A good survey of the debates and evidence is provided by Jose Serra in his 'Three mistaken theses regarding the connection between industrialization and authoritarian regimes', in *The new authoritarianism in Latin America*, ed. by David Collier, Princeton University Press, 1979.

27. For an account of the peasants' leagues see E. DeKadt, *Catholic Radicals in Brazil*, Oxford University Press, 1970.

28. René Dreifuss, *1964: A Conquista do Estado*, Editora Vôces, Petrópolis, 1981, p.55.

29. What follows is based essentially on Dreifuss's patient and pathbreaking work in tracking down the interconnections of the Brazilian and foreign elite, first presented as a Ph.D. thesis at the University of Glasgow in 1980 *(State, Class, and the Organic Elite: The Formation of An Entrepreneurial Order in Brazil, 1961-1965)*. References are to the published Brazilian edition.

30. IBAD, Instituto Brasileira de Acao Democrática, was a political organization created by local entrepreneurs to oppose Goulart in the late 1950s (Dreifuss, p.101ff.). IPES, Instituto de Pesquisas e Estudos Sociais, was a supposedly more academic institution, perhaps a little like a British Centre for Policy Studies, uniting Brazilian businessmen who were associates of multinational interests, retired army officers such as the crucially important military theoretician, General Golbery do Couto e Silva, and other local entrepreneurs. Essentially, it provided a centre of strategic studies and a cover for short-term planning, on the part of those responsible for the coup.

Among the contributors to the Rio branch of IPES were local subsidiaries of the Chase Manhattan Bank of New York, American and British insurance companies, Esso Brasileira de Petróleo, Hoechst do Brasil, Bethlehem Steel, Coca-Cola Indústria e Comércio Ltd, British tobacco interests, the British Match Corporation, and Remington Rand do Brasil (Dreifuss, Appendix H). Most finance, however, was channelled through local business organizations in which the multinationals participated.

31. Dreifuss, p.138. The report was prepared by a local firm of management consultants.

32. Dreifuss gives details of the creation of a Rockefeller think-tank on the area in the late 1950s and early 1960s, in which European interests were deeply involved, notably the Atlantic Community Development Group for Latin America, ADELA. In 1972, the list of ADELA's shareholders included such major British interests as Lloyd's, the Bank of London and South America, ICI, Royal Dutch Shell, Unilever, Rio Tinto Zinc, and such major continental European firms as Fiat, Nestlé, Pirelli, Ciba-Geigy, Saab-Scania, Metallgesellschaft and Farbwerke Hoechst. See Dreifuss, Appendix A.

Rockefeller's interest in strategic plans for the continent is however well known, through the Rockefeller Report on the Americas (1969) which recommended the end of the existing local emphasis on industrialization and a switch towards the production of primary products which enjoyed a 'comparative advantage' in relation to the American and world economies — the kind of economic strategy since put into effect in Chile, and now being undertaken in Argentina, at the cost of dismantling large sections of the existing industrial structure.

33. Dreifuss, p.87.
34. Royal Dutch Shell would of course have been a potential beneficiary of any move to privatize the state's existing oil company, Petrobrás, or limit its activities.
35. Dreifuss, p.78. Italics added.
36. The Brazilian state has taken steps in all these directions since the coup, more particularly since the upheavals in the world economy during the 1970s. But it has done so in the interests of a development strategy which essentially rests on foreign capital and thus as part of its own responsibility for safeguarding foreign capital's local interests. No foreign powers have thus been offended, nor have the international banks.
37. Dreifuss, p.80. Military officers were already playing a certain role as directors of private companies and local shareholders in foreign-owned firms by 1964. Volkswagen, Mercedes Benz and Schering all had generals sitting on their local boards (*ibid., p.78).
38. Italics added. Dreifuss, p.81.
39. R. Bonelli and P. Malan, 'The Brazilian Economy in the Seventies: Old and New Developments', *World Development*, 5, 1-2, 1977.
40. Serra, p.146.
41. See Carlos Filgueira, 'Consumerism and the New Orthodoxy in Latin America', *IDS Bulletin*, 13, 1, December 1981. It takes an economist deeply steeped in the dogmas of free consumer choice to ignore the effects of company advertising campaigns and the careful fostering of consumerist values through the media, and assert that such patterns are evidence of popular support for this pattern of development.

    Meanwhile, the concentration of income in the hands of the upper middle classes continues to increase, with the numbers living below official definitions of the poverty line swelling from 77 per cent of the labour force in 1976 to 80 per cent in 1978. See *Latin American Regional Reports: Brazil*, 12 September 1980.
42. Serra, *op.cit.* E. Bacha suggests that for the Brazilian economy to operate at full capacity, the country would have had to run a commercial deficit of 45 per cent of the value of its total exports between 1964-1974, compared to a mere 11 per cent under the conditions of 1952-1963. See *World Development*, 5, 1-2, 1977.
43. *Latin American Regional Report: Brazil*, 8 February 1980.
44. In 1979, the four biggest privately-owned companies in Brazil were controlled by British or German interests: Mercedes Benz, Souza Cruz (controlled by British American Tobacco), Volkswagen do Brasil and Shell do Brasil.

    In 1980, according to the Banco Central, the US share in foreign capital's accumulated stake in Brazil amounted to 29 per cent, followed by West Germany with 15 per cent and Switzerland and Japan with 10 per cent each. These figures cover investment in all sectors.

    See *Latin American Regional Reports: Brazil*, 2 January 1981 and 17 April 1981.
45. *Latin American Regional Reports: Brazil*, 1 January 1982.
46. See NACLA's survey of these developments, 'Car Wars', *NACLA Report on the Americas*, XIII, 4, July-August 1979.
47. *The Economist*, 16-22 January 1982, p.62. See Rhys Jenkins' article elsewhere in this collection.
48. *Idem.*
49. *The New International Division of Labour, op.cit.*

# LATIN AMERICA AND WESTERN EUROPE: TOWARDS A NEW INTERNATIONAL SUBSYSTEM?

*Wolf Grabendorff*

Latin America belongs to the 'latecomers' in the international system. There are good reasons for this, in particular the overwhelming hegemonic role the United States played in the foreign relations of most Latin American states. However, there can be no doubt that at the beginning of the 1980s, in spite of the United States' efforts to re-strengthen its hegemony in Latin America, this hegemonic power can no longer be seen as the link between Latin America and the rest of the world. Latin America became an active participant in international politics at the end of the 1970s, through an ongoing process which includes such factors as reactions to economic necessities, the shift of balance in international politics which places a greater importance on the Third World in the international system, and finally, the reaction to the other actors in the international system which began to take a greater interest in Latin America.

This analysis will examine to what extent Western Europe can play a meaningful role in the process by which Latin America, both as a region and as individual states, will become integrated into the international system. Internationally, this will not be an economic analysis, although obviously economic interests cannot be ignored in the study of international relations; rather, the aim is to point out that for many decades certain political affinities between Western Europe and Latin America have remained buried, in part because Western Europe was concerned purely with its own problems, but in part, too, because the United States had defined the idea of the Western Hemisphere in such exclusive terms that there remained little room for Latin America to form other close associations.

In order to evaluate the prospects for co-operation between Europe and Latin America, we shall first analyze the relative position of both regions in the international system. The expectations of both regions

41

can then be compared with one another. The analysis will then briefly address the question of the perspectives for further development of relations between the two regions. Finally, it will consider the possible advantages and disadvantages of closer co-operation for both sides as well as point out the external and internal obstacles to such co-operation.

## The Integration of Latin America in the International System

The changing role of Latin America in the international system can best be seen in a comparison between Latin American reactions to United States policies in Guatemala in 1954 and, 25 years later, in Nicaragua in 1979. Even without any broad interpretation of shifts in the international balance of power, it has become obvious that Latin America is playing a very different role at the beginning of the 1980s. The discussion about whether this is a result of the weakening of the hegemonic power of the United States, or of the strengthening of the bargaining power and economic and political influence of the Latin American states, is not as important as the fact that such a development is irreversible.

For most of the three decades since the founding of the Organization of American States (OAS), Latin America has been tied into the subsystem of the 'Western Hemisphere'. The inter-American system was simultaneously a source of irritation as well as a security umbrella for all Latin American states, including Cuba which, in spite of having left this subsystem, owes its international manoeuvrability precisely to the fact that geographically it remains a part of the system.

The 'Western Hemisphere' subsystem of international politics has, by now, been succeeded, and to a certain extent even replaced, by four new subsystems integrating Latin America into the international system:
1. Latin America-Western Europe,
2. Latin America-Pacific states, with emphasis on Japan,
3. Latin America-Africa and the Middle East,
4. Latin America-socialist states.

The political participation or integration of Latin America as a region or at least of several important Latin American states in these four subsystems is not necessarily a substitute for the previously dominant Western Hemisphere subsystem. Rather, in order to identify the particular emphasis which Latin America places on its membership in these various subsystems, one must consider what its priorities are, particularly in the economic field. Another factor is the political orientation of the domestic regimes of the respective Latin American states.

It is possible to be a member of several subsystems simultaneously. However, the individual Latin American states usually go through phases, shifting their priorities from one subsystem to the other. A good example is Brazil, which for most of the 1970s concentrated its political and economic interests on the Latin America-Western Europe subsystem, whereas by the beginning of the 1980s it had clearly shifted its priorities to the Latin America-Africa and Middle East subsystem.

The geographic situations and the specific economic and political requirements of each individual Latin American state make a choice of participation in the subsystem not only possible but also necessary. Apparently this increases the heterogeneity of Latin America, since, for example, Mexico, Peru and Chile are more involved in the Latin America-Pacific subsystem, while Brazil, Argentina and Venezuela participate more in the Latin America-Africa and the Middle East subsystem. Nevertheless, the case of OPEC — although this is exceptional — has shown that politically and economically effective subsystems are by no means limited to certain geographic regions. Of greater importance is that all participants in such a subsystem should share certain characteristics, both in terms of their alliance needs as well as with regard to their commonalities with other actors in the international hierarchy. This was, and to a certain extent still is true for the Western Hemisphere subsystem.

The ability of Latin America to become integrated into these new subsystems and to participate in their formation within the international system clearly demonstrates that since the mid-1970s the Latin American region at various levels has become ever more active and more competent in the field of foreign relations. Thus in any restructuring of the international system it finds itself in the position of being able to safeguard its own interests or at least to prevent them being ignored.

It is no mere accident that one can draw certain parallels with Western Europe's membership of certain subsystems. Similar to the Western Hemisphere subsystem, the Atlantic subsystem dominated the international ties of Western Europe for many decades. In the meantime, however, in spite of the continued dominance of membership in this system, other subsystems have taken their places in the international politics of Europe, for example 'Western Europe-Mediterranean', 'Western Europe-Arab states', 'Western Europe-ASEAN states' and in particular 'Western Europe-socialist states'.

The process of disengagement, that is, the shifting of sovereign decisions from the dominant subsystem to other subsystems in formation has been difficult for both the West Europeans and the Latin

43

Americans, and will remain so during the 1980s. It is a particularly difficult and slow process to switch structural transnational relationships from one subsystem to another. This can often be accomplished only through a change in ruling elites or a change in generation within the ruling elite. For this reason the advantages to be derived from membership of the various subsystems is rather limited. Apparently the diversification of foreign relations, or each switch of priorities, must be obtained at the cost of certain disadvantages in regard to the previous situation. One must also anticipate that the dominant partner, that is, the United States, will consciously try to hinder the 'drift' of either Western Europe or Latin America out of its own sphere of influence.

At the same time, and despite all setbacks, the process of growing diversification indicates a growing independence in the foreign relations of the individual Latin American actors. This independence almost automatically contributes to a constant acceleration of the process of emancipation. Since foreign policy in Latin America has always been a form of survival strategy, most Latin American countries could not have become more industrialized without strong foreign partners. This means that Latin America's experience of unequal international relationships has shown how important it is to diversify this pattern of relations in order to avoid the pressures of ties which bind it too closely to either one of the superpowers or economic spheres.

Latin America's specific problems may well be that its integration into the world market took place many generations earlier than its integration into the international political system. Thus its efforts to strike a balance between its international economic and its international political integration are both extremely important and at the same time understandable. Only the ability of Latin America to form new alliances in the international system can guarantee that classic North-South relations will be replaced by a multi-polar network of interdependencies on various levels.

## Characteristics of the Latin America-Western Europe Subsystem

The development of the Latin America-Western Europe subsystem did not begin in the mid-1970s. Rather, the historical and cultural ties between the two continents have remained intact since colonial times. In spite of the overwhelming political, economic and military influence of the United States in the past thirty years, certain patterns of

44

interaction with Europe were maintained. However, they found their expression more in bilateral and transnational terms than in the form of an inter-regional policy.

What precisely are the attributes shared by both partners with regard to their positions within the international system? The element they share most is probably their vulnerability to actions by the United States. This was true both for Latin America's relations within the inter-American system as well as for Western Europe's relations within the post-war Atlantic Alliance. For very different historical reasons, both regions assumed the role of a junior partner to the United States, and on both sides moves towards greater autonomy are accompanied by an awareness of their own economic, political and above all military vulnerability.

The process of forming close relations between Latin America and Western Europe was therefore pursued with an eye towards the possible reaction of the common hegemonic power. The fact that both sides have emphasized the economic aspects of their relationship is not least due to the assumption that the United States generally welcomes commercial relations between Western Europe and Latin America. Yet the US would certainly not tolerate a substantial increase in political relations, and would have strong objection to greater co-operation in the area of security policies. This is also the basis for the great sensitivity shown by the United States toward West European initiatives in Central America. The idea that medium powers within the Western system, in this case France and Mexico, take initiatives which are in direct contradiction to the global goals and security perceptions of the United States, will inevitably affect their respective relationships within the USA-Western Europe and USA-Latin America subsystems which have been dominated until now. So far the United States had considered both regions extremely important economically, but their political importance was regarded as secondary.

In addition, both Latin America and Western Europe share a total disinterest in hegemonic aspirations and place great emphasis on peace-keeping measures as well as on demands for world-wide disarmament efforts. A further common feature is the generally co-operative structure of each region. In contrast to the regional systems of the Arab states for example, they are not structured by or for conflict, but rather, are willing to live side by side with ideologically different power centres and neighbours.

In general, the characteristic shared by both regions in regard to their respective roles within the international system reveal an identical thrust toward the increased emancipation of the medium powers. The development of both Latin America and Western Europe into relatively independent centres of power has, however, only been possible because of the relative loss of hegemonic power by the United States. The common interest of both regions thus continues to be a decrease in the influence of the superpowers of the world, since only under such a premise would a further increase in their own manoeuvrability in international politics be possible — either as a joint actor or in regard to the foreign policies pursued individually.

If one compares the elements shared by both regions with the significant differences in their international positions, the differences between First and Third World looms particularly large. Although Latin America is today without doubt the most developed region of the Third World, there still exists a very basic difference between Latin America and the First World. It is characterized by the contrast between the status defenders and the status seekers within the international hierarchy. Western Europe's political identity is marked by the experiences of the East-West conflict. Its level of consciousness about the North-South conflict, in comparison to that of Latin America, is therefore relatively underdeveloped. Conversely, the same can be said to apply to Latin America's awareness of the determining influences of the East-West conflict on the international system. These basic differences, however, will become ever less distinct as the North-South conflict obscures the East-West conflict by increasingly drawing the Third World into the polarization between East and West.

The prevailing concept of viewing the Third World only from the perspective that it could be a threat, that is, as a 'security risk', or that it might be a source for profitable economic relations, is gradually being replaced in Western Europe by the recognition that the greater integration of Latin America must be accompanied by its greater participation in the decision-making process within the international system. Another difference, however, is that Western Europe is much more vulnerable as regards its security than is Latin America. Western Europe still finds itself at the centre of the conflict between the superpowers, as a part of the world where both superpowers attempt to make their ideological concepts prevail.

The resulting perceptions of the West Europeans in regard to certain events in the international system must necessarily be different from those of the isolated Latin Americans. To the extent, however, that Latin America itself increasingly globalizes its own foreign relations through participation in other subsystems such as Latin America-Pacific states, Latin America-Africa and Middle East, and Latin America-socialist states, this difference between Western Europe and Latin America in the international system will tend to become less distinct in the course of the 1980s.

Another difference may assume increasing significance in coming years, namely the fact that Latin America's share of world production

46

will continue to grow, while Western Europe's relative share will tend to shrink. The result will be that the crass economic differences evident until now will gradually diminish, if one takes into account the statistical averages rather than per capita income. This trend, however, cannot disguise the fact that the total number of differences will still far outnumber the commonalities within the Latin America-Western Europe subsystem. Such a subsystem will therefore continue during the 1980s to be characterized by its asymmetry. Even if efforts to create more interdependence between the two regions were to succeed, this would contribute to an improvement in the position of both regions within the international system, yet would, on the other hand, be of uneven benefit to both regions.

### Expectations of the Partners within the Subsystem

Without too much exaggeration it can be said that the way the subsystem has performed so far fulfilled most of the expectations of the West Europeans and disappointed most of the hopes of the Latin Americans. Although the 'European card' has in certain cases and in certain transactions proved to be a very useful instrument enabling it to assert some independence from the hegemony of the United States, the Latin Americans never felt that the Europeans had responded to their expectations. On the contrary, in some parts of Latin America, Western Europe is seen merely as a representative of the United States with almost no freedom of manoeuvre, particularly where questions of world order are concerned. Most Latin Americans are willing to recognize that Western Europe — as in the case of Japan — is in a position to offer conditions as good as the United States in certain important areas such as credits, technology transfer and market access, but is unable or unwilling to link these economic transactions to political preconditions.

The Latin American criticism is as follows: Western Europe is so strongly tied to the coalition of interests of highly industrialized countries and so thoroughly dependent in its foreign policy actions on the United States that, with only a few exceptions, Latin America cannot expect all that much from the West Europeans where a change in the international order — and this does not just mean in the international economic order — must be achieved.

### a. Latin America

A realistic evaluation of Latin American expectations regarding Western Europe cannot, however, be made at this generalized level. In view of the enormous heterogeneity of Latin America, one must differentiate between four Latin American actors or groups:

1. Regional foreign representative, originally the Special Commission for Latin American Co-ordination (CECLA), later the Latin American Groups (GRULAs) in New York, Brussels and Geneva and today in particular the Latin American Economic System (SELA);
2. Latin American regional powers such as Brazil, Mexico, Venezuela and Argentina;
3. Latin American medium powers;
4. Latin American small states.

Only such a differentiation permits an understanding of the whole spectrum of Latin American expectations, which can then be compared with corresponding European expectations.

1. *Latin America as a regional actor* feels it has been discriminated against by Western Europe in the form of the EEC. It bases this feeling on the EEC's large number of association agreements with and preferences granted to a multitude of other developing countries. The hopes created with the famous 'Charter of Buenos Aires' in 1970 for a political dialogue with Western Europe and, in consequence, for a long-term agreement between both regions, have so far not been fulfilled. It has been mostly a 'dialogue of the mute' and the renewed call of SELA in Montevideo in 1978 to establish a framework for the various relations between both regions went almost unanswered. The expecations of SELA, of Latin America as a region, are geared to Western Europe as a region. Thus, its partner in any dialogue was and remains the European Community. The expectations are somewhat unrealistic insofar as the political forces within the European Community which might advocate such a Latin American 'association', however constructed, by no means carry enough weight. On the other hand, Latin America as a region has until now not been able to call greater attention to itself in Brussels despite some sporadic attempts to apply pressure. But with the political crisis in Central America and in the Caribbean, the recognition has grown, not in Brussels, but in the European Parliament, that there must be stronger political ties between Western Europe and Latin America. For the first time then, there exists the possibility that Latin America's expectations of the European Community may find a more willing ear.

2. The interests of *the Latin American regional powers* are in part similar to, but also in part very different from those of the region as a whole. All four states — Brazil, Mexico, Venezuela and Argentina — have decided to seek integration into the international system primarily — but not exclusively — at the national and not the regional level. This means that they have been intensely interested in forming Euro-

pean ties. Almost all of these four states have laid down similar criteria for their bilateral relations, in particular with Western Europe. Accordingly, their foreign policy partners must be able to offer the following;

— access to a large and diversified market;
— access to raw materials;
— access to financial resources;
— access to modern technology.

Even the two oil-exporting countries, Mexico and Venezuela, cannot do without access to financial markets. This means that only a few states could be considered suitable for relatively close co-operation, based on developmental and economic policy criteria. Besides the United States and Japan, this leaves only Western Europe. Given their enormous economic potential, the position of Latin America's leading powers in relation to Western Europe is extraordinarily strong.

The German-Brazilian nuclear deal is a good example of their success in playing the various Western industrialized countries off against each other, when large contracts are at stake.

For historical as well as geopolitical reasons the relations of Brazil and Argentina with Western Europe have grown exceptionally during the last decade. This does not mean, however, that the expectations held by these Latin American regional powers in regard to Western Europe can all be fulfilled in the near future. On the contrary, the rapid industrialization of these states and the concomitant necessity of competing with West European industrial goods on the world market have tended to lead to a decline in co-operation, especially in the field of economic policy. With the exception of Venezuela, these countries have concluded agreements with the EEC but are by no means enthusiastic about the way these have been implemented. They have therefore expressed more interest in bilateral relations with significant West European partners.

3. *The Latin American medium powers* include Chile, Peru, Colombia and Ecuador, which until now have not been able to 'go it alone' in their relations with Western Europe and have therefore always been more interested in establishing closer relations between the subregional integration mechanisms, such as that between the Andean Pact and the EEC. During the past few years the potential for achieving such an arrangement seemed relatively good, but because of the political situation in Bolivia it has been put on ice. The expectations of these states regarding Western Europe are couched more in terms of development aid than trade preferences. Because of their limited economic capacity, their potential to play the 'European card' against the United States is quite small. Consequently, their opportunities for foreign policy diversification appear extremely limited.

4. *The Latin American small states* include the whole of Central America and the Caribbean as well as the smaller states of South America. Because of their limited economic potential, they are primarily interested in improved relationships with Western Europe in terms of development aid. Tying the Central American and Caribbean states into a Lomé-type arrangement would to some extent meet the expectations of these countries. They are, however, unable to undertake any greater initiatives within the Latin America-Western Europe subsystem because given their geopolitical situation, most of them are extremely closely bound to the United States. Only when they try — as in the case of Nicaragua or Grenada — to pull away from the influence of the hegemonic power through a change of regime will Western Europe become a particularly significant partner for them. To what extent a consensus between a strongly anti-American regime and West European partners can be maintained remains to be seen.

## b. Western Europe

What are the expectations of Western Europe within the subsystem? In the past three decades the West Europeans have developed only a limited awareness of the problems in the region. Only after the emergence of the regional powers and their policy of diversification of external relations did Europe's position in Latin America grow stronger. Given the conflict-laden developments in other parts of the Third World, Latin America seemed like a promised land for a Western Europe craving energy and raw materials.

Latin America, with its population of 350 million, is Western Europe's largest market in the Third World. It is considerably more differentiated and receptive than Asia, the Arab countries or even Africa. Latin America is furthermore a region of untapped mineral deposits and fantastic energy resources. Because of these conditions, repeatedly emphasized by both sides, Western Europe has become accustomed to a relatively high degree of complementarity of the production structures of the two continents.

The discussion about a European political strategy toward Latin America has only just begun. There is still general uncertainty as to how to integrate bilateral and transnational relations into a functional system of inter-regional relations. Given the endemic instability of the political regimes in Latin America, Western Europe as a whole has rather avoided any definition of its relationship on the political level. More conservative groups in Europe are generally prepared to lend support to 'law and order' efforts by authoritarian regimes as a necessary precondition for economic growth, while the more progressive groups view social change as the only basis for long-term development in Latin America. One result of these different perceptions is that Latin America has earned a reputation in Western Europe for being an area of political, social and economic experimentation. In Europe the widespread tendency to apply ethnocentric standards to development in Latin America has not exactly contributed to finding a politically acceptable basis for co-operation with Latin America.

This problem also helps to explain why bilateral governmental relations have retained a rather formal character, whereas intense political relations in the last years have shifted to a sub-governmental level of transnational actors. The co-operation between respective political parties is certainly the best known of these relations, but the unions, the churches, a number of interest groups and scientific institutions have also contributed a great deal to what has become the 'European connection' in Latin America. The willingness of these European institutions to transfer human and material resources to support the political and/or social interests of their Latin American partners has without doubt contributed to the strengthening of civilian elites in many Latin American countries. In Western Europe this development is consciously viewed as a necessary corrective to the support given by the United States to military elites in Latin America.

Both sides place relatively high expectations on these transnational elements within the subsystem. From the West European perspective, they present a chance to provide support to counter-elites who might be able to initiate changes in generally outmoded political systems. This would also strengthen the democratic capacities of individual countries, based on imparting the pluralistic concept of the West European political philosophy to the various groups being supported. At the same time it cannot be overlooked in Western Europe that the ruling elites in each affected country view this kind of partisanship as interference in the internal affairs of the country and thus as a very negative aspect of European-Latin American relations.

In order to identify the various expectations on the European side, it seems useful to introduce four subdivisions:

1. Western Europe as the European Economic Community;
2. Western Europe as Christian Democratic Actor;
3. Western Europe as Social Democratic Actor;
4. Western Europe as individual countries (France, West Germany, Spain).

Only with an understanding of the differences in the perception of these various political actors does the diffused picture of West European relations with Latin America gain some clarity.

1. *Western Europe as the EEC*. It is doubtless correct to point out that European integration has both served as an example to Latin America

and been considered in Europe as exemplary for other regions. The effects of European integration on third countries, particularly in the case of Latin America, have become quite evident:

— in protectionism, inherent in any economic community (the best example being the protection of agricultural markets);
— in the preferential treatment of certain parts of the Third World originating from former colonial ties, particularly in Asia and Africa, which caused automatic discrimination against other developing countries;
— in the co-ordination of foreign trade policy within the EEC states, which renders almost impossible any political influence on trade policies at the bilateral level.

Despite repeated efforts at negotiations, inter-regional co-operation, such as with ASEAN states, has not yet been established with Latin America. In contrast to the European-Arab dialogue and also to the Mediterranean policy of the EEC, Latin America has not yet, even in the broadest sense, been included in security policy considerations of the EEC's foreign and economic policies.

In addition, West European consideration of US interests has so far prevented the EEC from taking steps toward global agreements on association or co-operation with Latin America. Such agreements could act as political signals to the United States, for which Latin America is indeed waiting and hoping, but which Western Europe is reluctant to provide.

Thinking in terms of geopolitical spheres of influence seems to be part and parcel of the decision-making in Brussels. From the point of view of the EEC, it has until now fared rather well with its policy of evasion and appeasement. The strategy of seeking acceptable arrangements with Latin America's regional powers while not granting any general regional preferences has proved successful especially because Latin America has been unable to conduct important negotiations with Brussels as a bloc. The initiatives of SELA could do little to change this situation, because they were repeatedly frustrated by the policies of Brazil and Argentina.

2. *Western Europe as Christian Democratic Actor*

The ideological link with Latin America was first introduced by Christian Democratic parties. Shortly after World War II, Catholic intellectuals from Western Europe exercised an exceptional influence on Latin American intellectuals through Catholic social teachings. This influence gained political importance through the efforts of Eduardo Frei in Chile, beginning in the early 1960s. Following him, Rafael Caldera has, since the end of the 1960s, continued to hold high the banner of Christian Democracy in Latin America from Venezuela.

Due to the electoral victory of Allende in Chile, the United States began to view Christian Democrats as a 'Kerensky movement' which would pave the way to power for more radical political parties and seemed no longer willing to tolerate it. Since then, however, the United States has welcomed the help of the Christian Democrats in stemming socialist and Marxist movements, particularly in the Central American region. The Christian Democratic international movement, leaning primarily on the European and Latin American parties, played an important role in the crisis in El Salvador by supporting the US backed President, José Napoleon Duarte. It would, however, be a mistake to see this as a typical expression of the interests of European Christian Democracy in Latin America. The United States' regional policy is by no means supported by a majority of the Christian Democrats in Western Europe although when it comes to keeping Marxist movements out of the political scene, the affinities between Christian Democrats and United States policy are greater than between the Social Democrats and US policy. Nevertheless, it can generally be said that the Christian Democrats share a much wider understanding of the specific problems facing Latin America than can generally be found in the United States. This also has to do with the fact that the large majority of the Latin American Christian Democrat parties are to the left of the average political and ideological position of the European Christian Democrats.

The expectations of the Christian Democrats can be summarized by saying that they are aware of the fact that it is impossible to achieve political stability in Latin America under the terms of US policy, that they would like to prevent a growth in the power of socialist or communist models, and that therefore it would be preferable to let the Christian Democrats accomplish the task of securing political stability. In this way, western interests would be maintained, while at the same time gaining greater autonomy for Latin American initiative. The concept of being able to become a third force in Latin America is threaded in various forms throughout the expectations of European Christian Democrats.

*3. Western Europe as Social Democratic Actor*
Since the second half of the 1970s — more precisely, following the congress of the Socialist International (SI) in Geneva in 1976, which proved to be of great programmatic, political and personnel importance — the influence of the social democratic movement in Latin America has grown considerably. This is mainly due to the growing importance of the Third World in international politics, for the influence of the Socialist International as a whole grew at the very moment when it opened its doors to the Third World and absorbed new

53

impulses from those areas, especially from Latin America. The basic premise of the SI and the social democratic parties in Western Europe is that a new international order cannot be limited to the field of international economics, but rather that, instead of power politics, a stronger participatory orientation in the international system must be achieved. Some, not without justification, have come to regard this as a third way, as a mixture of political realism and idealism. Yet in many social democratic parties there is a large gap between aspirations and political reality because the parties' interest in closer co-operation with Latin American partners is by no means always reflected in the foreign policy of the West European states, even where social democrats are in power. One problem of social democratic attitudes towards Latin America is that they use Latin America as a field for progressive, and, in the Marxist sense, anti-imperialistic foreign policy, as a tactic for fulfilling demands of the left wings within their own parties. That social democrats succeeded in establishing welfare states and economic democracy in Europe in contrast to conservative capitalism (à la Reagan or Thatcher) has lent the SI a certain mythic credibility. It would seem, however, that the SI's role in Latin America has been reduced to one of performing mainly a braking function against the hegemonic interests of the United States. Examples of such efforts are the SI's urging Carter to ensure that the military respect the election results in the Dominican Republic in 1978, that a solution was reached in Nicaragua in 1979 and that in 1980 an attempt was made to promote discussions on a political solution in El Salvador.

Given the enormous international magnetism of Willy Brandt, president of the SI, and the success of its actions, the danger arises that Europeans, but perhaps even more so Latin Americans, will tend to overestimate the influence of the SI. Similar to Christian Democratic experiences in the 1970s in Latin America, the social democratic initiatives are likely to see their influence wane during the 1980s.

4. *Western Europe as individual countries*
One should not underestimate the fact that individual states of Western Europe have repeatedly attempted to develop a special profile in Latin America. Italy must be included here, and recently France and the Federal Republic of Germany have become more active in their relations with Latin America. In addition, the special role of Spain as a self-designated 'bridgehead' to Latin America must be considered.

Under De Gaulle, France had repeatedly emphasized its Latin roots and tried to play a special role in Latin America, as a way of asserting

54

its independence from the United States in international affairs. France's efforts to seek its own profile in Latin America has found its particular expression since Mitterrand's election in its attempt to pursue a 'leftist policy' in Latin America; in particular, it would like to acquire an 'anti-imperialistic' image without endangering its sizeable economic interests in Latin America. Given its general agreement with Mexico's assessment of problem areas in Central America, France faces few risks. The more traditional ties with Peru, Argentina and Brazil, based to some extent on France's weapons sales, are now overshadowed by the new importance of Mexico. Foreign Minister Cheysson's doctrine that the three most significant leaders of the Third World today are Algeria, India and Mexico reveals that common interests with Mexico go far beyond any initiative favouring the opposition in El Salvador. For this reason the rejection of this initiative by authoritarian as well as elected regimes in Latin America had little effect on France. Mitterrand's expression of solidarity with the 'wretched of the earth' created some confusion not only in Latin America but also in Europe. But France expects developments in Latin America to confirm its view that medium powers in the Third World will increasingly become drawn into the international decision-making process and it hopes to pave the way for such development in Latin America.

Compared to those of France, the initiatives of the Federal Republic of Germany (FRG) in Latin America appear rather modest. In general the tolerance level in the FRG for new development models in the Third World is considerably higher than that in the USA. For this reason developments in Peru under Velasco, in Chile under Allende, and most recently in Nicaragua have always found a good deal of support in the Federal Republic. On the other hand, in contrast to the activities of some political parties, governmental initiatives have been rather cautious.

The West German-Brazilian nuclear deal illustrated the limited extent of the Federal Republic's political freedom to manoeuvre in Latin America, despite all the economic possibilities. It seems safe to assume, therefore, that the Federal Republic would accept the significant political costs of satisfying Latin American interests only where important matters are involved. On the other hand, the Federal Republic is committed to efforts to keep the superpowers out of Third World conflicts and to further the emancipation and independence of Third World countries. Both in the Middle East and in Southern Africa, the Federal Republic clearly prefers a regional as opposed to a global solution. It attempts to pursue a similar policy in Central America and the Caribbean, but because of the specific sensibilities of the United States in this area, it does not voice its policy goals quite so loudly.

The specific profiles of the countries of Western Europe in Latin America would be incomplete were Spain not included. Since its democratization, Spain has repeatedly emphasized its role as bridgehead between Western Europe and Latin America. But even after its forthcoming entry into the EEC, Spain will not have the political or the economic power to initiate a revision of the EEC's foreign economic policy in favour of Latin America. The high expectations which some Latin American countries hold about Spain's membership in the EEC seem therefore quite misplaced. On the contrary, given its character as a partially industrialized country with an important agricultural sector, Spain's entry into the EEC will be likely to increase competition with Latin American products in the Common Market. This does not necessarily rule out the potentially important Spanish contribution to a Latin America-Western Europe subsystem, particularly in the sphere of cultural relations, partly because of historical ties, but partly also because it is politically more fragile than other EEC states, Spain is in a better position to understand political developments in Latin America and to stimulate Western Europe to co-operate with that region.

## Perspectives for the Development of the Subsystem

The prospects for the Latin America-Western Europe subsystem during the 1980s are by no means negative, despite the differences in expectations of and possibilities open to the two partner regions. In this context, however, two factors important for co-operation on an interregional level must be considered: first, the role of the state, and second, the question of patterns of bilateral relations.

The concept of the state as an engine for development and as a corrective mechanism for distortions in the social fabric which occur through economic growth is for the most part a West European invention. The new interdependence in the international economic system will tend to make the role of the state grow even more in the future. To the extent that contractual relations between various regions develop, the state must not only serve as an instrument of control and guarantees, but it must also try to compensate for undesired domestic developments where structural changes occur due to the new international economic order. How the new subsystem will function in the international system depends to a large extent on the role of the state as a well-functioning mechanism, able to exercise control. Such a state, in order to perform its duties, requires domestic legitimacy. For this reason, given the West European intention of forming stable long-term relationships with Latin America, the establishment of participatory democracies in Latin America is essential. The precise form such democracies might take must, of course, be left up to the Latin American societies themselves.

In building the Latin American-Western Europe subsystem, it is further necessary to reduce the scope of bilateral relations, since here the asymmetry of the relationship is most blatantly evident. Bilateral relations are advantageous to the industrialized states insofar as political pressure can more easily be applied. Thus investment and development aid can be tied to a specific code of behaviour, and different, normally unrelated elements can be linked to each other in order to achieve desired results.

In contrast, relations between regional blocs have the advantage that the bargaining power on both sides is, if not identical, at least similar. Certain countries or even regions are thus prevented from 'going it alone'; the pursuit of particular or strictly national interests is made more difficult by tying them into a regional bargaining context. Latin America's earlier negative experiences with international integration have furthered the tendency on the part of certain individual states, in particular the regional powers, to establish themselves in the international hierarchy. This, however, not only places considerably greater demands on their ability to form alliances, but also clearly limits their negotiating power at least with other groups of states such as the EEC. In that sense the prospects for a further development of the Latin America-Western Europe subsystem can be considered hopeful only if SELA were successful after all in becoming the leader in negotiations for the whole of Latin America, thereby also strengthening relations between the two regional blocs.

The subsystem will be affected in the future by the fact that, because of the different positions on both sides of the North-South axis, what is disadvantageous to Western Europe is often advantageous to Latin America in the pursuit of its interests. For that reason alone, an extensive harmonization of interests is certainly not a realistic goal for the relations between the two regions. On the contrary, a number of obstacles will remain in the future. Among these is the problem of mutual toleration of different political systems and divergent concepts of economic order. The relationship between Western Europe and the socialist states during the last decade has shown, however, that agreement on most political questions is by no means a necessary prerequisite for the relatively good functioning of a subsystem in the international system. This is especially true in cases where the system — and this should apply to the Latin American-Western Europe subsystem in the 1980s as well — is concentrated mostly on economic relations. The functioning of such a subsystem becomes problematic only when the willingness to improve both the quantity and the quality of the relationship no longer exists. For that to happen, it must be possible to question the existing rules of the game, while at the same time both sides must be aware that only together can they effectively change these rules and guarantee their observation.

In this analysis of the viability of a Latin American-Western Europe subsystem, little was said about what the various stages and forms of co-operation during the last decades actually looked like, because the prerequisites for such a subsystem did not yet seem to exist in the international system. All international relations, whether bilateral or inter-regional, are subject to fluctuations. In view of the relative loss of influence of Western Europe and the simultaneous gain in international status of Latin America, the 1980s seem to offer a good political prospect for the subsystem described here. The instruments and levels for such a subsystem must still be tailored to the needs of both partners. Both sides have benefited from putting the 'trial and error' phase behind them. Both sides, however, have until now neither shown the political courage nor found the political style necessary for overcoming the obstacles outlined here.

# ISSUE AREAS

# EEC-LATIN AMERICA RELATIONS AND THE GLOBAL ECONOMIC CRISIS

*Miguel S. Wionczek*

In an extensive paper presented at an international seminar on EEC-Latin American relations, organized exactly two years ago by the Institute of European Studies of the Université Libre de Bruxelles,[1] I insisted that the world economy has been passing through a major global crisis which was bringing havoc to both the European Economic Community and Latin America. Consequently, the economic and political relations between these two regions must be considered within the broader framework of that crisis. Nothing happened during the past two years to alter my opinion. On the contrary, world economic conditions are getting progressively worse, according to the World Bank, IMF, UNCTAD, GATT, regional development banks and the UN regional economic commissions.

Consequently, this paper has been divided into three sections: the first deals with the present condition of the Latin American economy and of intra-Latin American economic co-operation; the second deals with the economic problems facing Western Europe and with the most recent attempts by the EEC to develop a policy towards the developing countries (including Latin America); and the third discusses the preconditions necessary for the development of mutually advantageous economic relations between the EEC and Latin America. It is clear that such relations can only develop in the context of a global recovery from the present worldwide crisis, a recovery which depends to a considerable extent upon a basic reorganization of the international economic order.

## Latin American Economic Co-operation Attempts in the Post-war Period and the Region's Present Economic Position

In the late sixties a review was published of the post-war regional economic integration schemes in the developing world for the purpose of finding out why most of them had proved to be more fragile, conflict-ridden and short-lived than their initial proponents had expected.[2] In the case of Latin American economic integration during the sixties, ample factual evidence exists to suggest that the continent was drifting aimlessly under the mounting pressures of unresolved internal and external problems.[3] Under these circumstances it was extremely difficult to predict in 1970, where the region would find itself, not just by 1985, when according to the Latin American Free Trade Association's (LAFTA) agreement of 1967, a Latin American common market was to be established, but even by 1980, the deadline at that point for LAFTA's becoming a full-fledged free trade zone. The uncertainty felt 10 years ago was rooted in its failure to implement any long-overdue economic, social and political reforms successfully. Unable to resolve the underdevelopment problems it had inherited from the past, Latin America was poorly equipped to deal with the new problems that were emerging in a post-war world characterized by technological revolution, rising consumer expectations, and a demographic explosion. It is a pity that the post-1970 developments in Latin America proved the author's earlier pessimistic diagnoses to be largely correct with respect to the future of regional economic integration.

Progress in the field of Latin American economic integration during the seventies was slow. LAFTA, subject to a new series of 'review meetings' in 1980 after the failure of similar exercises in 1974 and 1975, continued to be a non-actor on the regional economic scene. In 1975 LAFTA was substituted as the locus for a regional development policy by a loose arrangement known as the Latin American Economic System (SELA). LAFTA's ambitious scheme for establishing the schedule for regional commitments on trade liberalization, industrial co-operation and the harmonization of other major economic policies was abandoned. SELA became no more than a limited co-operation mechanism for a few specific multinational investment projects and an informal regional co-ordinator for economic negotiation with the outside world. When compared to the scope of the proposals for regional integration which circulated in Latin America around 1960, SELA's achievements are very modest indeed. To date the achievements of LAFTA II, established in 1980 under the name of the Latin American Integration Association (LAIA) are negligible.[4]

In view of the growing obstacles to trade liberalization which led LAFTA's signatories to postpone, in 1969, the establishment of a Latin American free trade zone until 1980, and then forced them in 1974 to suspend its date indefinitely, two subregional co-operation schemes appeared in South America in the late sixties. The Andean Common Market was born in the north of the region in 1969 through the Cartagena Agreement, and the La Plata Basin Group was organized concurrently in the south. The first of these two subregional groupings placed emphasis upon the distribution of new activities in a few dynamic industrial sectors. The objective of the second was to improve subregional physical infrastructure. Although both co-operation schemes led to the emergence of new links among their respective neighbouring members, the new groupings had a very limited impact upon Latin America's growth rates and the direction and composition of its external trade. The same may be said about the Central American Common Market, which was established in 1958. Anyone cognizant of the present socio-political developments in El Salvador and Guatemala is aware that there is no meaningful economic integration in the Central American isthmus.

All five post-war integration schemes, therefore, contributed only marginally to the industrialization and structural transformation of Latin America. While some external observers claim that the region became the middle-class member of the underdeveloped world during the post-war period, this is only true when Latin America is compared with Africa and Southern Asia. In relation to the northern industrial countries, whether free-market or socialist economies, Latin America continues to be extremely underdeveloped. In addition the region's relative backwardness in terms of income, welfare, and social modernization has increased steadily.

It was clear ten years ago, therefore, that Latin America was unable, rather than unwilling, to elaborate a common economic policy.[5] Over the past thirty years, the development strategy of most, if not all, Latin American countries reflected a mixture of three different growth models, centred successively, but not exclusively, on import-substituting industrialization, regional trade integration, and efforts to export manufactured goods to advanced countries. The social and economic consequences of the absence of an integrated approach to internal and regional economic problems in post-war Latin America were serious: import-substituting industrialization proved very costly in political and social terms; regional co-operation schemes did not help to accelerate economic growth; and the latest strategy — giving high priority to manufacturing for export — also brought disappointing results as the world economic crisis developed in the mid-seventies.

Given the fact that many developing economies of the Far East and the less-developed countries of Southern Europe did better than Latin America during the post-war period in terms of economic growth and export trade, there are reasons to believe that the disappointing Latin

American performance was largely due to inherited political, social and technological backwardness and not to the traditionally defined productive factor endowment. If it is true that export possibilities depend upon the size, structure and growth of domestic demand, and that without changes in the domestic demand profile an industrializing low-income country runs rapidly into a 'structural-lock' dilemma, then it is the avoidance of the Latin American post-war economic strategies of internal socio-economic structural changes, such as the improvement of human resource quality and of forms of social organization, which explains Latin America's failures. The region's post-war experiences would give credence to two basic propositions of the modern political economy: the first that the major cause of sustained economic development is knowledge and not international trade, and the second, that the basic problems of a socially acceptable economic growth policy are not technical but political and institutional.

A long and impressive list of factors responsible for the failure of the integration efforts has been formulated by Latin American and foreign economists and political scientists.[6] The first obstacle was thought to be the ambitious geographical scope of LAFTA where in the name of a Latin American community of interests, economies all at different levels of development were put under the same roof in the naive hope that regional trade liberalization would do the trick. It is only fair to add that the conflicts of interests arising from the different levels of development also plagued smaller, subregional integration schemes.[7]

The second obstacle had its roots in the flaws of the doctrine put forward by the UN Economic Commission for Latin America (ECLA) that had served as the rationale for the establishment of a Latin American free trade zone in 1960. At that time, ECLA claimed that Latin American countries must integrate because import-substitution on the national level had run its course as early as the mid-fifties. But the experiences of the 'big three' (Argentina, Brazil and Mexico) and of some middle-sized Latin American countries over the past two decades have shown that national industrialization programmes can continue in the region for a considerable time even without an increase in the level of protection as long as the constraints upon industrialization for the home market are not too severe, some outlets for manufacturing exports are found, and the nationalist ideology remains strong.

The preference shown by the capital exporting countries in the sixties for bilateral tied public loans and private suppliers' credit, instead of untied foreign aid, and in the seventies for private banking lending via Euro-markets, in lieu of multilateral public funding, only strengthened the propensity of the Latin American countries to follow national inward-directed development and industrialization policy. Whatever their external payments situation might have been, Latin American republics were swamped in the sixties, and even more so in the seventies, with offers of external credit for those individual industrial projects which resulted in the export of capital goods to the region. This anarchic external financing was welcome in Latin America because it provided an excuse for not initiating the politically difficult modernization of the productive structure. Moreover, not only did it act as a brake upon the emergence of regional industrial policies, but it led to the accumulation of an external debt burden whose political and financial consequences went largely unnoticed by the borrowers in the less developed countries until the second 1979-80 oil price increase.[8]

The absence of co-ordinated aid policies towards Latin America among the donor countries, and the lack of interest on the part of the US in providing political and financial support for LAFTA and the two South American subregional groupings created another important obstacle to integration. The United States attitude to LAFTA was ambivalent in the sixties, fluctuating between a 'hands-off' policy and one of 'neutral benevolence'. After LAFTA went into a coma around 1970, US attitudes or for that matter the attitudes of any external actor toward LAFTA and its successor LAIA became irrelevant. The US was openly hostile to the Andean Group whose rule regarding the common treatment of foreign investment (Decision 24), agreed upon in 1969, was considered inimical to US private interest. Moreover, US policy towards Latin American integration schemes, including the Central American Common Market prior to its paralysis in 1968 reflected an unsettled conflict of interests among two groups of US-based transnational corporations (TNC); one that saw prospects for the expansion of their activities in the opening of a regional market and another that was fairly satisfied with the benefits of working under inward-directed national import-substitution schemes.

Finally, an intra-regional conflict of interests with regards to foreign private investment should also be mentioned. It involved, on the one hand, larger countries, which were worried about the possible entry of transnational corporations into the less-developed republics for the purpose of assemblying manufactured goods for the regional market and, on the other, smaller republics that were afraid the transnationals would be concentrated in the larger countries. It is easy to see, therefore, not only why no common policy towards foreign investment was ever successful in Latin America, but also why its establishment in the Andean Group brought about serious tensions within the Group and between the subregion and the US.

All the difficulties that arose in the Latin America integration schemes strongly suggest that, first, there is no cheap and painless way towards economic integration in the context of underdevelopment; second, that integration cannot be a substitute for reforms of the antiquated social and productive structures at the national level and, third that its success depends largely upon the ability and the willingness of the member countries to devise jointly a set of regional mechanisms providing for a reasonably equitable distribution of gains and losses from regional economic co-operation with due regard being given to the large initial differences in the development level of the participating countries. Since the equal distribution of gains and losses from integration is not only a political concept but a concept built around perceptions (and not trade statistics), it must be handled through constant negotiations involving the mutual abdication of certain aspects of national political and economic sovereignty. Such abdication is feasible only if the overall external conditions are propitious for the sustained economic growth of an integrating region and the individual partners perceive long-term political benefits from the integration. Since neither of these two conditions was present in Latin America, its integration attempts stagnated.

In short, economic integration is a political game and not an economic exercise, a point which hardly needs any elaboration in the capitals of the European Economic Community member countries. This is even truer in a generally underdeveloped region like Latin America, where the infrastructural links between its different parts are weak, differences in development levels are staggering, trade flows are directed mainly to the outside world, the distribution of economic power among the individual countries is extremely uneven, and all sorts of special bilateral quasi-colonial relations with the outside superpower are present.

The long-standing failure of regional economic integration attempts together with the global crisis of the seventies did Latin America a lot of damage. The evidence of the present close to disastrous situation is available in the 1980 report on *Economic and Social Progress in Latin America,* released in October 1981 by the Washington-based Inter-American Development Bank (IDB) and in the brief report by the Santiago-based ECLA Executive Secretary Enrique Iglesias, who in late December 1981 offered a review of the Latin American economic developments which occurred last year.[9]

Portraying the region as a victim of an international trade slowdown and other economic forces outside its control the IDB report made the following major points:

a. Although in 1980 the Latin American economies grew at a much more rapid rate than those of the industrialized nations over the last two decades, the gap in per capita product between the Latin American and the industrialized nations, the gross national product in relation to the size of the population, has widened.

b. Manufacturing growth has dropped from 7.2 per cent in 1979 to 4.6 per cent in 1980, a lower figure than all but two of those recorded in the seventies.

c. With an agricultural sector growth rate at 2.9 per cent almost totally offset by population growth, the region is turning increasingly to imported food.

d. Oil production in Latin America, led by Mexico, grew by 10 per cent in 1980, faster than that of any other region of the world. Latin America now produces 9.8 per cent of the world's petroleum output, up from 7.7 per cent in 1977.

e. Population growth, three times that of the industrialized countries, continues to be a serious obstacle, not only holding down the per capita product and offsetting agricultural development, but also contributing to the persistent social gap between the region's rich and poor.

Warning that the encouraging developments of the last 10 to 20 years in Latin America were threatened by international economic trends and market forces and noting the increase in external indebtedness and debt service payments — requiring countries to dip into reserves and reversing a three-year trend toward reserve accumulation — the 1980 IDB report concluded that

It is imperative for the region, especially for the medium and relatively less developed countries, to have external markets that will enable them to revitalize their exports and to obtain external financial resources consistent with their economic capacity and needs.

But imports of manufactured goods from Latin America by the United States grew by only 8.1 per cent in 1980, a precipitous drop from the 21.8 per cent growth in 1979. Exports to Western Europe have also declined. These export and import trends, coupled with the loss of foreign exchange in increased interest payments and profits leaving the region, led to a rise in the regional balance of payments deficit from $18.7 billion in 1979 to more than $27 billion in 1980.

One might have reacted to the IBD report, released in October 1981, that while the overall picture was far from good, the Latin American economy could easily have fared much worse in 1980. But less than three months later, in the final days of 1981, ECLA's Executive Secretary Iglesias provided evidence to suggest that what the IDB experts had considered as threats to the Latin American economic future in 1980 had become a dramatic reality one year later.

According to ECLA's preliminary data, Latin America's growth rate last year was the lowest for 35 years and average per capita income declined. Overall growth in the region was only 1.2 per cent, a large drop from the 5,8 per cent in 1980 and well below the rate of population increase. The average inflation rate in Latin America was 60 per cent, the worst figure ever recorded except for 1976. The balance of payments was in the red for the second year in a row. The current account was in deficit to a record $33.7 billion, nearly $6 billion up on the 1980 figure. The region's debt burden also became heavier. The disbursed foreign debt is estimated to have grown in 1981 by 15 per cent to almost $240 billion, four times the figure recorded in 1977.

The only major positive factor, according to Iglesias, was that the volume of Latin America exports rose by 11 per cent. This, he said, was 'extraordinary in view of the recessive conditions prevailing in the world economy and in international markets'. But Iglesias did not emphasize that this phenomenon was due principally to the fact that the volume of exports from Mexico (mostly oil) had risen by 36 per cent and that food exports from Brazil had risen by 24 per cent. In most of the non-petroleum exporting Latin American countries, however, bigger export volumes had been offset by a drop in unit prices such that the value of exports fell in all but six of the countries.

As in previous years, economic developments in Brazil and Argentina, two of the biggest economies in the region, had a major effect on the Latin American averages. In Brazil, GNP is estimated to have fallen by 3 per cent, against a growth rate of 8 per cent in the previous years. While manufacturing output dropped by 12 per cent, the inflation rate during the year reached 120 per cent. In Argentina, GNP dropped 6 per cent and industrial output shrank 15 per cent. The inflation rate was also running at 120 per cent.

Economic conditions both in Latin America and world-wide will continue to be difficult, Iglesias predicted, suggesting that to ameliorate the region's difficulties a new drive to bring in more foreign public and private finance was badly needed. But the question of who will bring capital to a stagnated and inflation-ridden region which owes the outside world US$240 billion was left unanswered. Other points on ECLA's agenda for action in the forthcoming years include: a) a better management of public expenditures, b) a sustained effort to increase non-traditional (manufacturing) exports to the rest of the world, c) an agricultural expansion policy and d) the design and implementation of a long-term energy policy aimed at achieving a major degree of regional autonomy in this sector. In some of these fields there may be room for EEC-Latin American co-operation.

# EEC's Policy towards Latin America and Other Developing Regions

Economic co-operation between Latin America and the European Economic Community has not been particularly close during the past twenty years, a fact which reflects not only the realities of global political life but also the short-term economic interests of both sides. Despite periodic dialogues between the two regions, involving economists and government officials, there is no evidence that Latin Americans as a group have made any advance towards establishing a coherent European policy, nor that the EEC member countries have designed a common approach towards Latin America. Although EEC-Latin America trade and investment links have expanded considerably of late, such links fall mainly under the category of private bilateral deals and not of inter-regional public matters, simply because, until very recently, both regions were of only marginal political and economic importance to each other. Moreover, there are three major obstacles built into the EEC system which hinder the expansion of economic relations between the two regions: EEC agricultural policy, the special trade regime for the ex-European colonies, and the persistent economic crisis conditions in Europe.

The EEC has concentrated its attention during the past fifteen years on the design of an African economic policy aimed at the establishment of an associated satellite free trade area.[10] During the same period, in spite of occasional statements regarding its relations with industrial Europe, Latin America has been working out painfully and with little success a common trade front in relation to the United States. Since the mid-seventies, the EEC's and Latin America's respective regional concerns were supplemented by the elaboration in the EEC of a general policy framework towards the LDCs and by Latin America's participation at the United Nations in the Group of 77, in the definition of the LDCs' common position on the major North-South issues.

During the seventies the EEC-Latin American contacts were few and far between and consisted mainly of expressions of Latin American concern over disadvantageous trends in the region's trade relations with the Community, and included criticism of the EEC's association policies. Such expressions which were contained in the Declaration of Buenos Aires, issued jointly by 22 Latin American countries in July 1970, were answered by the Community with the invitation to establish a permanent co-operation mechanism to be known as the Latin America/EEC Joint Committee. The creation of this body led, according to at least one observer, to the 'holding of periodic and uneventful meetings in which no improvement of the

long-expected (by Latin Americans) "dialogue" was achieved'[11] In
Latin American eyes this stagnation was due to the marginal interest
of the Community in the region, the priority given by the EEC to
Africa, and the development by the EEC member countries of relations with major Latin American countries on a purely bilateral basis.
The Community claimed, on the other hand, that Latin America was
unable to elaborate a global proposition for mutual co-operation, and
moreover, that Latin America was too heterogeneous a region to be
treated as a unity.

However, the EEC countries' have shown a slightly greater interest
in Latin America since 1979. It may well be that European initiatives
are directly related to the deepening international economic crisis and
to the EEC member countries' global search for new markets and
outlets for surplus investment funds. Also the very high degree of
European dependency on Africa for raw material supplies makes it
advisable to create alternative links with Latin America. It should be
noted that the EEC's initiatives have taken place parallel to its approaches to other developing regions such as the Association of South
East Asian Nations (ASEAN) and the Arab Middle East.

Thus, after some ten years of largely ceremonial relations between
the EEC and the Andean Group, the EEC Commission was reported
in February 1980 as having suggested to the Council of Ministers the
advisability of opening formal negotiations with the five Andean
countries along the lines of an agreement signed with Mexico in 1979
and another under negotiation with Brazil and finally signed in early
1980. According to an official EEC statement, the EEC contemplated
a basic non-preferential economic and trade co-operation agreement
with the Andean countries for the duration of five years which

in spite of the development level differences between the two parties, will put
them on an equal footing. In the commercial sphere, it will include the most-
favoured nation clause and the parties will commit themselves to fostering
trade expansion and diversification. With respect to economic co-operation,
the agreement will be forward-looking without excluding a priori any subject
which falls under the competence of the European Community. With a view
towards facilitating the implementation of the agreement, a mixed co-
operation committee will be set up to explore and to define the fields of possible common action and to act as a forum for consultations about the measures
which might have negative impact upon mutual trade.[12]

In May 1980 at a meeting of foreign ministers of the Andean Group
and the Community in Brussels it was agreed to initiate negotiations
on the so-called framework agreement. By the end of 1981 no such
framework agreement has been reached. Whatever limited purposes
this approach to the Andean Group may have, parallel EEC initiatives

directed towards the Third World do not seem to be getting very far either. The ASEAN-EEC meeting, held in Kuala Lumpur in March 1980, called to approve an economic co-operation agreement, dealt primarily with international politics and not with trade. According to one observer,

at the meeting the two parties occasionally wondered whether they were speaking the same language. And the economic agreement did little more than put on paper the minor concessions ASEAN had received from its European big brother over the years. These concessions are much less generous than those the Nine grant under the Lomé convention to countries in Africa, the Caribbean and the Pacific (ACP).[13]

Although it began in 1975 in the wake of the dramatic oil price increase the Euro-Arab dialogue has not made much progress either.[14] The EEC countries saw it as a means to forge stronger economic ties with the Arabs and to gain privileged, or at least stable, access to their oil. The Arabs' main objective was political: to push the EEC to take a more pro-Arab line in the Middle East dispute and to secure recognition for the PLO. As the EEC has consistently refused to allow the dialogue to encompass the Palestinian question and the Arab League has not been willing to discuss exclusively economic and technical matters, i.e. oil supply and pricing, the Euro-Arab dialogue at a senior political level was suspended in early 1979. It was reported later that the consultative mechanisms established for the Euro-Arab dialogue will not be the main forum for the EEC's economic initiatives with regard to the Middle East.

These examples of the EEC's approaches to different Third World subregions illustrate the difficulties arising from piecemeal dealing with specific LDC groups in the absence at Brussels of an agreed-upon framework for external policy toward the LDCs, containing both political and economic elements. What is worse, they are perceived in the Third World — perhaps injustly — as attempts to play small LDC groups against one another at a minimal political cost and optimal economic benefit for the Community. While the EEC's inability to work out a general policy framework for its relations with the developing world may be due to the conflicting national political interests of the member countries, the uneasy state of relations between the Community on the one hand and the United States and Japan on the other, and the recent intra-EEC economic conflicts, must be kept in mind when one looks at the future of the EEC-Latin American relations.

An ambitious example of the possibilities of economic rapprochement between Western Europe (especially the EEC) and Latin America has been offered in a recent study by a Belgian economist,

Bernard A. Lietaer.[15] The study suggests the development in Latin America of a new 'redistributive' development strategy based upon agricultural modernization, development of the hinterlands of the individual Latin American countries, and industrial sector specialization, all of them to be supported by European transnational capital and technology.

Such an economic strategy would not be aimed at inward-directed growth but 'at growth through specialization in sectors in which Latin America has a clear long-term structural advantage and which would be complementary to the major world markets'.[16] The political appeal of such a joint EEC-Latin American strategy for Latin America should arise, Lietaer suggests, from the fact that 'by choosing an ally which is geopolitically too weak to have illusions of hegemony, Latin America could improve its chances of being able to institute its own truly unique style of development'.[17] This position represents a step back from the ideas advanced in some Community circles in the late sixties which suggested that the EEC and Latin America might form a useful alliance in moderating US economic domination of the Western Hemisphere.[18]

Assuming that a mutually acceptable agreement could be reached concerning the code of conduct of European transnationals in Latin America, certain ideas contained in the Lietaer study may sound appealing to some sectors of Latin American public opinion. It is less clear, however, whether such a 'diagonal' arrangement would substantially help Latin America to get out of its depressing socio-economic situation for which both structural underdevelopment and the growing difficulties of the world economy are responsible. In the present international situation, it seems highly unlikely that Latin America can expect much external short-run relief. This is illustrated by the present 'beggar your neighbour' economic policies of the major industrial countries, as witnessed by the EEC countries' continued increase in their protectionist measures.

It has been reported that the EEC Commission is about to decide that certain LDCs, specifically the so-called newly industrializing countries (NICs), are so developed and competitive that access for some of their products to the Community should be more tightly regulated. If recommendations to that effect were implemented, imports from countries such as South Korea, Hong Kong, Brazil or Mexico would be subject to stricter quotas or tariff ceilings, allegedly to allow the less competitive developing countries to sell these goods in the European market. What is thought to be aid to the poorest LDCs, is in reality a threat to exclude the imports from those LDCs which are in the position to compete with Community industries.

As a matter of fact it is far from sure whether the access to the EEC markets gained by Latin America and other developing regions under special preference arrangements can be preserved for much longer. The issue of preferential access for developing countries' manufactures to the EEC markets leads inevitably to the question of the EEC financial development aid to the Third World at a time of paralysis in the North-South global economic negotiations. The readers of this essay are strongly advised to look into the European Court of Auditors report for 1980, released in early 1982, on the subject of the administration of EEC aid to the LDCs. The content of this document, as an important British newspaper put it, 'will be seized with enthusiasm by advocates of a restructured and more disciplined political and administrative approach to development aid'.[19]

## Preconditions for Mutually Advantageous Economic Relations between the EEC and Latin America

The world economic situation is much more serious than most politicians and the establishment economists want to admit. It is time to accept, in the light of overwhelming evidence, that what happened in the seventies was not a succession of the accelerated business cycles, but a gestation of a protracted structural economic crisis whose end is still not in sight. One of the most outstanding economists of our times, Michael Kalecki, used to say that the capitalist world learned enough from the dramatic experience of the Great Depression of the thirties, not to permit it to happen again. Kalecki has been proved wrong on that key point. The world economy (including the socialist economy this time) is repeating the painful performance of the thirties. There is little need to repeat the factual and statistical evidence available from the OECD, GATT, UN agencies, the World Bank and the IMF.

According to the most recent OECD survey (released in late December 1981) most industrial market economies, except Japan and perhaps West Germany, will register no growth in 1982, while a slight decline in inflation (to 8.75 per cent from 9.5 per cent in 1981) will be offset in social terms by continued increase in unemployment from 7.25 per cent to over 8 per cent. In the US the Reagan administration's predictions of 5 per cent real GNP growth in 1982 belongs, to use the mildest language possible, to the 'science fiction' category. It is certain that unemployment will rise to about 10 per cent, a sustained level of joblessness unknown in the US since the Great Depression. Paradoxically, the record arms spending on both sides of the Atlantic is not helping the economic recovery as it did in the late thirties but instead is accelerating the crisis. The reasons are relatively simple: the frightening technological progress in the armaments field has completely

73

divorced the armaments' industry from the peacetime economy. Consequently, growing expenditures on the sophisticated means of mass extermination have lost their multiplier impact upon employment levels and commodity prices. If traditional policy makers and establishment economists, whether monetarists or supply-siders, are unaware of such simple facts of life it is because they are completely ignorant of the nature and socio-economic implications of the present advancement in military technology, which in addition to threatening the world with total destruction, feeds inflation, creates unemployment by mechanization and consumes the scarcest high-level technologically innovative human resources.

The adjustment policies followed by the advanced industrial countries (including all EEC member countries) during the seventies amounted to plans for a major economic slowdown as the only remedy to accelerating inflation. Under conditions of considerable and growing unemployment of both labour and productive capacity in the whole OECD area, the present global crisis will be deeper, more severe and perhaps longer than the Great Depression of the thirties. Warnings to that effect multiply. The most recent evaluation of the world trade and economic situation, made public by UNCTAD in Geneva in July 1981 has the following to say about the world-wide prospects for the eighties:

... The problems facing the world economy are not cyclical in nature but rather reflect deep-seated and long-term phenomena. While there are basic differences in the economic environments in which different countries and groups of countries find themselves, nevertheless there are a number of common factors which point to slower growth in the 1980's than in the previous three decades.[20]

The UNCTAD global report points out five major factors behind the expected slowdown of growth in the developed countries:
1. the unprecedented rates of growth of productivity of the post-war years cannot be maintained indefinitely,
2. labour force growth in the developed countries including socialist Europe will decline significantly,
3. the developed market-economy countries as a group have become increasingly dependent upon external sources for many of their raw material requirements, with energy being the most obvious example,
4. many of the developed market-economy countries have increasing difficulties in controlling their domestic price levels because the underlying causes of inflation are to be found for the most part in domestic economic and social structures, and
5. significant shifts are taking place in the nature and dimension of

74

the economic problems confronting the developed Western economies and their solutions generally call for the creation of a new social consensus before the requisite changes in economic policies can be made; restrictive monetary policies as the major policy tool in attempts to control inflation will not do the job.

Growth in developing countries in the 1980s under the most optimistic assumption, would only reach about 4.2 per cent per annum on average. Given the high level of population and labour force growth and the income distribution patterns in the LDCs, this slow rate of growth in the developing world will almost certainly increase political and social instability. This in turn will contribute to increase international tensions, and stimulate a further diversion of scarce national resources from productive capital investment to military expenditures.

History provides few examples (ends the UNCTAD report succinctly) where sustained and rapid increases in apparent military prowess have not led to opportunities to test that prowess. Such a patern of resource allocation hardly represents a practicable means of adjusting to unfavourable economic conditions nor would it be self-sustainable. It is essential that attention be given to the implications for the world economy of accelerating growth in developing countries of a kind which bears some relations to their development needs.[21]

The UNCTAD's deep concern with world economic prospects is shared by other international agencies such as GATT. The preview of GATT's annual report on international trade in 1979/80, released in early 1980 insists that the re-establishment (in the near future) in the industrialized countries of 'conditions in which investment activity can expand rapidly is vital in order to prevent very serious international economic difficulties'.[22] Under the policies, presently being followed by the US, the EEC and Japan, this expansion of domestic investment capacity in the Western industrial countries cannot be expected for quite a time. In the absence of such recovery, initiatives for economic rapprochement with some regional LDC groupings, including Latin America, will be largely irrelevant for the immediate future of both the EEC and the LDCs. They would be tantamount to traditional 'too little and too late' measures, in a situation calling for a global response to the combination of protracted structural stagnation and the downward phase of the trade and investment cycle.

One of the reasons why Latin America can expect few results from the latest EEC proposals on EEC-Latin American rapprochement stems not from their limited nature but from their lack of originality. The non-European industrial countries are thinking about Latin America along similar lines. Japan, for example, in early 1979, established a private consultative council to the Prime Minister 'to study how to enhance regional co-operation and harmonious relations within the Pacific basin region', including Latin America, or at least the Latin American Pacific coast countries from Mexico to Chile.[23] The Study Group, presided over by a leading Japanese economist, Saburo Okita, attempts to put new life into the idea of the Pacific Trade and Development Area launched in the late sixties. The Japanese scheme for the Pacific free trade and capital transfer area seems strikingly similar to those which are presently under discussion in some EEC countries. Thus, the best that Latin America can expect in the very near future is a race among the EEC, the US, and Japan for its natural resources and for its markets for capital investment, technology and capital goods. While such a race may offer major Latin American countries an opportunity to strike better commercial and financial deals with the industrial nations, it once again leaves unanswered those questions which relate to Latin America's basic underdevelopment problems and their political and social consequences.

All these considerations lead to the inescapable conclusion that in the absence of global economic stimulation there is no way to cope either with the stagnation in the advanced industrial countries or with the underdevelopment in Latin America and the other parts of the Third World. In that context, however, a set of proposals was made public in 1980 by a very respectable international independent commission, headed by the former West German Chancellor, Willy Brandt.[24] What the Brandt Commission wants to see on a world scale is the sort of radical change in the relations between rich and poor countries that has already occurred between rich and poor people in individual developed countries since the Industrial Revolution. What is more, the report argues, the proposed massive transfer of resources from rich advanced countries to the poor South is in the North's interest, and the North clearly includes the European Economic Community. Furthermore, the report insists that the governments of industrialized countries must be far more prepared than at present to open their markets to the exports of the developing countries for two reasons. First, technological change inside Western industrialized countries has caused far more unemployment than Third World exports and, second, in any case, the developed countries cannot live under the illusion that protectionism against the LDCs will solve their domestic problems. The industrial countries are going to have to come to grips with the industrial adjustment process sooner or later. The later it is, the more difficult it will be.

Although signatories to the Brandt Commission's report included such well-known EEC personalities as the former Prime Minister of the United Kingdom, Edward Heath, the former Prime Minister of

Sweden, Olaf Palme, and the former French Minister of Agriculture, Edgar Pisani, it did not get the support of the EEC member countries. Informally, it is reported that there are many people at the EEC who deplore its very poor timing and insist that in view of the present economic difficulties of the industrial countries the LDCs will have to wait for even a partial implementation of the Brandt Commission proposals. It is also reported that the prevailing view in Brussels is that it is up to the OPEC countries — responsible for the so-called oil crisis and for practically all other difficulties of the world economy — to help the non-oil exporting LDCs. There are also those who hopefully expect that the Brandt Commission proposals will die a natural death because inevitable strains are bound to appear not only between oil exporting and oil importing countries but also between the NICs and the least developed countries as well.

Independent from the fate of the Brandt Commission's proposals, global negotiations on North-South issues that were to be started at the UN in autumn 1980 did not move a single inch forward because of the US administration's veto and the indecision and ambivalence of the EEC positions confirmed at the so-called North-South mini-summit, held in Cancún, Mexico in October 1981.

The limited commitments which the Community is reported to offer for the North-South negotiations, if they are ever held, contrast sharply with Latin America's expectations. In the words of one major LDC participant in the debates on the agenda of these negotiations, while

the purpose of global negotiations is two-fold: to ensure the sustained growth of the world economy, and to attack the structural aspects of the existing economic order, behind the interplay of conflicting positions one finds two different concepts of international economic co-operation. One only contains a series of marginal concessions which do not basically affect the links of dependency and inequality; the other is concerned with the rational and equitable distribution of resources and the transformation of the existing order.[25]

As this writer put it some time back, the transformation of the existing order is urgently needed not because it is wicked, immoral or unjust, but because it is full of contradictions. In the long run it does not bring real benefits to anyone, due to its inadequacy in the rapidly changing international political, social and economic conditions.[26]

The best proof that the present international economic order is inadequate is that it has not prevented the world economy from falling into the present serious crisis, it has made a large contribution to the chaos pervading international financial relations, and has brought international political relations to a state of quasi-war among Western industrial countries, the Soviet bloc and the LDCs. At a time when even the future of the EEC seems to be endangered by the destructive political forces originating in both global and regional stagnation, it is really difficult to postulate any sort of mutually advantageous economic rapprochement between the EEC and Latin America along traditional lines.[27] It is hard to visualize how Latin America, or for that matter any other underdeveloped continent, can be thought able to provide the stimulus for economic recovery in the industrial countries by supporting the entire burden of such recovery. Conversely, endogenous economic recovery in the industrial world, accompanied by progress in the negotiations on the major North-South issues, offers a great deal of scope for co-operation between Latin America, rich in resources and potential markets, and the European Community. However, at present the prospects for such a new international framework are very bleak indeed. A large degree of responsibility for this sad state of affairs falls unfortunately on the EEC authorities in Brussels. The EEC Council of Ministers at its Luxembourg meeting in June 1981 did not accept the need to stress to the US and Japan the link between the economic and political security of Europe and 'the reestablishment of international economic relations offering sufficiently attractive prospects to its developing partners'.[28]

Reporting these and other developments in the European Community's relations with the developing world, the same source concluded that

The net result is that 1981 has seen yet more nails driven into the coffin of the hopes of the poorer countries for any major shift in the world's economic balance in their favour.[20]

 Under such conditions what can one really expect with regard to the future of the EEC-Latin American economic relations?

**Footnotes**

1. Miguel S. Wionczek, 'The Relations between the EEC and Latin America in the Context of a Global Economic Crisis', *La Communauté Européenne et l'Amérique Latine*, Institut d'Etudes Européennes, Editions de l'Université de Bruxelles, 1981.
2. Miguel S. Wionczek (ed.), *Economic Co-operation in Latin America, Africa and Asia: A Handbook of Documents*, Massachusetts Institute of Technology Press, Cambridge, Mass. and London, 1969.
3. Miguel S. Wionczek, 'The Rise and the Decline of Latin American Integration', *The Journal of Common Market Studies* (Oxford), IX, 1, March 1971.
4. Miguel S. Wionczek, 'La Evaluación del Tratado de Montevideo 1980 y las Perspectivas de las Acciones de Alcance Parcial de la ALADI', *Integración Latinoamericana* (Buenos Aires), 5, 50, September 1980.
5. Miguel S. Wionczek, 'Latin American Growth and Trade Strategies in the Post-

      war Period', *Development and Change* (The Hague), V, 1, 1973-74.

6.   See, for example, Edward Milenky, *The Politics of Regional Organization in Latin America: The Latin American Free Trade Association*, Praeger, New York, 1974 and Eduardo F. Lizano, *La Integración Económica Centroamericana*, 2 Vol., Fondo de Cultura Económica, México, 1975.

7.   Rafael Vargas-Hidalgo, 'The Crisis of the Andean Pact: Lessons for Integration among Developing Countries', *Journal of Common Market Studies*, XVII, 3, March 1973.

8.   George C. Abbott, *International Indebtedness and the Developing Countries*, Croom Helm, London, 1979.

9.   'La Evolución Económica de América Latina en 1981', *Notas Sobre la Economía y el Desarrollo de América Latina*, Servicios de Información de la CEPAL, 355/356, Enero de 1982.

10.   Sam Olofia, 'ECOWAS and the Lomé Convention: An Experiment in Complementary Conflicting Customs Union Arrangements', *Journal of Common Market Studies*, XVI, 1, September 1977.

11.   Blanca Muñiz, 'EEC-Latin America: A Relationship to be Defined', *Journal of Common Market Studies*, XIX, 1, September 1980.

12.   Comunidad Europea, 'Comisión Europea Propuso Abrir Negociaciones con Grupo Andino', *Comunicado de Prensa* 6/80, Santiago de Chile, Marzo de 1980 (the writer's translation from Spanish).

13.   'Asean and EEC: Politics before Business', *The Economist*, 15 March, 1980.

14.   David Allen, 'The Euro-Arab Dialogue', *Journal of Common Market Studies*, XVI, 4, June, 1978.

15.   B. Lietaer, *Europe + Latin America + Multinationals: A Positive Sum Game for the Exchange of Raw Materials and the Technology in the 1980s*, ECSIM/Saxon House, Brussels and London, 1979.

16.   *Ibid.*, p.159.

17.   *Ibid.*, p.155.

18.   Douglas Evans, *The Politics of Trade*, McGraw-Hill, New York, 1974.

19.   Larry Klinger, 'Why EEC Aid for the Third World Runs into Snags', *Financial Times* (London), 15 January 1982.

20.   UNCTAD, *Trade and Development Report 1981* (Report by the UNCTAD Secretariat), Geneva, 31 July 1981, TD/B/863 (mimeo), p.185.

21.   *Ibid.*, p.193.

22.   GATT, 'International Trade in 1979 and Its Present Prospects', *GATT Press Release*, 1256, Geneva, 15 February 1980.

23.   The Pacific Basin Co-operation Study Group, *Interim Report on the Pacific Basin Co-operation Concept* (translation), Tokyo, 14 November 1979.

24.   *North-South: A Programme for Survival, The Report of the Independent Commission on International Development Issues under the Chairmanship of Willy Brandt*, Pan Books, London, 1980.

25.   United Nations, *Report of the Committee of the Whole Established under General Assembly Resolution 32/174*, A/34/PV 104, New York, February 1980.

26.   Miguel S. Wionczek, 'The New International Economic Order: Past Failures and Future Prospects', *Development and Change* (The Hague), 10, 4, October 1979.

27.   On the growing intra-EEC problems see 'Saving the EEC' (editorial), *The Economist* (London), 28 November 1981.

28.   David Tonge, 'Trade Competes with Aid on North-South Relations', *Financial Times* (London) Special Supplement on Europe, 7 December 1981.

29.   *Ibid.*

# EUROPEAN SOCIAL DEMOCRACY LATIN AMERICA: THE CASE OF WEST GERMANY

*Tilman Evers*

## Introduction[1]

Amongst the many protagonists and policies which make up *the* European policy toward Latin America there is a new arrival: social democracy. It has a supranational co-ordinating body, the Socialist International (SI), which is active in Latin America representing the whole of international social democracy. But European social democracy still operates mainly as a supplement to national politics through its many constituent parties which share some common concerns but at times are at variance with each other and even in conflict. Within this spectrum, West German social democracy plays an influential role through the West German Social Democrat Party (SPD), the governing party of Europe's strongest economic power. The SPD has vast financial resources, long experience and a solid infrastructure, and is the only member party of the SI which can count upon a network of permanent representatives in Latin America through the Friedrich Ebert Foundation.

In my attempt to provide some kind of explanation for and analysis of the operation of European social democracy in Latin America I shall limit myself to the case of West German social democracy as this is the case I know best, and also because it plays a central role.

Strictly speaking the presence of the Socialist International in Latin America dates from 1955 when, a few years after it was re-founded in Europe (in 1951), a Latin America secretariat was installed in Montevideo. The SPD has had a permanent presence there since 1966 when the Friedrich Ebert Foundation, through which it works, founded the Latin America Institute for Social Research (ILDIS) in Santiago, Chile.[2] Nevertheless, this European presence acquired little political importance and for many years it limited itself to the role of observer.

80

The move towards more active political involvement came suddenly, in the mid-1970s. One can almost put a date to it: a meeting in Caracas from 23-25 May 1976 called the Conference of European and Latin American Leaders for International Democratic Solidarity. The initiative came from Willy Brandt, the former West German chancellor, president of the West German SPD and winner of the Nobel Peace Prize. The leading European social democrat and socialist leaders (Brandt, Kreisky, Palme, Soares, Gonzalez and others) met together with representatives from a wide range of Latin American political groupings united only by their disapproval of the number of military dictatorships in the region. In November of the same year, Brandt took over as president of the Socialist International at its 13th Conference in Geneva with the declared aim of revitalizing that 'venerable circle of friends' to include new participants from the Third World, and in particular from Latin America.[3]

In the following years the Socialist International sponsored an uninterrupted flow of conferences, meetings, political missions and declarations. These activities developed as much through the Socialist International as at a party to party bilateral level. The Socialist International dedicated a growing part of its attention to Latin America and has organized a number of special conferences. In 1979 it created a Socialist International Committee for Latin America and the Caribbean under the presidency of the Dominican, Pena Gomez, breaking with the historical Eurocentrism of the organization. In November 1980 a Committee in Defence of the Nicaraguan Revolution was created under the presidency of Felipe Gonzalez.

The most concrete financial and organizational support, however, is still organized first and foremost at a bilateral level, party to party. At this level, the most effective instrument is without doubt the Friedrich Ebert Foundation of the West German Social Democrat Party. Founded in 1925 'to facilitate a reasonable education for talented proletarian youth', it has turned into an operation the size of a government ministry with more than 600 collaborators (much more than the SI). Of these, 200 are permanently based in the 'developing' countries of Southern Europe, Africa, Asia and Latin America. Precisely because of the Foundation's non-official and apolitical image, they are able to carry out active political work which would normally be prohibited to any official foreign organization. Although it is formally separated from the state and the party it is in fact intimately involved in both and constitutes a multifunctional instrument in the hands of the West German SPD, uncontrolled by the party activists, parliament, the government or the general public. In the same way as other, less prominent, party foundations,[4] it receives vast state funds through the Ministry of Economic Co-operation (with the 'developing countries') which exercises little accountability.

The kinds of activities which European social democracy is developing at these two levels could not be more varied. They range from political and material help for the armed struggle in Central America to 'marketing' for European multinational companies, together with public declarations, seminars, grants, technical training and advice in the trade union and co-operative field, adult education, mass communications, planning, agrarian reform, credit systems etc, plus direct organizing and financial help to political parties and their electoral campaigns.

In organizing these activities, it does not link up just with parties of a similar ideological or organizational character nor is recruitment of new members to the Socialist International the prime objective. Some of its most politically relevant contacts (like the Mexican PRI, the Nicaraguan FSLN, the Peruvian APRA) do not have any formal relation with the Socialist International but prefer to stay in an undefined periphery of 'friends and associates'.

The 'eruption' of the Socialist International in Latin America around 1976 could not have been so rapid and successful unless a large number of political forces within the region had been receptive towards it. It is difficult to conceive of any other international party organization gathering together in its meetings such dissimilar groups, movements and parties as guerilla organizations engaged in the armed struggle, self-declared Marxist organizations, parliamentary socialist and social democratic parties, personalistic movements, descendents of the old populism, parties which follow the model of the British Labour Party (such as those in the English-speaking Caribbean), liberal-conservative groups, and a single party in control of the state like the PRI in Mexico. It is difficult to find any point of coincidence between all these groups, other than that the military dictatorships in the region constitute an obstacle or a threat to their own accession to power and it suits them to broaden their room to manoeuvre in relation to the United States.[5]

Undoubtedly the political, economic and social conjuncture in Latin America in the second half of the 1970s played an important role in this. I shall not attempt to analyse in depth the attraction for social democracy from the Latin Americans' perspective. It is a subject which should be looked at primarily by Latin Americans themselves. Nevertheless it does constitute the other side of the coin without which an analysis of why there is a social democratic offensive would not be complete. To give a provisional idea, I will sum up some arguments which have been put forward on this subject.

a. The Socialist International offers the Latin American elites an opportunity to deepen their economic and political ties with Europe, thus modifying their subordination to the United States. The crisis of US supremacy after Vietnam and Watergate provides a favourable moment for stressing the 'European option' (which in principle is not new).

b. The internationalization of the world economy means that any party aspiring to government has also to internationalize its political links in order to gain access to international centres of decision-making. Amongst the few available alternatives, the social democratic connection has the advantage of conceding a high degree of autonomy without presenting an openly imperialist image. For the traditional populist parties in particular, European social democracy presents them with an acceptable cover for collaborating with multinational capital without openly betraying their anti-imperialist traditions.

c. The Latin American left has not yet recovered from the failure of its earlier bid for political power. In order to gain some political space, it is obliged to collaborate in broader political fronts whose immediate objectives, such as human rights, basic social needs and political freedom, are shared both by the left and by social democracy. This is seen as an opportunity to consolidate *tactical* alliances without losing *strategic* autonomy. But there are also organizations of the left which, through lack of their own political project, are attracted to the social-democratic proposition of a 'third way', either as a transitional or definitive project. This also reflects the clear inadequacy of the previous theoretical and practical formulae in the face of new mass movements which don't fit into the classic mold of the class based or populist movements of the past.

d. For those left groups who are fighting under conditions of il-legality and repression or through the armed struggle, the Socialist International is almost the only international link which can offer them political and material help, in view of the known limitations of the different world headquarters of 'proletarian internationalism'. The link with the Socialist International gives a non-communist legitimacy in the West and gives certain opposition groups working under military dictatorships protection against repression.

e. Even to some sectors of the Latin American right, the military dictatorships do not seem very reliable or permanent. The SI therefore appears as an acceptable agent of controlled transition.

f. Rapid industrialization in various countries has created complex social structures to which individualist and amorphous party organizations have not yet adapted themselves. European social democracy seems therefore to have the 'know-how' for modernizing their own political methods and structures.

g. Finally, Willy Brandt's prestige as a Nobel Peace Prize winner is not insignificant for those politicians who have their own prestige in mind.

These are strong reasons for thinking that the social democratic offensive in Latin America is as much a 'Noah's Ark' for the most varied Latin American political forces, as it is a 'Trojan Horse' for European interests.

It is no coincidence that in the same second half of the 1970s other proposals emerged aimed at political and ideological internationalisation. Thus the Christian Democrat Organization of America (ODCA), reactivated its international links. In the United States some liberals in the US State Department during the Carter presidency sought to relegitimize US hegemony, using the theme of 'human rights' — a sideline of the Trilateral Commission which at the same time proposed a political and ideological internationalization at the level of the industrialized capitalist centres. In October 1979, a Permanent Conference of Latin American Political Parties (COPPPAL) was founded, similar in its composition and focus to the Latin American wing of the Socialist International but led by the Mexican PRI.

Although until now international social democracy has worked mainly in a rhetorical and ideological way, its presence has already had important practical effects in a number of instances. In 1978 it helped its member party in the Dominican Republic the PRD, to win the election and to force the armed forces loyal to Balaguer to respect this result. The most important case is without doubt its support of the FSLN in Nicaragua, both materially and — even more important — in gaining international recognition at the end of 1978.

On the other hand, social democracy has also suffered setbacks. Parties allied to the SI lost elections in Venezuela and Costa Rica in 1978 to their Christian Democrat opponents (the SI affiliate regained the presidency in Costa Rica in 1982), and in Jamaica and Peru in 1980 against candidates supported by the United States. In Bolivia, it was the 'international' of the southern cone military dictatorships which in 1980 snatched electoral triumph from a coalition of parties, the UDP, linked to the SI.

At present, the civil war in El Salvador for the first time creates a situation of direct confrontation between the SI and the United States. For West German social democracy, this conflict is a touchstone for all other relations between the Federal Republic of Germany (FRG) and its principle ally, the United States, under the Reagan administration. Although El Salvador is one of the smallest countries in the region, the Latin American commitment of the FRG for the first time has come to bear upon the country's global politics. This is due to the high symbolic significance which the anti-communist obsession of the Reagan administration has given to El Salvador. The behaviour of

West German social democracy in this conflict will without doubt define its whole political future in the region. Will it risk conflict with the United States in order to maintain its anti-dictatorial image?

Ultimately this raises a question about the interests which the German SPD pursues with its incursions into Latin America. It is also the key question for the different forces of the Latin American left which are establishing contacts with international social democracy if they are to reach a realistic assessment of the possibilities and limitations of this contact.

There are a number of problems with such an analysis. In the first place we know relatively little in concrete terms about the contacts between European social democrats and their Latin American colleagues. The major part of existing documentation is confidential. During public meetings, the most relevant conversations take place out of the reach of microphones, and without doubt, some of the most significant contacts are unknown.

In the second place, social democracy's diffuse activities and attitudes give the impression of pure pragmatism and empiricism that is impossible to trace to a few underlying causes and objectives. The actors themselves put forward no theory for their actions but, furthermore, suggest that the absence of theory is in itself one of the prerequisites of success in practice. There is no coherent ideological discourse except for a general anti-dictatorial posture and support for a political and 'social' democracy. There is no definition of the level of combativity required to achieve this end, nor is there any definition of the common reference point of 'democratic socialism'. In practice this usually does not go beyond a very general conception of Keynesian economic policies together with a verbal commitment to a 'welfare state' ('socialism').

In political terms it is limited to a system of representation which links a level of mass legitimacy with a bureaucratic form of decision making firmed rooted in the state structures of existing bourgeois domination.

During the 1960s it would have been unthinkable for the Latin American left to enter into any contact with European social democracy. It was considered almost the other face of US imperialism — and not without reason. Throughout the Cold War years, the Socialist International had allied itself with the United States, anti-communism being its main creed. In Latin America this was reduced in the 1960s to a united effort to contain 'Castro-communism', and the Socialist International was not very distant from institutions and individuals associated with the CIA. In 1966 for example, the Socialist International gave political backing to the Accion Democratica (AD) government of Venezuela for the suppression of the guerilla forces active in the country. Twelve years later the survivors of the guerillas have become parliamentary deputies for the Socialist Action Movement (MAS) and People's Electoral Movement (MEP) parties which take part in the meetings of the Socialist International. And the Minister of the Interior responsible for the repression in the mid 1960s, Carlos Andres Perez, as president of his country in the late 1970s gave material and moral support to the armed struggle of the Sandinista guerilla forces in Nicaragua. Obviously the Socialist International has changed from what it was in the 1960s, but so has the Latin American left. The epoch of the great popular movements and of the guerilla *foco* with a strict anti-capitalist ideology was closed militarily, but at the same time the undisputed hegemony of the United States was brought to an end in the capitalist world after the Vietnam war.

Even the traditional enmity between the pro-Soviet communist parties and social democracy no longer prevents occasional contacts between them, following the experience of joint action against the military dictatorship in Chile. In 1977 Brandt participated together with top leaders of the Chilean Communist Party in a conference in Rotterdam about the Chilean situation. In March 1980 the Friedrich Ebert Foundation joined with the Nicaraguan FSLN in organizing a solidarity conference in Managua, at which representatives of the Cuban Communist Party were also present. Fidel Castro himself in his speech to the 2nd Congress of the Communist Party of Cuba saw the social democratic presence in Latin America as a 'positive sign' in the present conjuncture.

How much is it a positive sign, and what defines the present conjuncture? Here we return to the case of West German social democracy.

## A Political Complement to the Economic Offensive by West German Capital in Latin America?

At first sight the most obvious explanation for the social democratic offensive after 1976 is to consider it as a political complement to the expansion of West German capital in Latin America. The volume of trade and the importance of West German investments in Latin America would not be compatible with the relative lack of political interest in the 1950s and 1960s. This 'lack of interest' was in fact only apparent: it meant an acceptance of the *status quo* and the hemispheric dominance of the United States. But with the rise of West German transnational capital to the stature of a serious competitor with US capital, West German interests could no longer shelter comfortably under the political roof of its rival, and would have to begin to build their own political links in the region. This step from minor partner to serious competitor is marked definitively by the 'nuclear deal' with Brazil in 1975, in which West Germany entered into a serious conflict with the United States for the first time, winning a US$5 million order for its strategic nuclear industry.

This is the most commonly accepted explanation amongst political analysts of all sides. To cite one North American, one Latin American and one German voice: '. . . West German social democracy is involved in Latin America so that it can create a political base for West German capital . . . It is difficult to escape the conclusion that the pink flag of social democracy will give way to the green light for West German capital'.[6] 'The loss of competivity of US industry in strategic sectors, the increasingly apparent capacity of European economies to compete with it for markets, also allows the "export" of European policy'.[7] 'The attempt to transform economic power into world political ascendency increasingly characterizes the basic feature of official West German policy, as much in relation to its Western "allies" (including the United States) as to the countries of the Third World'.[8]

This argument is supported by the statements of the politicians responsible for official West German policy. Helmut Schmidt, for instance, social democrat and head of government since 1974, has said: 'We have now gained world economic importance and relevance which demands that we prove ourselves up to the task. In effect we are making a real effort in that direction and we believe that until now we have managed to cope with this responsibility'.[9] The representatives of the social democrat-liberal coalition have even received the backing of the conservative opposition in this. The newspaper *Frankfurter Allgemeine Zeitung*, voice of the West German upper bourgeoisie, wrote at the time of Schmidt's visit to Latin America in 1979: 'A certain rivalry with the United States (ought not to be) the motive for over-cautious behaviour in South America . . . as if there was a desire to show all the world that (West Germany) is a political dwarf'.[10]

Also, in the economic data there is a strong basis for this explanation of the social democrat offensive. The German Federal Republic is the second largest exporter in the world, only a little way behind the United States. In 1977 for example it exported almost as much as France and Great Britain together. This commercial ascendency is part of the history of reconstruction and prolonged capitalist prosperity — at a world level and especially in West Germany — after the Second World War until mid-1970. Since 1950, West German external trade has shown a constant surplus, reaching a record of DM23 million in 1978.

This dual trade dominance between the United States and West Germany is not a new fact — it has not changed since 1959. But the difference between the volumes exported by them has been getting less and less (see Table 1). This commercial success is connected with the composition of West German exports. Machinery, vehicles, chemical and electrical products account for 56 per cent. In other words, the Federal Republic has specialized in the production of those capital goods whose global demand was bound to grow in the post-war expansionist phase of capital and which involve the use of the most advanced technology. The Federal Republic occupies first place as world exporter of manufactured products, surpassing the United States by the end of the 1960s (see Table 2). West Germany's trade surplus produced a constant pressure to revalue the Deutschmark which increased its value spectacularly in relation to the US dollar and other currencies, and has become the dominant currency in Western Europe.

The commercial power of West Germany is without doubt impressive. But is there a direct relation between this and the Latin American political context which interests us? In the first place, there are no sharp changes in global trends in the first half of the 1970s which could explain the emergence of a new political strategy. In the second place, looking at the distribution of West German foreign trade by regions, the relation with the 'developing countries' is clearly secondary to trade with industrialized countries (73.9 per cent), and especially with other members of the EEC (48.3 per cent). In percentage terms, exports to 'developing' countries (according to the terminology of the Development Assistance Council) represent only 19.8 per cent; excluding the 'developing countries' of Southern Europe, exports to the Third World are 14.3 per cent, and Latin America takes last place after Asia and Africa with only 3.1 per cent (1979 figures). The tendency for Latin America and for all 'developing' countries is a decrease in its relative position despite a constant increase in absolute terms.

Competition with the United States is therefore mostly for markets in the industrialized countries themselves. But Third World markets are considered 'markets of the future'. Their raw materials continue to represent a vital interest that is not reflected in the quantative relations of the world market. The composition of West German trade with the 'developing countries' by sector shows the classic pattern: manufactured products in exchange for raw materials and foodstuffs.

There was a sharp change at the beginning of the 1970s with the drastic rise in the price of various raw materials, in particular that of oil after 1973. In one year this reversed all the advantages which the Federal Republic had accumulated in its terms of trade over the previous decade.

To what extent has Latin America itself participated in the subsequent redefinition of the commercial relationship of the Third World with West Germany? Statistics from the 'critical years' 1973-76, show that the increase in value of Latin American exports to West Germany was modest and was due in part to products such as copper and sugar whose rise in 1973-74 was short-lived. In fact the increase in trade during these years with Latin America is *less than the increase with respect to all the other regions of the world*. The largest increase — as one would expect — was with the oil-exporting countries (from 1974, oil and its derivatives represent over 50 per cent of German imports from the Third World). The relative participation of Latin America in the external trade of the Federal Republic tended to decrease throughout the 1970s despite an increase in absolute terms (see Table 3). No Latin American country reached even 1 per cent of the imports or exports of West Germany. Latin American imports do signify important 'inputs' for some sectors of the German economy. Its imports of coffee and bananas come entirely from Latin America. There is an important Latin American contribution in copper (Chile), tin (Bolivia, Peru), some special metals (Brazil) and cotton (Guatemala, Colombia). On the other side, trade with West Germany takes either first, second or third place from the Latin American point of view. From Latin America's perspective there is therefore enough of a basis for a growing interest in closer relations. But from the West German perspective there is no new aspect to trade relations which can explain the seemingly sudden 'discovery' of Latin America by the Socialist International.

With respect to direct investment a different picture emerges. The continuing rise in the external value of the mark increased the price of its exports but facilitated the export of capital. Annual external investment increased constantly from the 1950s to 1970. It leapt sharply to a new level of DM5 million as an average annual outflow after 1973. The devaluation of the dollar in 1972 influenced this, as did the context of the economic crisis and competition within the capitalist world in 1973-74. Since 1979 there has been a new leap to DM8 million a year. From a net importer of capital, the Federal Republic became an exporter (1968-70, and definitively after 1974). It has been estimated that in 1980 the total amount of accumulated West German investment abroad surpassed for the first time the amount of foreign investment in West Germany.

But if there was an important advance in the Federal Republic, it still had not yet challenged the clear leadership of US and British capital (see Table 4). In comparison with them, the Federal Republic is a 'giant in exports and a dwarf in investments'. Whilst the external production of US transnational affiliates is more than four times the value of US exports, and in the case of Britain the relationship is double, the West German economy produces scarcely a third of the value of its exports outside the Federal Republic. In relation to Latin America, West German imports as well as exports are worth more every year than the total accumulated from investments since 1952. As to the sectors preferred by West German investment, there is a similar picture to its exports: chemicals, banking and insurance, electrical engineering, iron and steel metallurgy, machinery and cars. This reflects the high degree of concentration in these strategic sectors of the West German economy, where a few giant enterprises dominate exports as well as foreign investment.

The regional distribution of this investment clearly favours the industrialized capitalist countries. Amongst the three big regions of the Third World, Latin America is by far the favoured destination of West German capital, with 12.3 per cent of total external West German investments. This is due in the first place to the importance of Brazil which alone takes 9.1 per cent, and is the fourth largest recipient of West German investment after the United States, Belgium/Luxembourg and France (1978) (see Table 5). The importance of Brazil reflects the preference of West German investors for the industrial sector (see Table 6). Their penetration of the raw materials and agriculture sectors is miniscule. This corrects the impression of the relatively minor importance of Latin America for West Germany in the field of trade. As by far the most industrialized and 'wealthy' (in terms of gross *per capita* product) region of the Third World, Latin America's economic relations with West Germany are not only through trade but also now largely through direct industrial investment, which demands a developed internal market and an extensive material and social infrastructure. This is expressed also in the external structure of employment by West German capital, 20 per cent of which is concentrated in Latin America. In Brazil alone, West German capital employs more people than it does in the US (16 and 14 per cent respectively in 1978).

However, despite the increase in absolute terms, the relative weight of West German capital invested in Latin America has decreased with respect to the 1960s, and only remained more or less stable during the 1970s (see Table 7). But these global statistics do not show with sufficient clarity the significant change in the direction of outflows during the 'critical years' under discussion. This does confirm that there was a clear increase in West German interest in direct investment in Latin America at the same time as the SI launched its political incursion into the region. But is this a sufficient explanation for the offensive?

Was the economic expansion of West German capital in Latin America during the 1970s so dramatic that it can explain the simultaneous export of a new political strategy? If this is the case, why were the social democrats especially active in small countries such as Nicaragua or the Dominican Republic where the interests of West German capital are negligeable?

But more important, how do we explain the social democratic character of this strategy? Why were the political expedients most available to West German capital not just intensified? For instance, government to government contacts, the chambers of commerce, the 'public relations' offices of the multinationals themselves might have been strengthened. Despite the wave of publicity centred around the entrance of international social democracy onto the scene, and whatever its future role might be, its practical support for West German business interests in the 1970s was minimal.

It was as a governing party that the social democrats played a political role of direct support for West German interests. The example of the nuclear deal with Brazil has already been mentioned. Since the assumption of the Social Democrat-Liberal coalition in Bonn, arms sales and the sale of equipment for their production increased spectacularly in Latin America as in the world as a whole, converting the Federal Republic into the fifth largest world exporter of arms. While as members of the SI the West German social democrats participated in many international acts of condemnation of the Pinochet dictatorship, as the government it furnished the necessary permission for the export of two submarines to the Chilean junta in 1980 (which it had to withdraw following protests from the grassroots of the party). In 1977 the *Bank fuer Gemeinschaft*, owned by the large unions, gave credit to the Argentine military junta which also had no problem in receiving 'its' two West German submarines. And while the SI condemned repression in El Salvador, in 1979 (still under the government of General Romero) the social democrat city council of West Berlin received a visit from officers of the Salvadorean Army, and the chief of police, also a social democrat, gave them a lecture on 'anti-terrorism'. In 1981, the West German navy participated in manoeuvres in the Caribbean, and organized joint exercises with the Brazilian navy, the first since the times of Hitler and Vargas.

To sum up, the interpretation of the social democratic offensive as the political counterpart to European economic interests, especially those of West Germany, has an element of truth if we go from the basis that there must be some relationship between those interests and the politics of international social democracy in Latin America. But to see the relationship as directly functional to these economic interests does not explain (or show the political significance of) what it is that gives this political position its specifically social democratic character, and distinguishes it from a straightforwardly imperialist policy. We must conclude that the relationship is more complex.

# A Strategy to Expand Internal Markets?

The mistake which from my point of view leads to this kind of simplification lies in identifying social democracy directly and exclusively with the safeguarding of the long-term interests of capital. Yet the historical roots of West German social democracy in the workers movement still affect its practice today, even if to a much lesser degree. Its political existence is not identified with capital, but rather with the *relationship* between capital and labour and with certain *methods* of resolving conflicts within this relationship. Could it be that in the present conjuncture in Latin America this particular quality is needed to further West German interests in the region?

According to one argument in the industrialized zones of Latin America, where West German interests are concentrated, there is an industrial proletariat which is too broad and experienced to remain controlled — in the workplace or in the national political arena — by purely repressive measures. Nor could the extreme forms of poverty be tolerated which might lead to massive social eruptions. But apart from preparing the social climate for West German transnational companies, there would also be a very concrete economic rationale. With its concentration in the production of manufactured goods for local consumption, West German capital could only benefit from a gradual improvement in the purchasing power of the wage earning class, and with the integration of the masses (supposedly) marginalized from the capitalist market. The model of accumulation based on the production of durable consumer goods is hampered by the structural limitations of internal markets, originating in the social organization of income with (also supposedly) precapitalist characteristics. Behind the rhetoric of 'social democracy', the defence of union rights and programmes of 'basic needs' would, according to the interpretation, be part of a strategy to enlarge internal markets for West German capital.[11]

To sum up, according to this argument the political project of international social democracy would have as its goal the formation of a *social bloc for associated industrialization*, bringing with it a subsequent stage of 'inward' industrial development. Such an internal expansion would interest all the social agents of the process of industrialization in Latin America, including transnational capital which would inevitably exercise hegemony within such a bloc. As a consequence (which is not stated explicitly) this interpretation visualizes the social democrat project as an historic recurrence of the class alliances which constituted the populism of the 1940s, adapted to the present conditions. The political implications of such an interpretation are no less one-dimensional than those of the previous explanation, but only give the opposite result: instead of appearing as European imperialism, social democracy appears now as the legitimate heir of Latin American populism and, as a result, as a *strategic* ally of the Latin American left.

There is also some economic basis for this argument. Latin America has a gross per capita national product of US$1,775 — two and a half times the average for all the countries on the capitalist periphery (US$791), and also of the apparently new rich oil-exporting countries (US$968)). It is by far the richest region of the Third World.[12] Amongst the ten 'developing' countries with the largest absolute gross product, there are four Latin American countries (Brazil, Mexico, Argentina and Venezuela). In the list of the Newly Industrializing Countries (NICs) which represent the aristocracy amongst the countries of the Third World, there are already twelve Latin American countries. In the eyes of the West German investor, this means that Latin America 'has risen to be a kind of middle class'.[13]

The regional and sectoral concentration of West German external investments shows clearly that they are mostly oriented toward existing and future internal markets. It is a constant feature of social democratic discourse with respect to North-South relations that the West German economy can have no interest in keeping the countries of Africa, Asia and Latin America underdeveloped. In 1969 the then Minister of Economic Co-operation, Erhard Eppler, said: 'We will still export less to the whole of Africa than to Switzerland. Certainly not because our machinery would not be of use in Africa, but because it can't pay for it. A trading "partner" is the more interesting for us the more developed it is, and the more purchasing power it has'.[14]

It seems certain that the degree of industrial development reached in various Latin American countries with their corresponding relations of production based on a wage earning and relatively well organized labour force, constitutes a social substratum without which European social democracy could not become an interlocutor sought after by a variety of Latin American political forces. It also seems certain that in the long term there is a correlation between the expansion of internal industrial markets and the social democratic type of politics.

But there is a long way between the existence of this economic rationale and the idea that industrial transnational capital might demand the intervention of social democracy in Latin America.

In the first place, it would be necessary to make much more specific the general proposition that 'the industrialization of the Third World benefits the West German economy'. What kind of industrialization in which group of countries in the periphery would today benefit which sectors of West German transnational capital? How does this kind of industrialization affect the relations of production and distribution of each respective country? Only on the basis of this information can an analysis be constructed of whether or not the external interests of West German capital are compatible with a social democratic political methodology.

We cannot enter here into a detailed analysis by country, but on the basis of the general information at our disposal, our hypothesis would tend to be negative. The economic principle underlying any social democratic policy is an evolution of real wages which allows the market price of the labour commodity to be seen as a 'just wage'. Without this economic precondition, the appearance of market relationships in which the contradiction between labour and capital appear not to be necessarily antagonistic cannot develop into a reliable mass ideology. This demands a context of relatively integrated reproduction in which the bulk of wages reappear in the market as demand, fuelling the circulation of capital including in its most advanced sectors.

In Latin America on the contrary, an 'associated' model of industrial accumulation predominates at present, the dynamic of which is actually not based on consumer goods but on the purchasing power of the high income sectors. For the foreseeable future we can discount the possibility of such a profound restructuring of the actual norms of income distribution that the demand for mass consumer goods would displace the demand for consumer durables from their dynamic role in the economy. This leads us to the first conclusion, that an ostensible broadening of the internal market in a social democratic project would be oriented exclusively towards those class fractions integrated into pre-existing urban-industrial systems, and would have little or nothing to offer economically to the majority of the population, who would continue in various urban and rural subsistence activities.

However, it seems unlikely that the transnational model of accumulation is really running up against a serious bottleneck in the internal market, considering its capacity to continue growing 'upwards', introducing new products, or exporting to other countries of the periphery or even to the metropolitan countries. That this could lead to the process of *de*-industrialization in other Latin American countries (e.g. Chile) does not invalidate the argument. The dynamic of capital accumulation takes place in geographic areas not identical with national boundaries.

In strictly economic terms, the margin for social democratic reformism is rather limited. This is seen by asking the question: Are there Latin American economies in which large national and international capital can improve its present conditions of accumulation through an enlargement of its present markets to include the relatively better-off of the poor? This question can only be asked with respect to certain subregions within Latin America, with very specific characteristics, i.e. those poles of industrial growth where the market for manufactured products already reaches an appreciable degree of diversification and saturation and where already the purchasing power of wages, as much in their level as in their total volume, represents a reasonable proportion of the existing market. The most typical region in this respect is the industrialized triangle of Brazil (Sao Paulo-Rio-Belo Horizonte). Here the incorporation of wage earners in the consumption of durable goods (radios, televisions, refrigerators etc.) is already taking place through a system of consumer credits. These were introduced in Brazil at the time of the economic miracle, when political repression was at its height, without any 'push' by social democratic forces. In 1978 the wage increases won by the metalworkers of Sao Paulo through their strikes effectively led to an additional growth in sales of simple consumer goods by about 5 per cent.[15] But these strikes were organized without any support from international social democracy,[16] and during the strikes in the following years the businessmen of Sao Paulo — far from considering any benefits from the increase in demand — mobilized all their repressive resources once again to reduce the real wage.

However, the resistance of the dominant classes themselves does not in itself invalidate the argument. West German social democracy still remembers its own historical experience that capitalists are never voluntarily convinced of the need to increase wages. Even in West Germany, the rise of real wages which ended up benefiting industrial accumulation was the result of hard social struggles.

It would therefore be necessary to strengthen the potential for protest of the lower classes, supporting their ability to organize through the formation of party and union organizations sufficiently strong to wring wage concessions from the capitalists.[17] But it would also be necessary to organize the other 'victims of underdevelopment', mainly agricultural workers and the sub-proletariat or marginal masses, in order for them to gain access to the market. Given their diffuse and precarious economic situation, this would require programmes aimed at meeting 'basic needs' with the 'participation of those affected'.

In the final analysis, West German social democracy would not be alarmed at the possibility that such a social mobilization might endanger the existing oligarchic regimes in some countries. It would be necessary to accept a temporary instability in exchange for stability in the long term.

These other social and political repercussions of a strategy aimed at expanding the market have in fact been discussed for some time amongst West German social democrats under the apparently innocuous title of 'dynamization of structures'. In 1970 the aforementioned Minister of Economic Co-operation, Eppler, said: 'We must start with a flexible, pluralist, perhaps even consciously contradictory manner, appealing for example to the future vision of dominant forces such as young and pragmatic managerial groups, at the same time as encouraging and supporting groups with reformist tendencies and continuing to talk to revolutionary elements. The decisive factor is the chance to dynamize structures effectively'.[18]

In an identical sense the then vice-minister, Matthoefer, stated one year later: 'It is a task of social democrat parties and the most lucid forces in the United States, first to organize the construction and continuous support of democratic-socialist parties and effective trade unions so that they can impose a programme of radical structural transformation and reforms ... secondly, it is necessary to give massive support through development aid programmes to reformist movements as they become governments'.[19]

Once again, if this strategy aims at encouraging the interests of West German capital, the latter doesn't perceive it in this way. In Latin America, the West German transnationals are as much or more opposed to the activities of trade unions as their counterparts in other metropolitan countries. Faced with the danger of social disruption by the 'marginalized masses', its perspective is to consider it a police question and certainly not as 'structures' for 'dynamizing'.

But is this just a failure to see their objective interests? If our economic argument was correct we have to concede a considerable degree of realism in the fear of the multinationals that in the foreseeable future higher wages mean less not greater profits. As for the 'marginal masses', sufficient has been said and written to believe that they are in fact integrated into existing markets in the only (and for this reason 'best') form compatible with the actual form of accumulation, and that the 'basic needs' programmes proposed by the World Bank and assumed by the official West German agencies tend to stabilize — also politically — this type of 'marginal integration' in the market rather than change it.

It is logical: as long as there is no real economic improvement to offer, any political mobilization of the masses is counterproductive. It could perhaps be considered as the mobilization of social pressure on behalf of the interests of others (e.g. in elections), but with the danger that this could rebound on the promotors within a short period, with all the weight of frustrated expectations. It is precisely this contradiction which has brought the downfall of all the reformist governments in the region, since the end of the 1950s, including governments led by member parties of the SI. As a result, in the actual practice of these parties, we find little or nothing to suggest that they are organizing or mobilizing a trade union movement amongst urban or rural workers. On the contrary, where such party unions remain from previous years, the present party leadership is collaborating instead in its *de*-mobilization. None of the Latin American parties which belong to the Socialist International was born historically from the workers' movement in its country (as is the case with the West German SPD) or has today the characteristics of a workers' party.

But neither does the present policy of the West German SPD with respect to the Latin American parties and trade unions bear much resemblance to the proposal for 'radical structural changes' put forward by Matthoefer in 1969. It is no accident that the proposal for 'dynamizing structures' was put forward in the initial phase of the social democrat government in Bonn under Willy Brandt, which was marked by a reformist euphoria. Today such positions have no place in government policy, where there has been a return to the discourse of the 'pragmatism' of 'mutual interests'. Thus the Friedrich Ebert Foundation in Latin America defines its own role — in the words of its director Guenter Grunwald — as 'social policy which assists relevant social groups such as trade unions and parties to moderate and channel their conflicts. This also means maintaining these societies in a socially tolerable, if precarious equilibrium, and finding viable compromise solutions (orig.: *tragfæhige* 'second-best' — *Loesungen*) to pressing social problems'.[20]

Certainly this static conception does not cover all aspects of social democratic policy in Latin America. But neither does the idealistic vision of a social bloc for associated industrialization which stimulates internal markets. All the indications are that for the foreseeable future the process of industrialization in Latin America will continue to base itself more easily on authoritarian and repressive political structures than on class conciliation.

Perhaps the most revealing example in this respect is that of Argentina. According to all the criteria, the country should have been destined for a social democratic policy, as it had the best-organized and most experienced working class in the continent, a well-integrated internal market, and a level of wages which allowed the higher-paid workers access to motor cars, etc. Nevertheless, in the same year in which social democracy launched its conquest of Latin America, in Argentina transnational capital unleashed a brutal offensive *against* all these advances which, according to the argument, would have been in its best interests.

Of course it is possible and even probable that a detailed, country by country analysis would be able to establish the margins for expansion in respective existing internal markets which a practical policy ought to try to take advantage of, however limited these may be. What we feel is unlikely is that there is sufficient margin to serve as a socio-economic support for class conciliation of the social democrat type.

Nor do we want to discount as mere ideology the objective of broadening internal markets so dear to social democracy on both sides of the Atlantic. Has the Latin American left any less illusory economic programmes to offer? In a sense it is a necessary historic illusion, expressing a *national* aspiration, as impossible to carry out as it is to abandon in the present period.

If this is so, the significance of the 'social democratic alternative' today must be found not in economic issues, but in the sphere of politics and ideology proper, including the symbolic. Otherwise it would be difficult to explain the prominence given to small countries without relevant markets: activities would have to be concentrated in Brazil, where up till now the presence of social democracy has been modest (although perhaps involuntarily), or in Mexico, where only recently, with the country's transformation into an oil power, has a greater effort been made.

In conclusion, the degree of Latin American industrial development, which is relatively advanced in various Latin American countries, constitutes without doubt a precondition for social democratic formulations, and in this sense helps to explain the warm reception given to international social democracy in Latin America since the end of 1976. But the actual contents of its Latin American policy, its geographic emphases and its timing are not explained by the thesis of the extension of internal markets. The disappointing experience of member parties of the SI in government, demonstrates that their 'democratic socialism' — useful as it may be as a common meeting ground for heterogenous opposition forces — does not have a model of development to offer suited to the reality of Latin America.

## A Project for Change in Bourgeois Domination?

If there is no direct economic rationale which links the penetration of Latin American markets by West German capital with the proliferation of social democrat activities, we must seek a more truly political explanation. Various interpretations centre on this theme, identifying social democracy as an alternative project for bourgeois domination in Latin America.[21]

These interpretations vary according to the degree of immediacy assigned to the project, whether the emphasis is on an immediate counterrevolutionary objective or on a more long term stabilization. A third version along the same lines considers the social democratic alternative even less related to the present situation in Latin America and interprets it as a strategy of coopting elites in the long term.

## a. A counterrevolutionary device?

According to this argument, European social democracy entered the Latin American scene to preempt radical protest movements which will emerge in Latin America in response to military authoritarianism. The United States is seen as incapable of performing this function, it is completely identified with the dictatorships themselves and its imperialist image would exacerbate the opposing forces rather than placate them. The economic competition between the United States and the Federal Republic is considered subordinate to their common interest in 'stabilizing' the region. Rather than rivalry, there is a division of labour.[22]

Portugal is the model for this experience. West German social democracy played a key role in reversing a social process which for a time had real anti-capitalist perspectives, and thus it preempted a direct US intervention. Through a party of its creation, the Portuguese Socialist Party led by Mario Soares, it managed to capitalize electorally on the legitimacy of the Armed Forces Movement of 1974 and to use it as part of an anti-communist strategy.[23]

This interpretation is especially widely held among representatives of the more orthodox left. But can the Portuguese case be transposed to the Latin American situation? Was there an urgent need to 'save capitalism' from mass anticapitalist movements? In fact, the year 1976 is the culmination of the defeat of such movements throughout the South American continent. None of the dictatorships appeared seriously threatened and in some countries the counterrevolutionary offensive was still in full ascendency (Argentina, Peru, Colombia).

When Willy Brandt brought together the Latin American political leaders in Caracas, Venezuela was like a liberal democracy marooned by the tide of military authoritarianism. From the period of the declarations issued in Caracas until the present, the rhetoric as well as the practice of international social democracy in Latin America has been openly anti-dictatorial and not openly anti-communist. In its Latin American relations, West German social democracy makes no attempt to avoid contacts with those organizations of the left which in West Germany itself would be abhorred as 'extremist' and 'terrorist'.

Only recently, after the 1979 revolution in Nicaragua, international social democracy has good cause to suspect an alternative anti-capitalist power in the region. Its response has been to support the *tercerista* fraction of the FSLN and recently a special committee was created within the SI whose most important function is to defend the Nicaraguan process against the international right, but also by implication to control the internal 'pluralist' process. In no other Latin American country outside Central America has the Marxist left been reconstituted after its defeats, nor does it have a revolutionary project capable of bringing together a material force with a possibility of gaining power.

## b. A project to reinstitutionalize bourgeois domination?

In the other variant of this interpretation it is not a question of an imminent anticapitalist danger, but of possible future disruptions if military governments don't 'become civilized' in time, giving way to more institutionalized bourgeois alternatives with a broader social base. Once they have fulfilled their main objective of repression and demobilization of the forces which threatened capitalism, the dictatorships will have no means to stabilize their rule. Their permanence in government will have become unnecessary and even counterproductive as they offer too obvious an image of the enemy, capable of uniting all the opposition forces. This applies to situations where they have succeeded in strengthening capitalist economic development (Brazil) as much as to situations where their economic and social projects have failed (Peru, for example).

This strategy implies re-establishing a parliamentary system with parties and elections, to give state power a certain legitimacy and to make the relations of social domination more anonymous and less open to attack. The degree of institutional liberalization would be adapted to the relationship between the forces in each country, resulting in a 'relative' or 'restricted' democracy. This change of image would also facilitate international economic and political relations with the metropolitan capitalist countries, which are organized politically according to these bourgeois 'civilized' norms. For reasons of internal politics, the European and US governments are uncomfortable dealing with 'fascist-style' governments.[24]

The counterrevolutionary and anticommunist aspect is not absent from this variant of the argument, but it is more as a preventative measure and at the level of ideological struggle. This perspective sees an ambiguous relationship of co-operation and competition between the United States and Europe. In principle, it is a transformation supported and sought after by 'liberal' sectors within the United States which temporarily gained governmental positions within the Carter administration. The European social democratic presence is required to 'flank' US interests. While the United States calms the military regimes and even puts moderate pressure on them through the rhetoric of 'human rights', the Europeans establish the contacts with the opposition political parties which because of their anti-US traditions and rhetoric would be prevented from having direct relations with the US. At the same time, social democracy would be the guarantee that the political transition does not exceed the limits of the transnational economic model, and that 'liberalization' does not lead to uncontrollable social eruptions.

A united operation of this type was effectively carried out with the transfer of power in the Dominican Republic from Balaguer to Guzman, with the simultaneous presence of the Organization of American States (OAS) and the SI. Elements of this joint strategy appeared in a less clear-cut fashion in other cases of bourgeois-democratic reinstitutionalization (for example, Ecuador in 1978). But subsequently there has been a sharpening of the competitive elements between both metropolitan powers, coinciding with the conservative turn of the Carter government after 1979. The US was by then not prepared to concede any interference from the SI voluntarily. In Nicaragua both lost control and came together almost involuntarily because of the lack of alternatives. In all the elections from mid-1978 onwards more pro-US candidates were opposed by a candidate supported by the SI (Costa Rica, Venezuela, Peru, Jamaica). Finally in El Salvador after 1980, the two international strategies ended in public confrontation.

In essence, the United States suspects that the Europeans — especially the West Germans — will take advantage of the common task to create more durable forms of domination, in order to place *its* political personnel in positions to ensure an economic advantage. This is how one could explain why the US as an established hegemonic power, ends up by giving priority in critical moments to the stability of the *status quo* to the detriment of 'human rights' (for example with the Pinochet regime in the Letelier case), while social democracy develops an almost 'subversive' relationship with this *status quo*.

This interpretation certainly points to some key elements of the 'political climate' into which the social democratic offensive has been inserted. Undoubtedly, the 'crisis of the dictatorships' in Europe and the success of West German social democracy in influencing the Portugese and (to a lesser degree) the Spanish process, gave a considerable stimulus to the SPD to extend its international thrust and on the other hand raised the expectations of anti-dictatorial forces in Latin America. The fact that these greet social democracy as the only alternative source of international support, explains *their* interest, but what is the West German interest?

It seems that this interpretation only fits into a limited time scale. It begins in 1977 with the resurgence of massive popular protest (Peru, Brazil, Chile, Bolivia, Guatemala, Nicaragua) and ends in 1979 when the United States departed from the project of a change in bourgeois domination in order to give priority once again to its imperial role. The interpretation therefore does not account for the starting point of the Caracas offensive, nor for the situation of conflict between the US and the SI after 1980.

To sum up: although European social democracy played a role in the sense of proposing and implementing strategies for a change in bourgeois domination, in the present Latin American situation it does not seem to have been an essential actor, either for the capitalist system in itself or as a safeguard of the economic and political interests of West Germany in the region.

## An Open Forum for the Assimilation of Political Elites

Up to now we have not found that West German social democracy has an immediate interest of its own which might explain its offensive in Latin America. Instead we have found various objective and subjective conditions which from the Latin American perspective have facilitated its acceptance. Can it be that there is no such immediate interest with respect to Latin America, but rather a sense of seizing the opportunity to occupy the political spaces as they present themselves for some future use? If this is the case, the present activities would have more of a preliminary function aimed at establishing relations with present or future political leaders, in order to form personal acquaintances and to create loyalties. A change in bourgeois domination in several countries would not then be the focus of attention, but would rather characterize a conjuncture in which the formation of new elites was the order of the day. In a long term perspective, it would mean forming a political personnel and party structures oriented toward West Germany which would guarantee access to the centres of political and economic decision making in the respective countries in the future. The optimum result would be that some day this political leadership be in the position of government, but also as the legal opposition they would be useful intermediaries.

This interpretation was suggested by one of the most perceptive observers of social democracy in Latin America, Daniel Waksman Schinka. In an article published shortly before his premature death, he compared the present phase of social democratic penetration in Latin America with the 'opening gambit' in chess. It is not yet a question of engaging in battles, but of occupying the best strategic and tactical positions for any future contingency.

In my judgement, this interpretation has not received the attention it deserves amongst political observers who strive to link the *present* anti-dictatorial practice of social democracy with the present interests of West German capital. It is my impression that the left — Latin American and West German — shows rather less vision of the future than social democracy, by not giving sufficient consideration to this long term strategy.

It is not a question of something as crude as 'buying off' leaders with grants, travel to Europe, golden handshakes and funds for their party activities (although this is also done). Nor is it a question of ideologically indoctrinating them with a defined social democratic ideology. Political assimilation has a much more subtle effect: it works at the level of non-verbal behaviour which we could call the *political unconscious* (and indeed it is probable that many of the representatives of West German social democracy have only a vague consciousness of their own *modus operandi*). This political unconscious is characterized by the personalization of politics around political leaders who are increasingly professionalized and detached from their base; the practice of seeking political support amongst other leaders and not in the capacity for initiative of the group itself; thinking in terms of 'factors of power' and not forces, interests and social processes; the notion of politics as a transaction between elites which arbitrate interests and conflicts which are not their own; perspectives for change which do not question the social relations of domination in themselves, by excluding from their field of vision all the 'microstructure' of power in the personal behaviour of daily life and by putting forward the state as the only place and agent of transformation; a detached and technocratic discourse which prevents the immediate representation of interests; the conception of political organizations as hierarchical apparatus and the clearly hierarchical practice amongst the leaders themselves. In other words, it is not a question of directly inculcating a specific political content, but of transmitting a bureaucratic political *style*. By this indirect and often unperceived means, the political content filters through in the attitudes even of those forces who believe that they can 'use' social democracy with no danger to their own distinct political identity.

As a long term strategy there is no need for a complete economic and social project at the present time. On the contrary, any premature definition would only limit the options for the future. Besides, an element of ambiguity and inconsistency forms part of the 'offer', maintaining a kind of 'neutrality' in the open forum which is being presented to the Latin American interlocutors. For the moment all that is required is the *image* of having a distinct development project — the art consists in knowing up to what point you can take the ambiguity without losing 'credibility' — a favourite expression of Willy Brandt.

From this perspective, it is not lack of sincerity but part of an impeccable logic that leads West German social democracy to knock on several doors at the same time, for example supporting a friendly governing party but at the same time keeping up contact with opposition groups either of the left (for example in Venezuela, AD and MAS) or of the right (e.g. in Nicaragua, apart from the FSLN, with the MDN of Robelo and the non-socialist leaders of the ex-*tercerista* fraction).[25]

With this interpretation, it is already less incomprehensible that the activities of West German social democracy are not necessarily concentrated in the same Latin American countries as West German capital. If it is a question of co-opting elites, what counts during the initial phase is more the symbolic than the practical value of these activities. As a result, social democracy has to locate itself in those areas where struggle symbolizes the conflicts and aspirations of the leaders with whom it wishes to establish relations — which without doubt during these last years have been the countries of Central America and the Caribbean.

The counterrevolutionary interpretation which was basic to the previous interpretation of a change in bourgeois domination, is not absent from this long term perspective, but just latent at the present time. It also strengthens the aspect of competition rather than co-operation in US-West German relations with Latin America. Without an imminent danger to capitalism, the US can have no interest in the West Germans building up their 'own' political personnel in the region. This interpretation thus clarifies many of the apparent contradictions in the social democratic offensive.

But some doubts remain. If it is just an opportune moment for co-opting elites, why was such a sudden thrust required? The explosive character of social democratic activities in Latin America implies a stronger impulse, more directly linked to essential interests. Also, it cannot be denied that the Willy Brandt team took certain risks in entering into conflict with the United States and seeing itself flooded by the nationalist or even anti-imperialist tendencies which it drew around the SI — a risk which politicians are not used to taking without being forced into it in some way. If it is impossible to find an explanation for this eruption from within the context of relations between Latin America and West Germany, we have to seek it in other contexts.

## The Project of a Conciliatory West German Posture toward the North-South Conflict

By focusing the argument for economic rationality behind the social democratic offensive exclusively on the economic relations between Europe and Latin America, a whole series of dramatic developments which shook the world capitalist economy in the first half of the 1970s are left aside, for example the world crisis of 1973-74, the rise in the price of oil, the crisis of the dollar, etc. These may not have originated in Latin America but they have strongly affected Europe-Latin American relations. I do not believe we can understand the revitalization of the SI without situating it in the more all-embracing context of the 'North-South conflict' over the reordering of the world economy which surfaced at that time.

For the dominant classes of West Germany, the period of crisis forced them to consider how modifications in the international division of labour could be influenced in their favour and how they could adapt to these in the most advantageous way possible. Against this background, the sudden thrust of West German social democracy in Latin America can be explained largely as a projection of a conciliatory position in relations between West Germany and the Third World in general.

In this broader context of the crisis of the first half of the 1970s, there are many threatening indicators for the West German economy. In 1975, for the first time in post-war history, there was a fall in the real value of West German exports. In that year, the first 'synchronized' crisis in all the industrialized economies, the export of capital goods and basic consumer goods fell by 17.6 per cent. As an external expression of the crisis, inflation reached a record 7 per cent and unemployment tripled in three years (1973: 1.2 per cent, 1975: 4.7 per cent). The favourable trend in the terms of trade with the 'developing' countries was reversed, with the spectacular increase in the price of oil and other raw materials.

The crisis highlighted the fact that the other side to the West German economy's strength in exports is its extreme dependence on these exports, and as a result its vulnerability to any disturbance in the capitalist world market. There are few industrialized countries in which external trade represents such a high proportion of Gross National Product (Great Britain: 31 per cent, West Germany and Italy: 26 per cent, France: 20 per cent, Japan: 14 per cent and the United States: 8 per cent).[26] In the leading industries, between a quarter and a third of production, on average, is destined for export. The dynamism of the West German economy depends for its privileged position on the world market, the leading individual West German enterprises export on average over 50 per cent of their production, and the trend has been for this to increase rapidly (see Table 8).

This means, amongst other things, that a good part of the West German labour force depends on exports. In 1974 it was calculated that 2.4 million of the economically active population worked directly and another 2.2 million indirectly for exports, which means 36.6 per cent of those economically active in the manufacturing sector of the West German economy. About a fifth of those work on exports to the 'developing' countries.

As a result, with the 1973-74 crisis, the West German ruling class saw its only salvation in securing and even accentuating the exporting base of the West German economy. This strategy was made explicit in 1975 in a book by two of the leading SPD economists.[27] The authors proposed a policy of 'active structural adaptation' to the 'critical modifications of the national and international economic context'. It meant consciously reinforcing the advantages of West German industry in the capital goods sector through multimillion state subsidies, and increasing the country's specialization in products involving the most advanced technology (research, automation, nuclear and solar energy, recycling, communications, transport, etc.). Internally this strategy demanded a process of rationalization, automation and concentration. It would be necessary to tolerate and even stimulate the transfer of less competitive industries with a higher labour coefficient to countries on the periphery, although this meant sacrificing jobs in West Germany.

This was exactly what happened. The value of sales from West Germany to the OPEC countries grew even more rapidly than its purchases, tripling in a few years. Whereas in 1973 it represented scarcely 3.2 per cent of West German exports, in 1978 this had increased to 8.4 per cent. This 'recycling' of petrodollars was complemented by the aforementioned expansion of direct West German investments after 1973, in cases where the proximity of markets, the cheapness of the labour force or other factors made this the best way to secure a market. The high rates of growth of investments in 'developing' countries — 20 per cent and more in the years around 1975 — give an idea of the extent to which the thinking of capitalists and politicians must have been obsessed by the desire to reserve opportunities for themselves in the Third World. This policy effectively enabled the West German economy to survive the crisis with less damage than occurred in other economies and even with the highest trading surplus in its history.

The presupposition of this strategy was that the world capitalist system should basically be maintained as a system of open markets, with free access to the sources of energy and raw materials and without excessive national protection. However, throughout the 1970s threats to this system kept the economists and politicians of the 'free world' awake at night. In the words of a high level West German diplomat, 'the most serious threat to the economic security of the German Federal Republic and the West comes from events in the Third World. Because of them, the supply of raw materials and energy in particular have become a central problem'.[28]

For the first time, after 1972, semi-official studies by the 'Club of Rome' and others began to glimpse the possible exhaustion of raw materials, sparking a rush by the industrial powers to secure — even militarily — 'their' zones of supply. Amongst some nationalist leaders of the Third World the idea spread that raw materials ought to be the exclusive patrimony of their own nations which should be used in accordance with their own interests. At the end of the 1960s, under the inspiration of Latin American nationalism, the countries of the periphery had come to dominate international forums such as the United Nations and UNCTAD, with their demands for a 'New International Economic Order' (NIEO). In 1973 OPEC was activated, and in 1974 the 'Charter of Economic Rights and Duties of Nations' was approved in the UN with 130 votes in favour, 10 abstentions and 6 votes against, among them the US and West Germany.

The defeat of Portugese colonialism in Africa paved the way for the revolution of 1974 in Portugal and the arrival of Soviet and Cuban military personnel and advisers in several African countries. Through the success of the anti-colonial struggle, and the victory of the anti-imperialist forces in Vietnam and Kampuchea, the 'non-aligned' movement reached its closest approximation to the positions of the Soviet camp with the election of Fidel Castro as president of its conference in Havana in 1979. For the countries of the periphery which import oil and other raw materials, the rise in prices sharpened economic problems and social conflicts, creating 'ungovernability and from there (tendencies) toward fascist or communist dictatorships'.[29] Added to this were various specific problems with countries of the periphery, such as the extension of maritime sovereignty to 200 miles and the problem of the migrant workers of Southern Europe and Turkey in the countries of the EEC.

As for the metropolitan countries, US hegemony was in crisis as a result of the defeat in Vietnam, the crisis of the dollar and the loss of internal consensus after Watergate. In Europe, with the rise of 'Eurocommunism', the Italian and French Communist Parties seemed one step away from participating in their respective governments. After initial confusion, the response of the capitalist countries of the metropolis to these threats to 'free trade' was to put up a strong resistance to any substantial modification in the existing world economic order, but at the same time to show willingness to engage in dialogue on mutual concessions on secondary points. Basically, the central countries were willing to 'concede' what in any case suited them or which they could not avoid: accelerated industrialization by some of the more advanced countries of the Third World, greater participation by the new financial powers of the Middle East in international bodies such as the IMF, more stable prices for certain raw materials, etc. These concessions would have to be matched by guarantees from the countries of the periphery to keep their markets as well as their energy resources and raw materials open to transnational capital. The catchword 'interdependence' emerged, suggesting to countries of the periphery that their interests were inexorably linked to the unhindered forward march of accumulation in the metropolitan economies (which is true, *within* the parameters of the present model of development and international trade). The internal social and political consequences of the existing world economic 'order' were detached from their structural causes. Low salaries, unemployment, miserable standards of living, were made to appear as endemic and preexisting evils which would become objects of a new form of aid geared to the concept of 'basic needs', thus controlling a source of cheap profits but also of possible political disruptions.

In essence, the strategy of confrontation and dialogue with which the industrialized countries resisted the demands for a NIEO are one and the same thing. This is reflected in the differentiated but complementary roles assumed throughout the 1970s by the twin institutions of the IMF and the World Bank.

Nevertheless, the dialectical tension between the strategy of dialogue and confrontation meant that the two were represented in distinct international institutions and competing political currents. In West Germany, the SPD was the receptacle through its ideological discourse for the line of 'mutual interests', while the Christian Democrat opposition party became the mouthpiece for a defence of 'legitimate self-interest' against 'unfounded demands'. The policy of the Liberal-Social Democrat government under Schmidt was a combination of both responses.

A point of conceptual reference for these policies is found in the historical trajectory of West German social democracy within the German labour movement, which it transposes to the present international context. In the words of Willy Brandt, 'Perhaps a part of what is happening today is explained by looking back at the process through which some of today's industrialized countries passed in the nineteenth and beginning of the twentieth centuries. A long and difficult process of apprenticeship was necessary until it was understood that higher wages for the workers contribute to a massive increase in purchasing power sufficient to give impetus to the entire economy'.[30] The idea is completed by quoting from Egon Bahr, a close collaborator of Brandt: 'Today we find ourselves in the same process on a global scale, with the difference that all of us, the entire Federal Republic, belong to the minority of the rich. We would be denying our history and conviction if we didn't encourage at a world level the process through which we ourselves have come . . . Whoever denies evolution encourages revolution'.[31]

By comparing the countries of the periphery to 'the workers' of

German history, they are assigned a role similar to that of the great — social democratic — union confederations in the Federal Republic: ideologically, politically and legally integrated into a corporative system of *Sozialpartnerschaft* (social partnership), they are considered 'co-responsible' for economic prosperity and social welfare. As such they have considerable power of negotiation for labour demands in exchange for subordinating them to the capitalist imperative for a 'satisfactory' rate of profit. The 'offer' which is implied in the conceptual transposition of this model to North-South relations is clear: material concessions and even certain political co-responsibility in exchange for not pursuing any modifications in the world economic system which the dominant countries find incompatible with their own interests. It is not by chance that after 1980 a tendency emerged to replace the term 'New International Economic Order' by 'International Development Strategy'.

The conceptual transposition of internal social relations to external ones reveals much about the social democratic 'mode of thought', which is classically liberal in the sense of going by the outward appearance of 'freedom and equality' in the market. By moving conceptually in the sphere of circulation while ignoring the underlying material differences between the agents of production, the antagonism between capital and labour seems just a divergence of interests. With the international transposition of this 'circulationist' ideology, class relations disappear completely from sight. By magic of analogy, those who occupy the roles of capital and labour are now the dominant classes of both groups of countries.

The purest expression of this line of thought and action is the North-South Commission, chaired by Willy Brandt, which due to its bourgeois composition and its results, reassert the essence of the existing international economic order.

The conciliatory West German position encompasses various other non-explicit 'messages':

— to the countries which export raw materials, that 'fair' prices can be obtained without creating cartels like OPEC.
— to African countries, that in their confrontation with South Africa they have no need to take on an anti-West or anti-white posture.
— to the countries of the Third World in general, that 'economic development' is synonymous with rapid industrialization which at the same time is the best method for absorbing internal social conflicts,[32] to which end West Germany is willing to co-operate with its machinery and experience of social integration.
— that there is no economic partner more respectful of political autonomy than the Federal Republic.

Let us examine this last point in more detail.

Faced with the threats to the metropolitan countries during the 1970s, the Federal Republic showed its total solidarity with the 'Western World' in the defence of 'market mechanisms'.[33] Nevertheless, the world economic crisis also sharpened competition between the different capitalist powers. In the midst of joint efforts to resist the demands for a NIEO, there was the first open conflict between the United States and West Germany over the nuclear agreement with Brazil in 1975.

Both competitors made use of their respective political resources. The position of the Federal Republic during the 1970s was marked by a strange inconsistency between its rapidly rising real influence and its *image* of international political modesty created in the previous decades. The crisis of US hegemony alone meant an advance of the Federal Republic as a factor in international politics. In the words of a well-known journalist: 'Vitally interested in the stability of its irreplacable raw materials supplies, (the Federal Republic) is about to take on some of the political responsibilities which until now it left entirely to its allies . . . the innocence of the economic giant dressed as a political dwarf has gone for ever'.[34]

Nevertheless the reputation of 'political innocence' seems to have remained throughout the 1970s. As a result, during the second half of the 1970s, West German social democracy was in the comfortable situation of being able to make use — in government policy — of all the real political weight of the Federal Republic in international matters, and at the same time — in its party diplomacy — deny that West Germany had pretensions or even capacity to assert itself as a world power.

There is another aspect to this inconsistency which is crucial to the international role of West German social democracy. The orientation of German industry toward the world market is as old as this industry itself — and has almost always been accompanied by political and military expansionism.[35] After the Second World War, an historical 'abnormality' occurs: on the one hand, the role of West Germany as an international economic power reaches a point never reached by the united Germany of the Second or Third *Reich*. On the other hand, it is inhibited from assuming an openly imperialist role in the political and military spheres. Divided, on the frontier between two power blocs, without its own atomic bomb and with the remnants of an antimilitaristic public opinion within the country, it could not become a military power able to operate on a world scale. Even legally, the *Bundeswehr* is firmly inserted in the US war system through NATO and prevented from acting outside the area of the alliance. Despite having become the fifth largest exporter of arms in the world (also toward 'developing' countries) as well as of military and police 'instructors' in Africa, Asia and Latin America, it has up to now been out of the question that the FRG could intervene militarily to 'defend' its economic interests in the Third World'.[36]

As a result, by conviction or lack of an alternative, the West German bourgeoisie puts on civilian dress rather than a uniform when it negotiates with governments in the countries of the periphery. It presents itself as the honest trader, respectful of contracts and laws, non-interventionist, even anti-racist. It defends — through self-interest — the principle of free world trade, opposing protectionism in other parts of the world, but also preserves the appearance of 'freedom' and 'equality' of all parts of the market. In this, it can count on the advantage that its colonial past is forgotten.[37]

To a certain extent, the FRG 'takes advantage' of the political-military control which the United States (and to a lesser degree France and Great Britain) exercises over the countries of the capitalist periphery in order to promote its own economic interests where they compete with the US, without bearing the burden of the financial and political costs of this control. In contrast to the widespread anti-Yankeeism in many parts of the Third World, there is (or was until recently) a positive feeling in favour of the 'West Germans'.

From the 1973 crisis onwards it seems that these symbolic advantages — until then unpremeditated — were 'discovered' as a possible 'public relations' element within an active export strategy. The conciliatory posture taken up by West German social democracy toward the Third World reflects two distinct but related interests:

1. the 'dialogue', part of a 'double' strategy of reducing the demands for a NIEO to secondary points compatible with its own interests;

2. the form of behaviour adopted by West German capital in the post-war period.

Both strands converge in the idea that North-South relations must be organized as *contractual market relations*, in which the different national economies participate as sovereign, free and equal. As Willy Brandt writes in the prologue to the report of the North-South commission: 'We must aspire to a world community founded on contracts rather than hierarchy, on consensus rather than coercion.' The advantages of such liberalism 'with a human face' over unrestricted liberalism are undeniable, but it is also undeniable that it leaves out the underlying structural inequalities.

The specifically social democrat ingredient of this liberal projection consists in accepting certain reforms of these inequalities, and distrust of 'market forces' as the only guarantee of free trade. Just as within countries — according to social democratic belief — the state must intervene in order to support 'the weakest' and to guarantee 'equality', and 'liberty' of the parts of the market, also in international relations it is necessary to create institutions — permanent or ad hoc to monitor and give structural support. Accordingly, the Caracas document affirms: 'the necessary application at the international level of the principles which we support within our countries'.

The revitalization of the SI after 1976 took shape, then, as a materialization of this conciliatory conception of North-South relations. That this concept is a concrete reference point for the social democratic 'offensive' is suggested by the fact that the central and most extensive paragraph of the declaration of Caracas is dedicated to the theme of the NIEO. The incorporation of parties and movements of the Third World as new associates of the SI also means a first step toward their integration into a non-antagonistic method of resolving this conflict. In this sense the international conferences of the SI also acquire a symbolic value as a style of international politics which it wants to project. The signals are sent out not only to Latin America but also to the Third World in general — or more specifically, to all those countries on the periphery which represent some special interest or danger for West German interests (the most industrialized countries, OPEC, national liberation movements, Southern Europe, etc.). A reading of the conversations and correspondence between Brandt, Palme and Kreisky which document the prelude to the 'opening up' of the SI, show that their interest is directed as much toward Africa and the Middle East as toward Latin America. The Caracas document ends by saying that the meeting 'must be continued in other meetings, in which related parties from other regions should gradually be incorporated'. The fact that the international social democratic 'offensive' has strongly concentrated on Latin America, may have corresponded more to the 'pull' of factors within the region than the 'push' of European social democracy — factors which belong as much to the political conjuncture as to the region's more 'mature' and familiar social preconditions in comparison with the majority of African and Asian countries. For many of these, Latin America is an example of industrialization and relative 'progress'. As a result, the aid of the SI to various Latin American movements struggling for radical social transformation counts as much for its symbolic value as for its practical effect in the respective countries. Thus its support for the Sandinista uprising and for the opposition in El Salvador created a progressive image not only amongst anti-dictatorial forces in Latin America,[38] but also amongst reformist movements throughout the world.

But as many of the governments in Africa and Asia which the SI wants to impress with a certain image of the FRG are more similar to Somoza than to the Sandinista Front, in what sense is it a recommendation to have allied itself with such a 'subversive' movement? Without doubt, the progressive behaviour of the SI in Latin America also raises distrust. Nevertheless, it works as a sign of 'non-imperialism', attractive for nationalisms of all types. A greater national self-determination, more industrialization ('progress'), also interests right-wing governments. It is precisely what unites them with those of the left in their demands for a NIEO and which implies the margin of possible concessions by the metropolitan countries.[39]

It is clear then that the progressive posture and practice of international social democracy in Latin America is not *the* European policy, but just the *ideological projection* of a conciliatory posture. The much more restricted catalogue of real concessions remains more authentically expressed in the Brandt Report. As to West German capitalism, its basic policy, implemented through the government and through the majority of international agencies, is still to limit to a minimum the inevitable concessions, defending by all means the essence of the present international economic 'order'.[40] As a top official in the Friedrich Ebert Foundation and protagonist of its Latin American relations has said, the art consists in 'discerning correctly between such distinct things as the SI, bilateral party relations, and government policy'.[41]

Implied in this is a division of roles which reflects the intrinsic ambiguity of West German social democracy. Until now, we have treated it as if its own interests were identical with those of West German capital which it promotes with its international policy. Nevertheless, the SPD does not consider itself the direct political representative of West German capital, nor does the latter accept it as such. There may be identification but not identity. The difference seems minimal, nevertheless, it is only this non-identity which creates the political space that allows social democracy in Latin America to be transformed into a political force of its own, and even into an ally of the left. Politically, then, all depends on a correct evaluation of the differences and interrelations between the interests of capital and the particular interests of the SPD.

### 'Flight forward' in Response to the Erosion of the 'German Model'

In discussing West German social democracy its historical roots in the labour movement must never be lost from view. It is a fact which continues to be present in its internal operations, its discourse and even in elements of its practical politics. We can understand social democracy better if we consider it not a political expression of the owning class

113

but as the *acceptance of their domination* by the working class. It is this that defines its character as a 'party of the people' in West Germany today.

But even in its other identity as *party of the state*, it does not directly represent the interests of capital but a *relationship between social forces*. This 'statist' character comes from a long conceptual tradition which since the origins of the party in the 19th Century, pinned all hopes of emancipation on the regulatory and redistributive action of the state, conceived of as a neutral agent which can be transformed into an instrument of liberation and 'social justice' in the hands of a workers' party. Thus the whole history of West German social democracy could be seen as a gradual rise from the status of slave to that of a master as against its former objective of a society without exploitation. The most important theoretical steps towards this were:

— to consider 'socialism' to be the same as 'centralized state economic planning';
— to see 'organized capital' as the stage supposedly preceding socialism, 'still' capitalist but 'already' centrally regulated;
— to see social welfare within a 'social market economy';
— and finally, the acceptance of the state's guarantee of fluid capital accumulation as a prerequisite for redistributive measures and social peace.

With the transformation of its former communitarian motivation into functions of the state, 'being in government' became virtually a substitute for a programme. *To continue in government*, even at the price of carrying out policies which are no longer recognizable as social democratic, appears almost as an historic mandate. Every decision, then, is shaped by the principle of remaining in power. With this, its central leadership is transformed into a *state personnel par excellence*. In order not to put its government in danger, it tries to provide administrative solutions to social conflicts, and to balance the existing relations of forces, but not to modify it.

Now, although the dominant interests within this relationship are logically those of capital, they are not the only ones. The interests of the subordinate classes which social democracy equally cannot ignore in its balancing act are also present, especially those of the main trade union organizations and the party's own salaried electoral base.

It is our thesis that this — always precarious — capacity to balance the different social forces is due to the specific conditions of West German society in a phase of its history which we can call the 'post-post-war'. The resignation of Willy Brandt as head of government in 1974 reflected the first symptom of crisis in the preconditions of social democratic government. The international activity of the SPD is to a considerable degree an *external* expression of its efforts to halt the collapse of these social preconditions *internally*.

The SPD referred implicitly to these preconditions when in its 1972 electoral campaign it coined the slogan the 'German Model'. In a drive to gain the votes of the right, it appealed with this slogan to nationalist pride in certain features of the German way of life which — of course — contrasted favourably with that of other nations. The SPD, according to this propaganda, would be, if not the creator, at least the best guarantor of this 'German Model'. Amongst these features are: sustained economic growth, accompanied by a proportional growth of real wages, full employment, a welfare state and social peace.

With the ascension of Willy Brandt to the government, the way was clear for a period of overdue reforms. Doors were opened to increased trade, also with the countries of the East, collective consumption was expanded, especially in the field of education, preempting the storm of student revolt in the 1968/9 years, and creating opportunities for the rise of the salaried middle classes. This policy of reformist integration had its counterpart in the modernization of the repressive apparatus, as a strategy for individualizing, isolating and repressing the groups which could not be integrated into the 'Model'. The funds for Internal Security were multiplied, to create special police forces and to install a sophisticated electronic system of political dossiers which accumulated confidential data on millions of persons. And activists of the Communist Party were legally prevented from taking up posts in public administration, either as doctors, teachers or railway workers, a form of professional proscription *(Berufsverbot)* still in force today.

The crisis of 1972/74 marked the end of the material and financial basis for such a Keynesian policy of reforms. In this sense, it is not accidental that Willy Brandt resigned as head of government in 1974 and the 'pragmatic' Schmidt took over. Since then the SPD has no longer dedicated itself to reforms but to easing and administering the crisis. Its efforts to preserve the 'German Model' were increasingly reduced to an attempt to shore up its two principal pillars: international competivity, and the level of wages and employment of the central nucleus of the working class, at the expense of the weaker sectors. It has already been shown that the privileged world position of German exports has its counterpart in a hugh vulnerability of the economy as a whole in terms of its external sector. In its strategy for survival, the SPD saw no alternative other than a complete identification of its economic policy with the interests of large-scale West German capital.

The revitalization of the SI after 1976 can be placed, as I see it, within this context. All that has been discussed so far in relation to its flexible posture on the North-South conflict as a strategy of 'good will' for West German exports, must be complemented by this internal political background. The 'forward flight' in the economic is complemented by a forward flight abroad in the political and ideological. The West German social democratic offensive in Latin America is revealed thus to be in good part an expression of a *defensive* internal policy.

It has already been pointed out that as we are dealing with social democracy, there must be some link with the relation between capital and labour. It is here, in the defence of the internal *status quo* that we once again find social democracy's traditional roots in what is the organized West German labour movement of today. Between this working class tradition and its support for forces of the left in Latin America there is no direct link except at the level of mutual ideological predispositions. The material link takes a long detour: it starts off from the zeal to remain in power, passing through the preoccupation with the wage and employment levels of its organizational support, its identification with the exporting interests of West German industry, and ending up in the propagation of strategies for 'associated' industrial development, the projection of a positive image for the FRG and the assimilation of modernizing elites. This latter element also serves to show the representatives of large West German economic interests that the SPD has better political contacts with the actual and future political leaders in the Third World than its Christian Democrat rivals.

Finally, the spectacular international progressive stance also played the important role of balancing the different political wings within the SPD. It served as a field of action and a 'receptacle' for the popular and reformist element in the party, removed from the tasks of government as a consequence of the crisis. Similarly, it was able to satisfy, albeit symbolically, the aspirations of the left-wing currents of its electorate within and outside of the party, who are very sensitive on (some) Latin American subjects since the Chilean coup in 1973. Later, as the divergences between the West German foreign policy and that of the United States under Carter and Reagan increased, the policy of West German social democracy toward the Central American conflicts was definitively established as a subject of internal controversy, becoming an indicator of the degree of independence from or servitude to the US.

In general terms this strategy succeeded during the years 1975-79. Exports soon recovered their upward rhythm. The loss of jobs in the key sectors of industry were kept at a minimum at the enormous cost of unemployment in the peripheral sectors. Between 1973 and 1975 the level of unemployment rose from its traditional low level of around 1 per cent to a new structural parameter of about 5 per cent. Despite this, the stability of the Schmidt government was not in doubt; in 1980 without great problems he defeated the candidate of the right. This coincided with the expansionist phase of the SI in Latin America. However in 1980/81 the symptoms of the crisis began to sharpen once more, touching on the basic consensus of the 'German Model'. The new doubling of the price of oil in 1978/79 led for the first time in the history of the West German economy to a negative balance of payments. Unemployment reached its highest level since 1954, surpassing 7 per cent at the end of 1981. The massive process of marginalization of labour threatened to go beyond the social democratic resources for social integration, beginning with the financial resources. The astronomic costs of unemployment subsidies has created a permanent drain on the federal budget which is already, for other reasons, in full fiscal crisis.

The renewed tensions in the East-West conflict after the Soviet intervention in Afghanistan was used to justify enormous additional military expenditure as well as huge credits to strengthen the military junta in Turkey. In order to finance the growing fiscal deficit, the state resorted to borrowing beyond any level of Keynesian rationality, and this can only cause additional financial problems in the future. There are already cuts in various sectors of collective consumption, especially in education and social services which have partly cancelled out the reforms introduced during the 'euphoric' phase of the social democratic government under Brandt. Drastic cuts are planned in 1982 even in the politically sensitive areas such as unemployment subsidies, housing etc. In carrying out these austerity plans it is doubtful that the union confederations can continue giving unrestricted support to the government.

In this situation the SPD is retreating before a conservative ideological offensive which proposes to solve the crisis in accordance with the ultra-liberal recipes of Friedman. Schmidt and his liberal allies are visible incorporating elements of this monetarist creed into their own economic policy. Such a strategy, leading to increasing marginalization and social polarization, will definitively end the 'German Model', except the hegemony of export capital.

However, on the left as well, there are groups which have openly rejected the consensus which is the basis of the 'German Model'. Unlike the student movement of 1968, the new social movements no longer base their expectations on the state. What unites the diverse ecological, pacifist, neighbourhood, feminist, youth, 'alternative' lifestyle and spiritual movements, despite the differences between them, are their grass-roots democratic structures, and the demand for autonomous control, which implies a rejection of the bureaucratic forms of social democracy, and makes their integration into the existing corporative system impossible. The electoral blocs formed by

117

these movements are in the process of establishing themselves definitively as a fourth force in the West German party political spectrum, and are even beginning to contest third place with the liberal party, with their 5-9 per cent of the votes, taking vital percentages from the SPD.

A bitter internal dispute within the SPD over economic and social policy, energy and disarmament, has led to speculation since the middle of 1981 about a possible split in the party. It is continually losing local and state elections. It seems certain that there will be no social democrat to succeed Schmidt as head of government, and even that Schmidt himself may lose the elections in 1984, if the social democrat government has not already fallen by then, due to the desertion of its coalition partner, the Liberal Party.

One of the most acute observers of West Germany, the French political scientist Alfred Grosser, summarized the situation at the end of 1981 in the following way: 'It may be that Helmut Schmidt remains as Chancellor until the elections in 1984. But it could also be that he will fall from power shortly, brought down by the right or the by the left (. . .) It would not be impossible for the pacifists and the Christian Democrat opposition to win at the same time, creating an explosive situation (. . .) The conditions for destabilization are numerous. It would at least be premature to argue that the firmly-rooted stability of the Federal Republic over the past thirty years has been buried (. . .) But the present crisis is without doubt the most serious so far.'[42]

Given the severe deepening of the crisis, a renewed 'forward flight' would be as useful and urgent as after the 1973/74 crisis. Nevertheless, it seems that the SPD's economic and political space has been reduced so far that there is no longer sufficient capacity for this, and that this time the flight is backwards. Under the duel pressure of its defensive internal position, and the renewed and aggressive hegemonic ambitions of the Reagan government, West German social democracy ostensibly lowered the tone of its Latin American sorties during 1981. In the interests of a favourable climate in its relations with Washington over the central question of arms limitation, parts of the SPD and of the government at one point even seemed disposed to abandon the international resistance to the US policy of repression and intervention, sacrificing basic principles of its Latin American policy which it had defended up till them.

What is clear is that the international social democratic offensive in Latin America has stagnated since 1980. On top of this there have been growing factional struggles within the Latin American Committee of the Socialist International. This indicates that its role in the region may be of a rather more conjunctural and limited nature than its forceful opening gambit might have suggested.

## Political Perspectives

What then are the consequences and perspectives which can be derived from this argument for the left in Latin America — but also in West Germany — in its contacts with social democracy?

To my mind, our analysis ought to start from the basis that the Latin American policy of the SPD and its strategy of assimilating elites and supporting nationalist tendencies is *in the final instance* — that is, tendentially, in the long term, independent of the intentions of any of the individual actors — made in the context of the competivity of West German transnational capital. But is this point of departure also perhaps the end of the debate? Is it enough to maintain that the activities of the SPD in Latin America are just the 'smiling face' of West German imperialism?

This would be the same as saying that all those forces of the Latin American left which entered into contact with West German social democracy had been deceived. On the contrary, it is my impression that they realistically made use of the space offered for temporary and limited co-operation, in view of their own weaknesses and the very reduced alternatives for potential allies. This is not to rule out the possibility that in the search for a new revolutionary identity after the failure of militaristic and vanguardist strategies, illusions may have been created in some sectors of the left as to how far the coincidence of interests could be maintained, and that the price of these illusions could well be the loss of their own identity.

On the other hand, neither is the progressive image of the policies carried out to date by the SPD in Latin America a mere fantasy. As part of its historic legacy, the social democratic credo contains some of the essential principles of the workers' movement, such as the defence of the right of workers to organize in trade unions, the demand for a 'fair wage', the belief in the parliamentary system and in free elections, and the responsibility of the state for the common good.

While in West Germany this set of principles has been converted into a basis for social appeasement and of the *status quo*, in the present Latin American context it has taken on a very different colouring. It represents a direct challenge to the dominant models of capitalist development in the region, and a common platform for all opposition forces.

In other words, West German social democracy is at one and the same time promoting the transnationalization of the Latin American economies, and on the other hand supporting the political forces which struggle against the effects of this associated development!

In essence, we find here the contradiction at the heart of social democracy, which is that it wants to be the defender of the working class without questioning bourgeois domination, a contradiction which, in the Latin American political arena, shaken as it is by the extreme social conflicts, is seen in all its inherent crudeness.

But as long as it can avoid a definition, the contradiction functions as the space created by this ambiguity, allowing the Socialist International to offer itself as the projection screen for very diverse interests and objectives.

In conclusion, it is a game of 'who uses whom', which both sides are consciously playing. Perhaps the basic rule of the game can be summed up as follows: Give me opportunities to think that I am using you, and I will give you opportunities to think that you are using me.

## Footnotes

1. The subject of this article has been matter of discussion by a number of working groups in Berlin, in which the author had the opportunity to participate, in particular: the ad hoc group of the Centre for Research and Documentation Chile-Latin America (FDCL); the editors of and contributors to the annual *Lateinamerika — Analysen und Berichte* (Latin America — Analysis and Reports) Berlin; and two seminars at the Latin American Institute of the Free University of Berlin. Without these discussions, it would not have been possible to write this article; my thanks to all those friends and colleagues who participated. In particular, the suggestions of Manfred Fassler, Wolfgang Hein, Klaus Meschkat, Urs Mueller-Plantenberg, Theo Rathgeber, Stefan Saarbach and Erich Suessdorf have left their mark on the text.

   Some minor cuts have been made and some footnotes and tables omitted for reasons of space. Complete German version in: FDCL (ed) *Sozialdemokratie und Lateinamerika*, Berlin, 1982; Spanish version in preparation.

2. Two years earlier, its rival party inside Germany, the Christdemokratische Union (CDU — conservative) gave financial and technical assistance to ensure the electoral victory of the Chilean Christian Democrat Party (PDC) under the leadership of Frei. Thus from its very beginnings the Latin American commitment of West German social democracy also had its internal political dimension.

3. The conceptual birth of this initiative is documented in the conversations and correspondence between Willy Brandt, Bruno Kreisky and Olaf Palme, between 1973 and 1975, which has been published in a book entitled *La Alternativa Socialdemócrata*, Blume, Barcelona, 1977. See also the account of Daniel Waksman Schina, *América Latina y la Crisis Europea: Rol de la Socialdemocratica Europea*, Mexico: the Permanent Seminar on Latin America, conference, August 1977, mimeo, and by the same author: 'La IS en América Latina', in a series of four articles in *El Dia*, Mexico, April 1980, and the three subsequent editions.

4. Of the Christian Democrat Party (CDU): Konrad Adenauer Foundation; of the Liberal Party: Friedrich Naumann Foundation; of the Bavarian section of the Christian Democrat Party, which is formally constituted as a party in its own right under the leadership of Franz Josef Strauss (an extreme right-wing neo-liberal): Hans Seidel Foundation.

5. Among those who have been visitors to the SPD headquarters in Bonn are Mario Firmenich, the leader of the Argentine *Montoneros*, but also, Admiral Massera,

who was formerly, as a member of the Argentina military junta, one of those who hunted him with the greatest determination. ARENA, the official party of the Brazilian military regime, renamed itself the 'Social Democrat Party' at the time of a recent reform of political parties, plagiarizing a name which it clearly saw as having attractive connotations. In 1978, the, till then, official candidate, General Figueiredo, said at one point that he considered himself to be a social democrat.

6. James Petras, 'La Social-Démocratie en Amérique Latine', in *Le Monde Diplomatique*, June 1980, pp.15-17.

7. Irina Bucher, 'La Socialdemocracia: ?Alternativa Política Para América Latina?' in *Uno mas uno* (Mexico), 27 November 1979.

8. Dieter Boris, Dietrich Busch, and Rainer Falk, 'Dritte Welt-Expansion der Bundesrepublik Deutschland', part 3, in *Antiimperialistisches Solidaritaetsbulletin* (AIB) 10, 1978, pp.6-10.

9. *Modernization of the economy — guaranteed employment*, special Social Democrat conference in Bremen (Bonn 1976, p.20).

10. *Frankfurter Allgemeine Zeitung*, 4 April 1979.

11. 'The rhetoric which talks of "basic needs" and "dynamizing structures", and which maintains an apparent neutrality with regard to social systems . . . at its best is able to remove those precapitalist and in many cases feudal barriers which get in the way of dependent capitalist development in the Third World. In consequence, it represents almost an essential element for the stabilization of the neocolonial system, in spite of containing a high degree of political risk (revolutionary tendencies).'' Boris, Busch and Falk, *ibid.*, part 1, 7/8, 1978, p.58.

12. World Development Report 1980, p.11.

13. Bundesministerium fur Wirtschaft (Ministry of Economy), in *Frankfurter Rundschau*, 25 April 1978.

14. Erhard Eppler, 'General approaches to development policy', in *Die Zeit*, 4 April 1969; in this sense also Harmut Elsenhans, 'Overcoming underdevelopment', in Nohlen and Nuscheler, eds, *Handbook of the Third World*, vol.1, Hoffman and Campe, Hamburg, 1974, pp.162-189. And by the same author: *Algeria: Colonial and Postcolonial Policies of Reform*, Hamburg, 1977.

15. Tilman Evers, Thomas Hurtienne and Urs Mueller-Plantenberg: 'Laenderbericht: Brasilirn', in the annual: *Lateinamerika — Analysen und Berichte*, vol.3, Olle and Wolter, Berlin, 1979, pp.222-239.

16. Because of pressure from its base, the German metalworkers' union (IG Metall — the biggest trade union in the world) gave its support *a posteriori*.

17. One interesting side effect of this from the perspective of West German social democracy might be that this kind of increase in salary levels in the peripheral countries would lessen the temptation for West German capital to emigrate solely to take advantage of the cheap labour force and thus creating employment in West Germany.

18. Erhard Eppler, 'Entwicklungspolitik und ihr Beitrag zum Strukturwandel', in Ministry for Economic Co-operation, *Mitteilungen*, IV, Bonn, April 1970, p.26.

19. Hans Matthoefer, *Frankfurter Rundschau*, 11 June 1969.

20. Guenther-Grunswald, 'Einige Grundsaetzliche Ueberlegungen und Andregungen der FES zur Lateinamerika Politik', in *Friedrich Ebert Stiftung Informiert* 5, September 1980, p.3.

21. Luis Maira, 'Fuerzas Internacionales y Proyectos de Recambio en América Latina', in J.C. Portanteiro, L. Maira, Liliana de Riz, et al: *Proyectos de Recambio y Fuerzas Internacionales en los 80*. Edicol, Mexico, 1980, pp.21-66; D. Wahl,'Zur Rolle Sozialdemokratischer Entwicklungskonzeptionen in der Neokolonialistischen Strategie des Imperialismus Gegenueber den Entwicklungslaendern unter Besonderer Beruecksichtigung Lateinamerikas'. *La-*

*teinamerika*, Wilhelm-Pieck Universitaet, Rostock, 1978, pp.5-40; Stefan Saarbach, 'Einige Aspekte der Aktuellen Lateinamerikapolitik der Sozialdemokratie', in *Lateinamerika — Analysen und Berichte*, Vol.4, 1980, pp.120-60; Heinz Dietrich, 'Die Socialistische. International und die Amerikanische Revolution', in *Links* 132, March 1981, pp.11-12.

22.     'An increased West German effort (in Latin America) also suits Washington's interests, because historical anti-American resentments mean that it is not best qualified to win sympathy for the West in that continent'. *Frankfurter Allgemeiner Zeitung*, 4 April 1979.

23.     The Portugese Socialist Party was founded in Bonn during a seminar held by the Friedrich Ebert Foundation. The fact that the anti-communist policies of Soares prepared the ground for a return to power by the right-wing in Portugal is seen as an unfortunate accident by West German social democrats, which they attribute to the short-sightedness and self-satisfied posture of Mario Soares, and not to any structural process. Whatever the case may be, this result was not yet apparent in 1976.

24.     Petras, *ibid.*, p.16; and in general for this interpretation, see L. Maira, *ibid.*

25.     Erich Suessdorf and Klaus Dieter Tangermann: 'Von Carter zu Reagan' in 'Zentralamerika: ein Vulkan', *TAZ-Journal*, 2, Berlin, 1980, p.126.

26.     *Fischer Weltalmanach* 1981 (1977 statistics). For 1981, exports were 28 per cent of GNP and for 1982 a record 30 per cent is expected; *Frankfurter Rundschau*, 3 December 1981.

27.     Volker Hauff and V.W. Scharpf, *Modernisierung der Volkswirtschaft: Technologiepolitik als Strukturpolitik*, Europaeische Verlagsanstalt, Frankfurt, 1975.

28.     For example, the enormous secondary effects which are derived from the adoption of a particular system of industrial norms, of a particular electronic technology for 'soft-ware' etc.

29.     Volker Hauff and V.W. Scharpf, *ibid.*, p.28.

30.     Commenting on the results of the North-South Commission, drawn up under his presidency, in the Brandt Report. The idea was already present in his speech in Caracas.

31.     Egon Bahr, cited by Wahl, *ibid.*, p.19.

32.     'Either industrial development in all parts of the world, or an accumulation of economic, and with them political, catastrophes in this, the largest part of the world'. Kalbitzer, an SPD deputy in the Bundestag (the German parliament), cited in *Entwicklung und Zusammerarbeit*, 10, 1976, p.4.

33.     See Urs Mueller-Plantenberg, *ibid.* This assertion is based on the restrictive position taken by the Federal Republic in all international conferences which have been held on the subject: a negative vote on the 'Charter of Economic Rights and Duties of States' in the United Nations in 1974; the Conference on International Economic Co-operation in Paris, 1975-1977; UNCTAD Conference in Nairobi (1976) and Manila (1979); special conferences, such as the 9th Special General Assembly of the United Nations in New York, 1980, and others.

34.     Kurt Becker: 'Kein Zwerg Mehr: Bonn Wird International Gefordert', in *Die Zeit*, 9 June 1978.

35.     With good reason Samir Amin sees the two world wars which have taken place during this century as one 'thirty years war' (with a truce of 20 years in the middle), in which Germany attempted unsuccessfully to ensure that it would succeed the British Empire as the first imperialist world power; in: 'Reflexiones sobre la Teoría del Imperialismo', in *Nueva Sociedad*, 50, Sept-Oct 1980, pp.5-23.

36.     Nevertheless, recently the West German right-wing has been making efforts to 'make conceivable' the idea of a West German military intervention — side by side with the North Americans — in the oil regions of the Middle East.

37. In fact, Germany lost her colonies in the First World War, and tried unsuccessfully to regain them in the Second.

38. 'The reaction of the international and national social democratic forces to the Sandinista revolution and the revolutionary popular state in Nicaragua will be a *thermometer indicating* the true nature and project of social democracy . . . Our attitude toward social democracy will, in these circumstances, be conditioned by the attitude it takes toward the Sandinista revolution'. Declaration of the Guerilla Army of the Poor (EGP — Guatemala), in *Nueva Sociedad*, 45, Nov-Dec 1979, pp.300-316 (emphasis ours).

39. This reflects the ambiguity of the notion of 'dependency' — the conceptual origin of the demand for international economic reforms. In speaking of the emancipation of 'countries' or 'peoples', it is not made clear whether the reference is solely to nation-states, or whether it refers also to the class struggle within the nation. The great symbolic value of the Nicaraguan example for social democracy comes from precisely this fact, that Somoza is synonomous with dependency, and Sandinism with liberation, as much in a class interpretation as for a bourgeois understanding of these words.

40. In the words of the Minister for Foreign Relations, Genscher: 'This new order (NIEO) will not be achieved by throwing out the old and experienced. On the contrary, we must permanently evolve existing structures and adapt them flexibly to new needs and conditions. It is a question of maintaining the efficiency of the regulating mechanism of the market economy, and offering the developing countries participation in the world economy with equal opportunities, as well as more than proportional growth'. Cited in: Ministry for Economic Co-operation, *Politik der Partner,* 5th edition, p.126.

41. *Der Spiegel*, 4 August 1980. On various occasions, Brandt has expressly distanced himself from Schmidt's policies, e.g. as early as his speech in Caracas: 'I am aware that the attitude of my country during different negotiations in recent years has not always been easy to understand. I do not intend to evade a critical discussion on the subject'. *Ibid.,* p.72. Talking about his election as president of the SI, he said: 'I am not one of those who believe that the North-South problems can be resolved simply by means of the market economy . . . (I want to) make it clear to the countries of the Third World that the SPD at least takes a more generous position than the Common Market countries under the dictates of the Bonn free-market economists'. *Der Spiegel*, 6 December 1976, p.49.

42. *Der Spiegel*, 43, 1981, pp.34-5.

# TABLE 1:

## Major Participants in World Trade
Percentages of world trade (ranking in brackets)

| Imports | 1950 | 1955 | 1960 | 1965 | 1970 |
|---|---|---|---|---|---|
| United States | 13.8 (1) | 11.7 (1) | 11.1 (1) | 10.8 (1) | 12.2 (1) |
| German Federal Republic | 4.2 (5) | 6.2 (3) | 7.5 (3) | 8.8 (2) | 9.1 (2) |
| Japan | 1.5 (17) | 2.5 (10) | 3.3 (9) | 4.1 (5) | 5.8 (4) |
| France | 4.7 (3) | 5.1 (4) | 4.6 (4) | 5.2 (4) | 5.7 (5) |
| Great Britain | 11.0 (2) | 10.8 (2) | 9.3 (2) | 7.9 (3) | 6.6 (3) |
| Exports | | | | | |
| United States | 16.6 (1) | 16.4 (1) | 15.9 (1) | 14.6 (1) | 13.6 (1) |
| German Federal Republic | 3.2 (5) | 7.0 (3) | 8.9 (2) | 9.6 (2) | 10.9 (2) |
| Japan | 1.3 (19) | 2.1 (9) | 3.2 (7) | 4.5 (5) | 6.2 (4) |
| France | 5.0 (3) | 5.4 (4) | 5.4 (4) | 5.4 (4) | 5.7 (5) |
| Great Britain | 10.0 (2) | 8.8 (2) | 8.0 (3) | 7.1 (3) | 6.2 (3) |

Sources: Handbook of International Trade and Development Statistics 1972; Statistisches Jahrbuch fuer die Bundesrepublik Deutschland 1977.

*Synopsis prepared by: Urs Mueller-Plantenberg,* 'Die Bundesrepublik Deutschland und-die Neue Weltwirtschaftsordung', *in* Lateinamerika — Analysen und Berichte, vol.2, Olle & Wolter, Berlin, 1978, p.85.

# TABLE 2:

## Major Exporters of Manufactured Products
Percentages of total world exports

| | US | Japan | FRG | France | Italy | Britain |
|---|---|---|---|---|---|---|
| 1964 | 21.5 | 8.1 | 19.3 | 8.7 | 6.3 | 14.4 |
| 1970 | 18.5 | 11.7 | 19.8 | 8.7 | 7.2 | 10.8 |
| 1974 | 17.2 | 14.5 | 21.7 | 9.3 | 6.7 | 8.8 |
| 1975 | 17.7 | 13.6 | 20.3 | 10.2 | 7.5 | 9.3 |

Sources: National Institute Economic Review, *78, November 1976, p.60, cited by Ernest Mandel and Winifred Wolf*, in 'Ende der Krise oder Krise ohne Ende? Bilanz der Wehtwirtschaftsrezession und der Krise in der Bundesrepublik', *Wagenbach, Berlin, 1977, p.81.*

## TABLE 3:

### Commercial Trade between the German Federal Republic and Latin America (1973-79)

| Exports to Latin America | 1973 | 1974 | 1975 | 1976 | 1977 | 1978 | 1979 |
|---|---|---|---|---|---|---|---|
| in billions of marks | 6.4 | 10.2 | 8.9 | 8.8 | 9.5 | 9.25 | 9.65 |
| as a percentage of total FRG exports | 3.58 | 4.42 | 4.01 | 3.42 | 3.47 | 3.24 | 3.06 |
| **Imports from Latin America** | | | | | | | |
| in billions of marks | 6.0 | 6.9 | 6.7 | 8.2 | 9.8 | 9.3 | 10.4 |
| as a percentage of total FRG imports | 4.12 | 3.83 | 3.63 | 3.69 | 4.15 | 3.83 | 3.55 |

Source: *German Ministry of Economic Co-operation*, Journalisten-Handbuch Entwicklungspolitik 1980 S. 176; *idem*, Politik der Partner: Aufgaben, Bilanz und Chancen Deutscher Entwicklungspolitik, *2nd ed. 1977, p.36: calculations our own.*

## TABLE 4:

### Percentages Held by a Number of Industrialized Countries of the World Direct Investments by Country of Origin

| | *1967* | *1971* | *1973* | *1975* | *1976* |
|---|---|---|---|---|---|
| Total held by industrialized countries | 100 | 100 | 100 | 100 | 100 |
| US | 53.8 | 52.3 | 51.0 | 47.8 | 47.6 |
| Great Britain | 16.6 | 15.0 | 13.5 | 11.9 | 11.2 |
| FR Germany | 2.8 | 4.6 | 6.0 | 6.2 | 6.9 |
| Japan | 1.4 | 2.8 | 5.2 | 6.1 | 6.7 |
| Switzerland | 4.8 | 6.0 | 5.6 | 6.5 | 6.5 |
| France | 5.7 | 4.6 | 4.4 | 4.3 | 4.1 |
| Canada | 3.5 | 4.1 | 3.9 | 4.1 | 3.9 |
| Holland | 2.1 | 2.5 | 2.8 | 3.2 | 3.4 |
| Sweden | 1.6 | 1.5 | 1.5 | 1.7 | 1.7 |
| Belgium/Luxembourg | 1.9 | 1.5 | 1.4 | 1.2 | 1.2 |
| Italy | 2.0 | 1.9 | 1.6 | 1.3 | 1.0 |
| Others | 3.8 | 3.2 | 3.1 | 5.7 | 5.8 |

Source: *UN*, Transnational Corporations in World Development: A Re-examination, *New York, 1980; cited by Marianne Mueller,* Die Entwicklung der Deutschen Direktinvestitionen im Ausland nach dem Zweiten Weltkrieg und Ansatze zu ihrer Erklarung. *Free University of Berlin, doctoral thesis, November 1980, p.35.*

## TABLE 5:

### Direct Foreign Investment of the Federal Republic of Germany, 1978, in order of Principal Countries of Destination

|  | Millions of DM | % |
|---|---|---|
| Total accumulated | 59.959 | = 100 |
| 1. US | 10.619 | 17.7 |
| 2. Luxembourg/Belgium | 6.420 | 10.7 |
| 3. France | 5.815 | 9.7 |
| 4. Brazil | 5.423 | 9.1 |
| 5. Holland | 4.042 | 6.8 |
| 6. Switzerland | 3.913 | 6.5 |
| 7. Austria | 2.469 | 4.1 |
| 8. Great Britain | 2.022 | 3.4 |
| 9. Spain | 2.000 | 3.3 |
| 10. Canada | 1.479 | 2.5 |

Source:   Monatsberichte der Deutschen Bundesbank, *January 1981, p.39.*

Note:   It should be remembered that the tables showing direct investment only account for annual transfers, but not reinvestment, and still less the real market value of these investments. According to OECD estimates, the real value stands at around 40 per cent more than the accumulated value of transfers; *H. Kragenau,* 'Umfang der multinationalen Unternehmen', *in: D. Kebschull and O.G. Mayer (eds),* 'Multinationale Unternehmen: Anfang oder Ende der Weltwirtschaft? *Frankfurt, 1974, pp.15-35.* In the case of Brazil, West german banks put their estimates as high as 100 per cent above the accumulated flows; *Boris, Busch and Falk,* ibid., 1st part *in*: AIB, *7/8, 1978, pp.54-65.* A second problem in understanding these figures is that the Ministry of the Economy and the Federal Bank use different statistical methods, and arrive at figures which do not correspond exactly to one another; in general, the estimates of the Ministry are lower.

## TABLE 6:

## West German Direct Investments in Latin America in Country Order
(on 31 December 1979)

|     |                                 | Millions of DM |
| --- | ------------------------------- | -------------- |
| 1.  | Brazil                          | 4996.4         |
| 2.  | Netherlands Antilles            | 1008.8         |
| 3.  | Mexico                          | 800.0          |
| 4.  | Argentina                       | 728.8          |
| 5.  | Panama (excluding Canal Zone)   | 195.8          |
| 6.  | Colombia                        | 136.8          |
| 7.  | Peru                            | 117.7          |
| 8.  | Venezuela                       | 109.6          |
| 9.  | Chile                           | 106.5          |
| 10. | Uruguay                         | 34.2           |
| 11. | Ecuador                         | 26.7           |
| 12. | Cayman Islands                  | 22.7           |
| 13. | Paraguay                        | 20.7           |
| 14. | Costa Rica                      | 16.6           |
| 15. | Guatemala                       | 14.9           |
| 16. | El Salvador                     | 14.8           |
| 17. | Bolivia                         | 9.6            |
| 18. | Nicaragua                       | 5.2            |
| 19. | Cuba                            | 5.2            |
| 20. | Dominican Republic              | 2.8            |
| 21. | West Indies                     | 2.4            |
| 22. | Jamaica                         | 1.5            |

Source: *Ministry of the Economy,* Runderlass Aussenwirtschaft, *10/80, 10 April 1980, cited in* Bundsanzeiger, 25 April 1980.

Note: The statistics provided by the Ministry of the Economy and those of the German Federal Bank are not entirely comparable, as they are based on different statistical methods; it would seem that the statistics given by the Ministry of the Economy are lower than those of the Federal Bank. The above figures do not take reinvestments into account.

## TABLE 7:

### West German Direct Investment in Latin America By Year
(Accumulated Amounts, as a Percentage of Total Foreign Investment)

| Year | 1955 | 1965 | 1970 | 1973 | 1974 | 1975 | 1976 | 1977 | 1978 | 1979 | 1980 |
|---|---|---|---|---|---|---|---|---|---|---|---|
| Millions of DM | 112 | 1579 | 3663 | 4081 | 4739 | 5483 | 6450 | 7466 | 8131 | 8745 | 9287 |
| % of World Total | 26.6 | 19.0 | 17.3 | 12.7 | 12.9 | 13.1 | 13.7 | 14.3 | 14.0 | 13.2 | 12.3 |

Source: Uberseerundschau 3, *May 1975, 5, October 1976, 4, October 1977,* cited by Boris, Busch and Falk, 'Dritte-Welt-Expansion der BRD', *1st part, in:* AIB 7/8, 1978, p.63; *Ministry of the Economy,* ibid; *Deutsch-sudamerikanische Bank, Kurzberichte 1/1978;* calculations our own.

128

## TABLE 8:

## West German External Sales as a Proportion of Total Sales (%)

*i. By Industrial Sector*

|  | 1950 | 1958 | 1967 | 1970 | 1974 | 1975 | 1978 |
|---|---|---|---|---|---|---|---|
| vehicles | 11.5 | 36.3 | 40.7 | 40.6 | 46.1 | 41.5 | 36.2 |
| machinery | 20.3 | 30.2 | 38.0 | 35.5 | 43.5 | 43.7 | 43.0 |
| metalworking (iron) | 16.4 | 17.8 | 30.3 | 24.0 | 35.2 | 34.0 | 33.6 |
| chemicals | 12.3 | 22.5 | 29.0 | 31.1 | 36.0 | 33.0 | 33.8 |
| metalworking (not iron) | 11.4 | 14.9 | 24.4 | 18.3 | 22.9 | 21.6 | 24.5 |
| coal | 27.3 | 20.8 | 22.7 | 22.8 | 27.8 | 28.4 | 24.5 |
| industry, average total | 8.3 | 15.1 | 18.7 | 19.3 | 24.2 | 23.6 | 24.1 |

*ii. By Corporation*

|  | 1970 | 1971 | 1972 | 1973 | 1974 |
|---|---|---|---|---|---|
| VW | 68 | 69 | 69 | 68 | 70 |
| Daimler | 45 | 43 | 47 | 49 | 55 |
| BMW | 46 | 41 | 43 | 46 | 46 |
| Hoechst | 56 | 56 | 59 | 58 | 63 |
| Bayer | 66 | 67 | 67 | 68 | 66 |
| BASF | 42 | 47 | 49 | 49 | 51 |
| Siemens | 41 | 42 | 41 | 43 | 46 |
| AEG-Telefunken | 29 | 30 | 32 | 33 | 37 |
| R. Bosch/Bosch-Gruppe | 40 | 40 | 40 | 48 | 52 |
| Thyssen | 21 | 26 | 26 | 30 | 34 |
| Mannesmann | 41 | 46 | 48 | 50 | 60 |
| Fried. Krupp | 34 | 31 | 34 | 33 | 37 |
| Metallgesellschaft | 20 | 25 | 26 | 28 | 28 |
| Kloeckner-Humboldt-Deutz (KHD) | — | — | — | 48 | 55 |
| Gutehoffnungshütte (GHH) | 37 | 31 | 30 | 42 | 44 |
| Salzgitter | 28 | 21 | 29 | 31 | 36 |

Sources: *i. Altvater, Hoffman and Semmler,* op.cit.
　　　　 *ii. Jorg Huffschmidt and Herbert Schui (eds.),* Gesellschaft im Konkurs? Handbuch zum Wirtschaftskrise 1973-76 in der BRD, *Pahl-Rugenstein, Cologne, 2nd edition, 1977, p.139.*

Note: 　External sales include both exports and foreign production.

# EUROPEAN TRANSNATIONAL CORPORATIONS IN LATIN AMERICA

*Rhys Jenkins*

## Introduction

The significance of transnational corporations (TNCs) in Latin America is well established. The debate over the impact of TNCs on economic development in the Third World has to a large extent focused on Latin America as the major underdeveloped area in which such firms have been active. The influence of TNCs in the region has extended beyond their economic activities into the social and political spheres. They have dominated key sectors in many countries in the region from the early past of this century, concentrating initially on the primary extractive industries such as copper in Chile and Peru and oil in Mexico and Venezuela. More recently they have gained control of the dynamics sectors of manufacturing such as chemicals, machinery and vehicles. They have played a major role in transforming patterns of production and consumption throughout the region. They have also been involved in diverse ways in local politics, including, on several occasions, attempts to overthrow governments in the countries in which they operate.

There is now a considerable literature on TNCs in Latin America from different ideological positions. Most of the literature, however, either treats the TNC as an undifferentiated phenomenon, paying little regard to the national origins of different TNCs, or focuses mainly on US TNCs. There has been little explicit consideration of European TNCs as a group and their impact in Latin America with the major exception of Lietaer (1979). This paper attempts to fill the gap. In doing so it will first be necessary to trace the increased competition between European and US capital for world markets. The extent of this competition in Latin America and the importance of the region for European capital is then considered. The identification of European TNCs as a group raises the question of whether these firms are in some significant ways different from US TNCs. If so, what are the implications of such differences for the host countries? After a brief discussion of the pattern of development associated with TNC expansion in Latin America, the impact of European investment is considered in greater detail.

Before looking at the operations of European TNCs in Latin America, it is worth considering the importance of foreign capital in the region as a whole. In the post-war period foreign investment has

---

**TABLE 1**

**Share of Manufacturing Industry Controlled by Foreign Firms c. 1970.**

| Country | Year | Foreign Share *(%)* | Basis of Calculation |
|---|---|---|---|
| Argentina | 1972 | 31.0 | Manufacturing production |
| Brazil | 1969 | 41.6 | Manufacturing assets |
| Central America | 1968 | 30.0 | Manufacturing production |
| Chile | 1968 | 29.9 | Capital and reserves of manufacturing limited liability companies |
| Colombia | 1974 | 43.4 | Manufacturing production |
| Ecuador | 1971-3 | 66.1 | Assets of public corporations |
| Mexico | 1970 | 34.9 | Manufacturing production |
| Peru | 1969 | 44.0 | Manufacturing production |
| Venezuela | 1975 | 35.9 | Value added in manufacturing |

Sources:

| | | |
|---|---|---|
| | Argentina: | *Sourrouille (1976), Table II.1.* |
| | Brazil: | *Newfarmer and Mueller (1975), Table 5.7.* |
| | Central America: | *Wilmore (1976), p.501.* |
| | Chile: | *Gassic (1971), Table 38.* |
| | Colombia: | *ECLA/UNCTC (1979), Table 19.* |
| | Ecuador: | *Mytelka (1979), Table 1.6.* |
| | Mexico: | *Fajnzylber and Tarrago (1975), p.256.* |
| | Peru: | *Anaya Franco (1974), Table 13.* |
| | Venezuela: | *Bitar and Trencoso (1981), Table 7.* |

come to be concentrated more and more in the manufacturing sector. With import substituting industrialization as the main development strategy in most countries the manufacturing sector became a key area of activity. TNCs were well placed to take advantage of the opportunities which this strategy offered and by the 1970s they controlled a third or more of the industrial output in most countries of the region (Table 1). However, such global figures tend to underestimate the strategic significance of TNCs in the Latin American economies. They tend, as already mentioned, to be concentrated in particular key industries within manufacturing where their share of output is much higher. They also tend to be concentrated amongst the largest corporations in each Latin American country. Moreover they exercise considerable control over markets because of the oligopolistic nature of many of the sectors in which they operate.

The high level of penetration by foreign capital in Latin American industry in the early seventies was the result of a process of denationalization initiated in most countries in the 1950s. By taking-over locally owned firms, increasing their market shares, and establishing themselves in the most rapidly growing branches of industry, TNCs extended their control over local industry within a decade. In the sixties and early seventies, the share of foreign capital in Argentine, Brazilian and Mexican industry increased from less than 20 per cent to around 30 per cent.


## The European Challenge to US Capital

In the immediate post-war period, the size and technological advantages of US TNCs placed them in an apparently impregnable position. Since the late fifties, however, there has been an intense struggle between US and European capital for world markets, a struggle that was joined in the seventies by Japanese capital. The surge of US investment into Europe in the fifties and early sixties, which was seen at the time as a major threat to European business (Servan Schreiber, 1969), has been countered by a major international expansion of European capital. Thus, far from the gap in terms of size and technology between United States and European firms widening, it has in fact narrowed. With hindsight US investment in Europe in the fifties and sixties can be seen as a response to the much higher rate of growth of the European economies and in this period European TNCs (Hymer and Rowthorn, 1970).

The relative decline in the position of US capital in relation to European capital can be illustrated in a number of ways. Large European firms have tended to grow at a faster rate than large US firms. Between 1957 and 1977, sales of US firms grew at an average annual rate of 7.8 per cent compared to 9.9 per cent for European firms and 12.8 per cent for continental European firms. As a result the number of US firms among the world's largest 100 companies declined from 74 in 1957 to 47 in 1979, while the number of European firms increased from 25 to 41 over the same period. The difference in size between US and non-US firms has narrowed considerably since the late fifties, particularly in cars, electrical machinery, iron and steel and non-ferrous metal. In a number of industries the leading position of US firms has been substantially eroded.

European capital expansion was directed at first to areas outside the United States, as the difficulties of entry were greatest in the US and high labour costs and low tariff barriers made exporting a more attractive alternative there. Not only did European TNCs grow more rapidly than their US rivals, but, by the seventies at least, their overseas operations were also expanding at a faster rate than those of US TNCs. One area which proved particularly attractive to German, Italian and French capital was Latin America, especially since the import substituting industrialization strategies, embarked upon in the region after World War II, presented opportunities for replacing goods previously imported from the United States by local manufacture of European products.

Although Latin America is often thought of as the preserve of US capital, such a picture is becoming increasingly less accurate. For the region as a whole the US share of accumulated direct foreign investment declined from 66 per cent in 1967 to 59 per cent in 1975. In a number of countries including Brazil, Colombia, Chile and Venezuela, the United States accounted for no more than a half of the total value of foreign investment by the mid-seventies. Whereas the United States continues to enjoy a pre-eminent position in Mexico and Central America, in South America it is more or less matched by investment from the other advanced capitalist countries.

## The Extent of European Investment in Latin America

The most important single source of non-US foreign direct investment in Latin America is of course Western Europe. In 1976 this group of countries accounted for 26 per cent of accumulated direct foreign investment, followed by Japan with 4.8 per cent and Canada 4 per cent. A similar situation existed in terms of the number of subsidiaries in Latin America controlled by non-US parent companies. European transnationals controlled 29 per cent of all foreign subsidiaries in the region.

While in aggregate US capital in Latin America clearly predominates over European capital, interesting patterns emerge at the sectoral level. Unfortunately the latest data on the value of foreign investment in Latin America by country of origin and by sector is for 1967. This indicates that at a time when the United States accounted for two-thirds of all investment in the region by OECD countries, it accounted for over 90 per cent in mining, over 80 per cent in commerce and over three-quarters in petroleum, while its share of investment in manufacturing was only 54 per cent. Whereas only a third of total US investment in the region was in manufacturing more than half of non-US investment went to that sector. Thus within the key manufacturing sector non-US foreign investment and particularly European TNCs appear to be of considerable importance in the region.

There are also significant differences between countries in the region. European capital has established a strong presence in the two most industrialized countries of South America, Argentina and Brazil, where more than 40 per cent of both the value of foreign investment and the number of subsidiaries is European. In the other Latin American countries European capital represents a less important proportion of total operations by TNCs (Table 2).

## TABLE 2

### Share of Western Europe in Direct Foreign Investment (DFI) and Number of Foreign Subsidiaries in selected LA countries

| Country | Reference year for DFI stock | Share of Western Europe in DFI stock | Share of Western Europe in number of subsidiaries |
|---------|------------------------------|--------------------------------------|---------------------------------------------------|
| Argentina | 1973 | 44 | 43 |
| Brazil | 1976 | 38 | 40 |
| Chile | 1964-68 | 25[1] | 35 |
| Colombia | 1976 | 20 | 16 |
| Mexico | 1975 | 16 | 21 |
| Peru | 1973 | 17[2] | 27 |
| Venezuela | 1977 | 15 | 19 |

**Notes**

1. Share of inflow of direct foreign investment in the period.
2. Manufacturing only.

Sources: *ECLA (1978), Table 38.*
*Lietaer (1979), Appendix D, Table IV.*
*MIT (n.d.).*
*ODEPLAN, (1970).*

## The Importance of Latin America for European Capital

At first sight it appears that Latin America is relatively marginal to the international operations of European TNCs. In the first half of the 1970s, 70 per cent or more of the net flow of direct foreign investment by France, the United Kingdom and West Germany went to other advanced capitalist countries. The share of the Latin American countries varied from 6 per cent for the United Kingdom to 11.5 per cent for West Germany. These totals amounted to slightly over a fifth of the net foreign investment by France and the United Kingdom in the underdeveloped countries and over a third for West Germany (Table 3).

### TABLE 3

### Share of Latin America in Flow of Direct Foreign Investment (DFI) from Selected European Countries

|  | % of total DFI | % of DFI in LDCs |
|---|---|---|
| West Germany (1971-76) | 11.5 | 34.6 |
| United Kingdom (1970-75) | 6.0 | 22.4 |
| France (1970-76) | 7.9 | 22.0 |

Source: *Billerbeck and Yasugi (1979)*.

The real significance of Latin America however is as a growing market for European TNCs and despite the relatively low share of direct foreign investment going to the region, the growth of investment is spectacular. In the early seventies both West Germany and United Kingdom investment in Latin America grew faster than in other parts of the Third World and far faster than in the advanced capitalist countries. In the case of France the growth was marginally lower than the rapid expansion of French investment in the developed countries but much higher than in other underdeveloped economies (Table 4).

There is little doubt that for individual European TNCs Latin America plays a crucial role in their international expansion strategy. The most clear example of this is Volkswagen (VW) which is not only the largest TNC in the region, but also the largest private corporation of any kind. Over a quarter of the company's vehicle production in recent years has been in Latin America. Even more significantly the region has been a crucial source of profit for the company. Between 1965 and 1975 VW do Brasil remitted US$280 million of profit to the parent company. This was of vital importance in the early 1970s when

## TABLE 4

### Average Annual Growth of Flow of Direct Foreign Investment from Selected European Countries by Area of Destination

|  | To Developed Countries | To Latin America | To Other LDCs |
|---|---|---|---|
| West Germany (1970-76) | 9.1% | 24.0% | 21.0% |
| United Kingdom (1970-75) | 9.4% | 19.0% | 13.2% |
| France (1971-76) | 26.0% | 24.0% | 4.2% |

Source: *Billerbeck and Yasugi (1979).*

---

the parent company's operations were in poor financial shape. In 1972 the Brazilian subsidiary accounted for almost half of the company's worldwide income and continued profitability in Brazil in 1974 and 1975 helped offset heavy losses elsewhere. Although Brazil is the centrepiece of the company's Latin American operations, VW is also a leading producer in Mexico where it is the largest manufacturer of small cars. It has also recently acquired the Chrysler subsidiary in Argentina, as well as being active in the Andean Pact countries.

Latin America thus plays a central role in VW's global strategy. More than three quarters of the company's foreign investment in the early 1970s was in Latin America and the region accounts for a quarter of the parent company's worldwide output. In recent years, under a combination of threats and incentives, VW has begun to export on a significant scale from both Brazil and Mexico. In Brazil the company, worried about the impact of the Ford Maverick on its market share, committed itself to exporting goods worth more than US$1000 million between 1974 and 1982 in order to introduce a new model. By the late 1970s VW was exporting more than 10 per cent of its Brazilian production.

In Mexico VW began exporting in the late sixties and in the early seventies the parent company allocated production of the Safari for sale worldwide to its Mexican subsidiary. In the late seventies with production of the Beetle being brought to an end in West Germany, Mexico became the major source of this model for the West German market. It also supplies some parts to its US plants from Mexico. The company is not only increasingly integrating Latin America into its international operations but also attempting to promote links between its subsidiaries within Latin America. There is some exchange of parts between Brazil and Mexico and the new VW subsidiary in Argentina will be supplied with parts and components from Brazil. With its strong position in the West German market coming under threat from

TABLE 5

## Sales and Employment by Major European TNCs in Latin America, 1978

|  | Sales | | Employment | |
|---|---|---|---|---|
|  | US$m | % of worldwide sales | '000s | % of worldwide employment |
| Volkswagen | 2,200[1] | 26[2] | 52[1] | 25[1] |
| BAT | 2,900 | 23 | 32 | 21 |
| Nestlé | 1,600 | 14 | 34 | 22 |
| Daimler-Benz | 1,500 | 11 | 26[3] | 13[3] |
| Olivetti | 1,800 | 13 | n.a. | n.a. |
| Philips | 1,100 | 7 | 27 | 8 |
| Fiat | 700[4] | 7[2] | 9[4] | n.a. |
| Dunlop-Pirelli | 800[5] | 19[4] | 16[5] | 10[4] |
| Shell | 700[5] | 2[4] | 11 | 7 |
| Saint Gobin | 800[5] | 11[4] | 17 | 11 |
| Bayer | 900 | 8 | 14 | 8 |
| Hoechst | 700 | 6 | 14 | 8 |
| BASF | 600 | 5 | n.a. | n.a. |
| Rhone Poulenc[5] | 600 | 10 | n.a. | n.a. |
| Unilever | 600 | 3 | 11 | 3 |
| L M Ericsson | 500 | 24 | 16 | 25 |
| Ciba-Geigy | 500 | 10 | 7 | 9 |

Notes: 1. Brazil and Mexico only.
2. Percentage of number of units sold.
3. Argentina and Brazil only.
4. 1974 figure.
5. Estimate obtained by applying Latin American share of worldwide total in 1974 to worldwide total for 1978.

Sources: *Stopford, et al. (1980).*
*Company reports.*
*Vaitsos (1978), Table 4.*

the Japanese, VW's Latin American operations, particularly the highly profitable Brazilian subsidiary, are likely to become increasingly important to the parent company.

The second most important European TNC in the Latin American motor industry, Daimler-Benz, enjoys a strong position in the regional lorry market. Although not as heavily committed to Latin America as VW, this region is still the most important sales area outside Europe for the company. Daimler-Benz dominates the Brazilian bus market and it is the market leader in lorries over three tons. Its other major subsidiary in Latin America is in Argentina. Brazil is increasingly being used as an export base not only for the rest of Latin America but also for Africa, Turkey and the United States where the firm's new assembly plant will be supplied with kits from Brazil.

Two other European TNCs with a major stake in Latin America are Nestlé and British American Tobacco. Nestlé is active in food and beverage processing in at least fifteen Latin American countries. It is the market leader in many of the product lines and countries in which it operates. For instance it dominates the markets for infant formula in Colombia, Peru, Mexico and Venezuela. British and American Tobacco is primarily a cigarette manufacturer but has in recent years diversified into other branches including food processing. It is the market leader in cigarettes in Argentina, Brazil, Costa Rica, El Salvador, Mexico, Nicaragua and Panama. Both these firms have over a fifth of their labour force in Latin America and in the case of BAT the region accounts for over a fifth of total sales.

A number of other European transnationals had sales in excess of US$500 million in Latin America in the late seventies (Table 5). Although insufficient data means that some companies have been omitted, the list is at least indicative of the extent of European involvement. For many of the firms included, Latin America accounts for a significant share of world sales and employment, particularly amongst those firms whose sales in the region are over US$1000 million.

## The Impact of TNCs in Latin America

The extensive penetration of the Latin American economies by TNCs in the post-war period has contributed to a pattern of growth which has been characterized by some authors as 'dependent development'. This 'style of development' which has predominated in Latin America in recent years and in which TNCs have played a leading role has a number of salient features. Penetration by foreign capital has been associated with high levels of industrial concentration, the denationalization of local industry through acquisitions by TNCs and the marginalization of both local capital and entrepreneurship, often reducing them to a *rentier* role.

The tendency of TNCs to introduce the capital-intensive techniques developed in their home countries, and the fact that local capital in order to compete effectively must adopt similar techniques, has tended to limit the employment creating effects of this type of development. At the same time the types of products marketed by TNCs are inappropriate to the needs of the bulk of the population, although not

138

of course to those social groups which control the greater part of purchasing power within the economy.

The marketing strategy of the TNCs is twofold. They intensively exploit the high income market introducing new models and new products in an attempt to increase demand for consumer durables through frequent replacement. They also attempt to extend the consumption of such products to lower income groups, often in the process displacing basic necessities from these groups' purchases, a phenomenon sometimes referred to as the 'empty refrigerator syndrome'.

A further characteristic of dependent development is the balance of payments pressure which it creates. TNC production is often highly import intensive so that, as the leading sectors of the economy come increasingly under their control, dependence on imported goods tends to rise. Moreover, repatriation of profits, dividends, royalties and interest payments contribute further to the outflow of foreign exchange. Unless, therefore, TNCs make a major effort at exporting from Latin America, they are likely to account for a substantial share of the region's balance of payments deficit.

*a. The case of European investment*
The question that must now be considered is whether European TNCs are in some ways different from US TNCs and, more specifically, whether such differences make their contribution to economic development in Latin America greater than that of US TNCs. The most explicit presentation of the argument that European TNCs are in some ways 'better' for development in Latin America has been put forward by Lietaer (1979). He identifies a number of key differences between American and continental European TNCs. In terms of sectoral distribution continental European TNCs are more heavily concentrated in manufacturing and specifically in the chemical-pharmaceutical and electro-mechanical industries. In technological terms innovation by European TNCs is concentrated on developing new production techniques rather than introducing new products, and on labour-intensive rather than capital-intensive production, thus making their products and technology more suitable for countries such as those of Latin America where labour is plentiful and capital is scarce. Lietaer also argues that European TNCs are generally more flexible in their overseas operations than their US counterparts, both in terms of their willingness to adapt products and production processes to local conditions and their willingness to enter into joint-ventures.

Other relevant characteristics of European TNCs which need to be considered include their performance regarding exports and imports and the ways in which they began their overseas operations. These questions are relevant to two of the major issues mentioned above, namely the impact of TNCs on the balance of payments of host countries and the denationalization of the Latin American economies as a result of takeovers of locally-owned firms.

Unfortunately the nature of most previous studies of TNCs in Latin America make it difficult to analyse these questions in detail since only fragmentary data is available. The best information is, however, on Brazil which has the double advantage of being both the Latin American country with the highest level of foreign investment and a fairly even division of investment between the United States and Europe.

Two studies have attempted to test the proposition that the production techniques employed by European or non-US TNCs in Brazil are significantly less capital-intensive than those used by US TNCs (Morley and Smith, 1977; Newfarmer and Marsh, 1981). Neither study was able to find very strong statistical support for this hypothesis on the basis of the available data. This suggests that far from the European TNCs having more labour-intensive production techniques particularly suitable for the Latin American countries, they employ very similar production processes to those used by US firms. Indeed there is reason to believe that the internationalization of capital is leading to a standardization of production technology amongst the leading capitalist economies, particularly as the substantial differential in labour costs between the United States and Western Europe has disappeared in recent years.

The argument that the products developed in Western Europe are more appropriate for low income markets than US products is rather more difficult to examine in quantitative terms. However an equally plausible case can be made for supposing that there is no substantial difference. Is it a coincidence that one of the largest European TNCs in Latin America is Nestlé, a firm which has created an international scandal as a result of the 'inappropriateness' of its powdered baby milk in underdeveloped countries? European pharmaceutical companies such as Hoffman La Roche and Ciba-Geigy have also been as involved as their North American counterparts in promoting inappropriate, ineffective and sometimes harmful drugs without suitable warnings, and often after such products have been withdrawn in the advanced countries because of the risks involved.

Even cases which are often quoted to illustrate the appropriateness of European products in Latin America turn out on closer examination to be ambiguous. One such example is Volkswagen in Brazil which became a market leader in the fifties and sixties with the cheap and reliable Beetle model. However, despite initial emphasis on a single basic model, VW do Brasil substantially expanded its range in the late sixties and seventies to produce more expensive models in competition with the subsidiaries of Ford and General Motors. Moreover given that the Brazilian car market is restricted to the richest 20 per cent of families, not even the Beetle could be regarded as an appropriate product for mass consumption in Brazil. As with production processes, the internationalization of capital is leading to increasingly similar products being produced by TNCs from the United States, Western Europe and Japan as recent developments in the car industry clearly illustrate.

The indicator that is usually presented to illustrate the greater flexibility of European TNCs compared to their US counterparts is their willingness to enter into joint-ventures often on the basis of minority ownership, compared to the traditional insistence of US firms on wholly-owned subsidiaries. Table 6 illustrates that there is indeed a clear distinction between the two groups of TNCs in this respect. This does not however prove that nationality *per se* is the crucial factor explaining differences in ownership patterns. As has already been indicated European TNCs in Latin America are relative latecomers. As such they faced established market positions held either by US exports or US subsidiaries. In order to gain a foothold in the region they were forced to be more flexible than existing dominant firms. This involved not only a willingness to take on local partners but also a greater willingness to begin local manufacturing operations.

## TABLE 6

### Distribution of Ownership Patterns of Subsidiaries of TNCs in Developing Countries, by Country of Origin to 1970

|  | Wholly Owned | Majority Owned | Co-owned | Minority-Owned |
|---|---|---|---|---|
| US | 50 | 19 | 10 | 20 |
| Western Europe | 30 | 20 | 9 | 40 |
| Other (predominantly Japanese) | 12 | 12 | 8 | 68 |

Source: *UNCTC (1978), Table III.24.*

Note: Affiliates of which parent firm own 95 per cent or more are classified as wholly owned; over 50 per cent as majority owned; 50-50 as co-owned; 5 to under 50 per cent as minority-owned.

The view that it was the need to challenge the dominant position of US capital that led to such flexibility is further supported by the experience of Japanese TNCs in the Third World. As even later arrivals on the local scene they have characteristically been more flexible than European TNCs (see Table 6). There is also evidence that US firms which are not market leaders have been willing to use joint-ventures in order to establish themselves in Latin America. Examples of this include American Motors and General Tires. This also suggests that it is the relative position of different firms within the international oligopoly rather than country of origin which is crucial.

Another aspect of the greater flexibility of non-dominant firms within the international oligopoly is illustrated by the development of the Latin American motor industry. When the Brazilian and Argentinian governments began in the late fifties to require greater use to be made of locally produced parts and components in vehicles assembly — with a view to full manufacturing within a few years — the Big Three US firms, General Motors, Ford and Chrysler, which have previously enjoyed a dominant position in the local market, were reluctant to engage in local car manufacture and concentrated on lorry production. European firms such as VW, Fiat and Peugeot had no such inhibitions and began car production since they were anxious to establish themselves in the region. Nevertheless the major difference was not between US and European firms but between the Big Three and other manufacturers. This is further illustrated by the activities of two small US producers, Kaiser in Argentina and Willys in Brazil.

One of the criticisms directed against TNCs in Latin America is that they tend to use a high proportion of imported inputs and thus limit the impact on local industrial development. Despite the evidence from the motor industry mentioned above, there is no overall tendency for European TNCs to make greater use of local inputs than for US TNCs. The study of Brazil already referred to, indicated that there was no statistically significant difference between US and non-US subsidiaries in terms of the ratio of imports to sales (Newfarmer and Marsh, 1981, p.101). A similar conclusion can be drawn from a sample survey of TNCs in a number of Latin American countries which indicated that both sales and imports by such subsidiaries are roughly equally divided between US and European firms in the region (Vaitsos, 1978, Tables 2 and 8).

The situation as far as exports is concerned is less clear-cut. The Brazilian study indicates that there may be a tendency for non-US TNCs to export a somewhat higher proportion of their output than US TNCs. This, it is suggested, is because of a less widespread network of subsidiaries of non-US TNCs which means that more export markets are open to them. On the other hand Vaitsos' data indicates that US subsidiaries account for a higher share of total TNC exports than of TNC sales, suggesting the opposite conclusion. The view that

US subsidiaries as a group tend to export more is reinforced by the observation that West German subsidiaries account for over 60 per cent of exports by EEC TNCs and that two firms (VW and Mercedes-Benz) account for most of West German exports.

A major criticism of TNCs in Latin America has been that to a large extent they have expanded through acquiring existing firms rather than setting up 'new' ventures. It is suggested that this has contributed to the denationalization of the economy, the displacement of local entrepreneurship and has generally limited the potential benefits of foreign investment for the recipient country. The question that therefore arises is whether European TNCs have been more willing than their US counterparts to set up new factories in the region. Evidence suggests that a similar proportion of both US and European subsidiaries were set up by forming new firms, 57 per cent of a total of 1,178 subsidiaries in the region were newly formed compared to 62 per cent of 321 European subsidiaries.*

## Conclusion

These comparisons of European and US TNCs in Latin America reveal that in general, differences are insignificant. Where differences do exist they are due to the position of different firms within the international oligopoly rather than their national origin. There is therefore little reason to believe that European capital will have more beneficial effects in Latin America than US capital as some authors have suggested. Indeed the internationalization of capital is all the time making differences in national origins less relevant as the world economy becomes increasingly integrated. The question of the impact of European investment in Latin America is not therefore distinguishable from the question of the impact of TNC activities generally in the region. Even more broadly it can be argued that the impact of the internationalization of capital is the dominant factor. This affects not only foreign firms but also locally-owned firms which also have to transform their production processes and products.

This is not to suggest that host governments in Latin America have nothing to gain from a diversification in the sources of foreign investment within their countries. Increased international competition between US and European (and of course Japanese) capital does make it possible for governments to obtain better terms in bargaining with TNCs. Such diversification may also enable governments to be less

* Calculated from Franko, 1976, Table 4. The difference was not statistically significant.

reliant politically on one country, in this case the United States, although of course European countries are not averse to trying to influence policies in the Latin American economies.

## References

E. Anaya Franco, *Imperialismo, Industrializacion y Transferencia de Tecnologia en el Peru*, Editorial Horizonte, Lima, 1974.

K. Billerbeck and Y. Yasugi, *Private Direct Foreign Investment in Developing Countries*, World Bank Staff Working Paper 348, 1979.

S. Bitar and E. Trancoso, *Venezuela y America Latina Industrializacion Comparada*. Paper presented to the First Conference of the Asociacion de Economistas de America Latina y El Caribe, Caracas, 1981.

F.H. Cardoso, 'Associated-Dependent Development: Theoretical and Practical Implications', in A. Stepan (ed.), *Authoritarian Brazil*, Yale University Press, New Haven, 1973.

V. Droucopoulos, 'The Non-American Challenge: A Report on the Size and Growth of the World's Largest Firms', *Capital and Class*, 14, 1981.

ECLA, Comision Economica para America Latina. *Tendencias y Cambios en la Inversion de las Empresas Internacionales en los Paises en Desarrollo y Particularmente en America Latina*, Division de Desarrollo Economico, Dependencia Conjunta CEPAL/CET, Documento de Trabajo 12, 1978.

Economic Commission on Latin America/Centre on Transnational Corporations, Joint Unit, *Foreign Participation in Colombian Development: the role of TNCs*, ECLA/UNCTC, 1979.

P. Evans, *Dependent Development*, Princeton University Press, 1979.

F. Fajnzylber, 'Oligopolio, Empresas Transnacionales y Estilos de Desarrollo', *El Trimestre Economico*, 171, 1976.

F. Fajnzylber and T. Tarrago, *Las Empresas Transnacionales: Expansion a Nivel Mundial y Proyeccion en la Industria Mexicana* (version preliminar), CONACYT/CIDE, Mexico, 1975.

L. Franko, *The European Multinationals*, Harper and Row, London, 1976.

G. Gassic, *Concentracion, Entrelazamiento y Desnacionalizacion en la Industria Manufacturera*, Documento de Trabajo, Centro de Estudios Socio-economicos, Santiago de Chile, 1971.

S. Hymer and R. Rowthorn, 'Multinational Corporations and International Oligopoly: the Non-American Challenge', in C.P. Kindleberger (ed.), *The International Corporation*, MIT Press,

Cambridge, Mass., 1970.

F. Lietaer, *Europe + Latin America + the Multinationals*, Saxon House, Farnborough, 1979.

M. Luiz Possas, *Employment Effects of Multinational Enterprises in Brazil*, International Labour Office, Geneva, 1979.

S. Morley and G. Smith, 'Limited Search and the Technology Choices of Multinational Firms in Brazil', *Quarterly Journal of Economics*, 1977.

L. Mytelka, *Regional Development in a Global Economy*, Yale University Press, New Haven, 1979.

R. Newfarmer and L. Marsh, *Industrial Interdependence and Development: A Study of International Linkages and Industrial Performance in Brazil*, mimeo, 1981.

R. Newfarmer and W. Mueller, *Multinational Corporations in Brazil and Mexico: Structural Sources of Economic and Non-economic Power*, Report of the Sub-committee on Multinational Corporations of the Committee on Foreign Relations, US Senate, 1976.

ODEPLAN, *El Capital Extranjero en Chile en el Perodo 1964-1968 a Nivel Global y Sectorial*, Version preliminar R/PL/70-007, Santiago de Chile, 1970.

A. Orlandi, *European Direct Private Investment in Latin America*, mimeo, Paper prepared for Latin American Bureau, 1981.

Ministerio de Industria y Turismo, *La Inversion Extranjera, 1971-73 en La Industria Peruana*, Lima, Peru, n.d.

B. Sepulveda and A. Chumacero, *La Inversion Extranjera en Mexico*, Fondo de Cultura Economica, Mexico City, 1973.

J. Servan Schreiber, *The American Challenge*, Penguin, Harmondsworth, 1969.

J. Stopford, J. Dunning and K. Haberick, *The World Directory of Multinational Enterprise*, Macmillan, London, 1980.

J.V. Sourrouille, *El Impacto de las Empresas Transnacionales sobre el Empleo y los Ingresos: El Caso Argentino*, International Labour Office, Geneva, 1976.

UNCTAD, *Marketing and Distribution of Tobacco*, TD/B/C.1/205, Geneva, 1978.

UNCTC, *Transnational Corporations in World Development: A Reexamination*, United Nations, New York, 1978.

UNCTC, *Transnational Corporations in Food and Beverage Processing*, United Nations, New York, 1980.

C. Vaitsos, *The Role of Transnational Enterprise in Latin American Economic Integration Efforts: Who Integrates and with Whom, How and for Whose Benefit?* Report prepared for UNCTAD Secretariat, 1978.

J.W. Vaupel and J.P. Curhan, *The World's Multinational Enter-*

*prises*, Harvard University Graduate School of Business Administration. Cambridge n.d.

L. Wilmore, 'Direct Foreign Investment in Central American Manufacturing', *World Development*, 4, 6, 1976.

# EUROPEAN FINANCIAL FLOWS TO LATIN AMERICA

*Alberto Orlandi*

## The Magnitude of Latin America's Foreign Debt and its Implications

Subsequent to the dramatic increase in petroleum prices of October 1973, Latin America as a whole, excluding Venezuela and Ecuador which are oil-exporters and members of OPEC, registered a large deficit in its current account balance of payments between 1974 and 1976: an annual average of US$13.6 billion. In 1977 and 1978 this deficit was reduced to the amounts, in current dollars of US$8.0 and 10.6 billion respectively. 1979 and 1980 have brought about, together with a new dramatic increase in fuel prices, an acceleration of current account deficits of non-oil developing countries. In 1978, this deficit amounted to US$50 billion for this group of countries as a whole and this figure is estimated to have grown to US$65 billion in 1980. Latin America alone incurred a deficit of US$17 million in 1979, which is equivalent to nearly one quarter of the overall OPEC surplus. In 1980, this deficit rose further to some US$25 billions.

Insofar as the import capacity developed by OPEC countries has mainly been directed to imports originating from developed countries, this compensator element has not been very effective in the Latin American case. As a result, total debt with official guarantee has suffered a five-fold increase between 1972 and 1980 in Latin America, and currently exceeds the amount of US$100 billion, which is double the amount of total Latin American non-OPEC exports to the world in 1978.

However, if debt without official guarantee is considered, which takes up an increasing percentage of Latin American loans from transnational banks, this figure is estimated to exceed US$140 and 170 billion in 1979 and 1980 respectively.

Brazil, Mexico and Argentina were responsible for the lion's share of this debt. Out of a total of US$140 billion in 1979, 54 were accounted for by Brazil alone, 38 by Mexico and 18 by Argentina. Peru and Chile, if account is taken of the smaller size of their economics are also to be considered heavy debtors, with US$8 and 7 billion, respectively, at the end of 1979.

These figures speak for themselves.

The problem of debt is a major obstacle to Latin American development, insofar as it endangers the attainment of basic development goals in many ways. Among these, the following may be listed:

— the countries are compelled to embark upon very harsh export strategies which tend to disregard the kind of production which might satisfy internal needs;
— dependence upon foreign capital, including transnational financial and manufacturing companies, is increased;
— national development strategies are often subject to the scrutiny of foreign lending bodies such as the IMF;
— given the erratic behaviour of the international economy, and its deep influence on internal indicators, long-term planning is made difficult.

## Functional and Geographical Origin of Financial Flows

Over the period 1966-1970, the composition of external financing to Latin America was the following: out of a total annual average of US$2.5 billion, 700 million were accounted for by direct investment, while the rest consisted of loans, almost equally distributed between net loans from official sources (multilateral and bilateral) and from private sources. Official sources, as a matter of fact slightly exceeded private sources over those years. In 1974-1976, the situation had already changed, with private loans taking up two thirds of total external financing with the rest being almost equally distributed between direct investment and official loans. At the same time, the absolute figures had grown tremendously, to US$13.6 billion, as an average, between 1974 and 1976. After two years of slight decrease (63 and 62 per cent in 1977 and 1978 respectively), the participation of private loans in total external financing increased again in 1979 and 1980. Available figures for 1979 indicate that, out of a total flow of US$25.3 billion, foreign private sources were responsible for over 76 per cent of it, that is US$19.3 billion. The rest was equally shared between direct investment and loans from official sources.

Commercial banks clearly predominate in the total flows from private sources although bonds and suppliers' credits are not negligible.

The first element to be noted, therefore, is a very definite trend away from direct investment and loans from official sources and in favour of loans from private sources, mainly commercial banks.

It is worthwhile to recall once again that only debt with official guarantee is considered here. Should debt without guarantee be taken into account, for which available figures are far less reliable, the role of private international banks would stand out as being even more important.

At the same time, bilateral and multilateral flows transferred to non-OPEC Latin America with a concessional element have dramatically been reduced. Between 1972 and 1978, according to the OECD *Development Co-operation Review* (1978 and 1979), these funds increased, in nominal terms, only slightly, from US$820 million to US$1.19 billion. By comparison, the same figure for Africa and Asia amounted to US$8.15 and 6.26 billion respectively in 1978. In relative terms, concessional flows represented only 8.2 per cent of total flows from OECD countries to Latin America in 1978, as opposed to 62.6 per cent and 64.1 per cent in the cases of Africa and Asia.

The second element to single out is, therefore, the virtual and apparently irreversible exclusion of the Latin American region as a whole, with the possible exception of Haiti and of the former European colonies of the Caribbean, from concessional financial flows.

The above is only partly explained by the deliberate trend, on the part of developed countries and multilateral development agencies, to concentrate official development assistance on lower income developing countries in Africa and Asia.

Two additional factors account for the drastic reduction in official assistance to Latin America. One is the sectoralization of aid, which has followed the same pattern as preferential trade relations. Europe has established very close ties with Africa, especially through the Lomé Agreement which covers both trade and aid, without any particular compensation for Latin America on the part of, say, the United States or Canada.

On the other hand, official development assistance as such, measured in terms of its ratio to the GNP of donor countries, has been reduced over the last decade.

Far from reaching the 0.7 per cent objective established in the framework of the International Development Strategy, official development assistance currently represents 0.33 per cent of the Gross National Product of OECD countries, down from 0.44 per cent in the sixties. In the case of the United States, whose behaviour is particularly important in the case of Latin America, this figure currently represents 0.2 per cent, and is not expected to grow in the foreseeable future.

Geographically speaking, however, the decrease in official development assistance flows to Latin America was less evident in the case of Western Europe than in the case of OECD countries as a whole. From 1969 to 1976, European assistance flows to Latin America were quadrupled (from US$87 to 342 million), whereas the OECD total practically stagnated over the same period around the figure of US$600 million. As a result, European participation rose from 14 per cent to more than half of total official development assistance received by Latin America.

However, it is important to note that the Netherlands, whose aid is concentrated on its former colony, Suriname, accounts for more than one third of the total flows, thus constituting the largest donor, ahead of the Federal Republic of Germany, which accounts for roughly another third, and, very far behind, the United Kingdom, Belgium and Sweden.

Latin America receives about 8 per cent of total official development assistance originating in European countries, with national percentages varying between 1.7 per cent in the case of Denmark to 24 per cent in the case of the Netherlands.

As to the qualitative aspects of this assistance, apart from the very special cases of former UK or Dutch colonialism in the Caribbean, the concessional character of this assistance is much lower in Latin America than in other developing areas. Broadly speaking, technical assistance absorbs a great percentage of total official development assistance flows.

Finally, European contributions to multilateral agencies operating in Latin America should also be considered, such as those made to the Inter-American Development Bank, either through its Inter-regional Fund or through its Fund for Special Operations. British contributions to the Caribbean Development Facility (US$20.9 million for 1978-79) are also worth mentioning.

However, the bulk of financial flows to Latin America, necessary to finance the growing current account deficit in the region's balance of payments, originates from private sources. The loans thus obtained in the international capital market, commonly referred to as the 'Euro-market', are provided by banks established in various parts of the world, often in Europe, but whose capital assets are in no way related to the country where the bank is established. As very often is the case, the role of an international bank is merely one of 'recycling' capital deposits originating in third countries (often petroleum exporting or other capital-surplus countries) by lending them, usually in syndicate with other banks, to overseas clients. These are the reasons why it is not very relevant to the scope of this paper (an evaluation of the European participation in total financial flows into Latin America) to give an account of the geographical distribution of such loans.

Nevertheless, a short description of such origins will be given.

According to the Bank for International Settlements, external assets pertaining to international private banks amounted at the end of 1978 to nearly US$893 billion. This enormous figure, equivalent to 75 per cent of total world trade flows for the same year, grew further still, to US$1,111 billion at the end of 1979. Out of this total, banks established in Europe accounted for US$776 billion (70 per cent of the total, or more than a four-fold increase since beginning of 1973), of which, in turn, US$640 billion were defined as 'Eurocurrency' assets, that is assets in foreign currency denominations pertaining to banks established in Europe. These few figures exempt us from further comments on the growing power of international private banks on a world-wide scale.

The participation of European based private banks in the flows of private loans to Latin America has been estimated at around 40 per cent by J.C. Sánchez Aranu, a consultant to CEPAL, in 1980 (see his *Las Relaciones Financieras entre Europa Occidental y América Latina*, E/CEPAL/R.224, Santiago de Chile, April 1980). Starting from the World Bank's debt tables, and using Europe's participation in one-bank loans as a proxy to its participation in syndicate loans, this estimate was put forth, which, as has been said above, is not very meaningful as to the ultimate source of the capital transfers.

Not much more can be said about international private bank loans, apart from the comments on the rapid deterioration of their terms and conditions which will be the topic of the next section of this paper. One of the characteristics of this relatively new, and predominant form of foreign financing is precisely its lack of clarity and uniformity in its way of functioning.

Increasing dependence on international private bank loans has led Latin America to a new kind of vulnerability in its external position. In the past, difficulties arose mainly from obtaining compensatory finance to cover balance of payments deficits. In recent years, massive movements of capital, connected with the upward swings in petroleum prices, have greatly increased international liquidity, making the access to private capital markets relatively easy. Besides, the granting of loans has not, by and large, been conditional upon the adoption of particular domestic economic policies, with the possible exception of the Peruvian debt renegotiation process in 1978. The dangers clearly seem to be elsewhere although the possibility of establishing such conditionality of loans is not to be discarded altogether. To a certain extent, the preference clearly given by private banks to 'certain' countries implicitly contains an element of approval of their economic policies.

As a consequence of both the increasing importance of external deficit and of the deterioration in the terms of financial flows received to compensate them, many Latin American countries already find themselves trapped in a 'debt spiral', in which an ever-growing share of new loans is pre-empted for the reimbursement of earlier ones. If one further considers that Latin American exports depend on the erratic behaviour of the prices of raw materials, which in this context function as an independent variable upon which exporting countries exert little or no influence at all, then the external vulnerability of Latin American economics can be judged in its entire gravity.

In a framework of growing international liquidity, such as the one prevailing in recent years owing to further increases in petroleum prices, the availability of new loans is not the central issue. However, apart from the consideration that the situation may change after all, namely in view of the 'risk factor' involved in a situation of spiraling debt, one wonders how much longer increasing external deficits can be sustained even from a purely internal point of view.

## Terms and Conditions of Financial Flows

As has been said in the previous section, the emerging predominance of international private banks in the total amounts of financial transfers to Latin America has been paralleled by a clear trend towards a deterioration in the terms of such flows. This is true of all developing areas, though the Latin American case presents characteristics of its own, which make the problem a particularly harsh one.

According to the World Bank, Latin America was confronted in 1977 with the shortest repayment and grace periods, and with the highest interest rates among developing areas. Among the six areas considered (Latin America, Mediterranean countries, Africa South of Sahara, Far East Asia and Pacific, Northern Africa and Middle East and South Asia) the deterioration is substantial for all of them except for South Asia, but in the Latin American case it is even more so. In 1969, for example, North Africa and the Middle East faced shorter repayment and grace periods than Latin America, whereas in 1977 the situation had been reversed.

As a result, the 'concessional factor', as calculated by the World bank, has been reduced from 18 to 9 per cent between 1969 and 1977 and is the lowest among the developing areas considered.

It is worthwhile to notice that even areas with a considerably higher per capita income than Latin America, such as North Africa, the Middle East and Mediterranean countries, enjoyed better financial terms than Latin America.

Finally, account should be taken of the fact that terms have suffered a further deterioration over the years subsequent to 1977.

## Other Sources: Bond Placements and Suppliers' Credits

*a. Bond placements*
This source of capital has been widely used by Latin American countries during the past century up to the time of the 'grant crash' especially for the financing of major public works. Between 1929 and the mid-sixties, this practice was discontinued. The scope of Latin American bond issues, however, has been increasing again especially since the stepping up of operations on the so-called 'Eurobond' market. These placements correspond to bonds issued in more than one market and/or with a currency denomination which bears no relation with the market in which the placement is issued.

Given the different nature of placements issued in European national markets and those issued on the 'Eurobond market', the two will be dealt with separately.

Placements in *national European markets* are regulated by domestic legislation with respect to maximum amounts, waiting lists and other elements.

These regulations tend to be rather strict, except perhaps in the Swiss and West German markets.

Between the sixties and 1978, Latin American countries and the Inter-American Development Bank had issued bonds on European national markets for an amount exceeding US$1.5 billion. Nearly two-thirds of these were accounted for by the IDB.

Among individual countries, Mexico was by far the most important user of this facility, with more than 80 per cent of the total (excluding the IDB). As to the European markets, Switzerland represented more than half of the total, followed by the Federal Republic of Germany, with nearly one quarter.

The issuing of 'Eurobonds' faces much softer regulations than that made on national markets, especially in terms of maximum amounts and information to be submitted.

On the other hand, countries with particularly strong currencies, such as Switzerland and West Germany, have a tendency to discourage the issue of bonds denominated in their currencies. This is the reason why most 'Eurobond' issues on European markets have been denominated in US dollars.

The distinctive feature of 'Eurobond' issues is that they are denominated in a currency which bears no necessary relation to the country or countries where the bonds are placed.

In the case of bonds placed on the Euro-market, as with 'Euro-loans' it is impossible to speculate as to the nationality of their ultimate buyer. It has been estimated by the OECD in *Financial Market Funds* that approximately half of the June 1977 total number of 'Eurobonds' end up being placed in Switzerland.

As has been said above, most bond issues on the 'Euro-market' (about 60 per cent out of a total of US$5.8 billion between 1966 and 1978) are denominated in dollars. However, over the same period, 'Eurobonds' issues for more than US$2 billion were also denominated in European currencies. Of these, over 90 per cent were in Deutschmarks, and the rest in European Units of Account and Dutch Guilders.

In 1977, quite exceptionally, issues denominated in European currencies amounted to nearly half of total issues on 'Eurobond' markets by Latin American countries.

The 'big three' of Latin America (Argentina, Brazil and Mexico) account for the greatest percentage of 'Eurobonds' issued both in US dollars and in European currencies (more than 90 per cent between 1960 and 1978), while Venezuela was also an important user of this source of financing.

To sum up, it seems important to notice that the placement of bonds, up to now, has been highly concentrated, on the users' side, around the Inter-American Development Bank on the one hand, and the largest Latin American countries on the other.

In view of the preference for this source of financing, with respect to loans from private commercial banks, it would be worthwhile to investigate whether there has been any overt discriminatory practice against medium- and small-sized countries in this respect. It may very well be so, although such an analysis goes beyond the scope of this paper. However, it seems that a more thorough knowledge of the whole process (waiting list, amounts involved, terms and conditions, etc.) of bond placements in recent years is a major feature where accurate analysis has been lacking in the study of financial relations between Europe and Latin America.

## b. Suppliers' credits

In 1970, net suppliers' credits (that is, disbursements minus amortisation payments) to Latin America reached the amount of US$550.4 million. This exceptional figure represented 11.6 per cent of total external financial resources received by Latin America in that year. Since then, the participation of suppliers' credit in the total has been decreasing steadily, and in 1976 it amounted to only 3.7 per cent of the total, for a total of US$583 million.

In order to estimate the participation of Europe in this total amount, the only possibility is to use World Bank data. These are quite complete, both by countries of origin and by destination, but have the disadvantage of not considering credits with a repayment period of less than one year. Although the latter are thought to be quite substantial, no quantitative estimate can be given of their amount. On the other hand, since the period of repayment is so short, their net effect on the total annual figures is rather limited.

With this limitation in mind, it is possible to evaluate European participation to the total, at least up to 1973. Between 1970 and 1980, European suppliers' credits represented between 66 per cent and 76 per cent of the total, since imports from the USA, financed through the Eximbank, are not included here, as they are considered as loans from official sources.

After 1973, it is more difficult to evaluate the participation of Europe in total suppliers' credits, due to the increasing importance of credits received from 'multiple' suppliers, that is where the origin is not specified. However, European participation seems to have diminished substantially, insofar as, even if the whole amount of 'multiple credits' received were to be attributed to Europe, the amount thus obtained would not exceed 50-55 per cent of the total.

From the point of view of individual countries, considering the years between 1971 and 1973, the Federal Republic of Germany heads the list of European sources of suppliers' credits, with 25.6 per cent of the total, followed by France (19.5 per cent), Italy (15.3 per cent), the UK (12.1 per cent) and Spain (8.7 per cent).

As to the countries of destinations, Venezuela (23.9 per cent) and Brazil (17.8 per cent) were the most important absorbers of European suppliers' credits between 1971 and 1973, followed by Argentina (13.6 per cent), Colombia (9.1 per cent), Chile (7.7 per cent) and Mexico (6.0 per cent). For all these countries, except for Mexico, the participation of Europe in the total of suppliers' credit received exceeded 50 per cent.

Subsequent to 1973, it is more difficult to give an estimate of European suppliers' credits, for the reasons explained above.

Comparing the gross suppliers' credits received by Latin American countries with total Latin American imports of machinery and transport equipment from Europe, one is confronted with the fact that, even in the most favourable hypothesis of calculating the whole amount of credits received from 'multiple' sources as pertaining to Europe, the ratio between the two decreases from 14.5 to 15.5 per cent between 1969 and 1973 to 7.5 to 9 per cent between 1974 and 1976.

Two unfavourable trends can therefore be pointed out, as a conclusion of this section on suppliers' credits:

a. their decreasing importance in relation to total financial flows;

b. their decreasing importance in relation to trade flows in capital goods as well.

Referring to export credits in general, it is also worth mentioning that, although no recent figures are readily available, these have probably increased their importance over the last two or three years, as well as export insurance. This is due to the fact that balance of payments difficulties encountered by many developed countries have led them to adopt more aggressive export strategies which have included competitive export credit policies.

In this respect, it is important to recall that export credits have not been considered as subsidies, regardless of their terms and conditions, unlike export promotion measures taken by developing countries (tax rebates and the like).

In view of the fact that developing countries are more and more confronted with protectionist measures, often based on the principle that subsidized exports should be hindered by levying 'countervailing duties' on them, one wonders why export credits have never been taken into account as being the 'developed' equivalent of the export subsidies granted by developing countries and so heavily taxed on developed importing markets. It is worth recalling also that GATT's Multilateral Trade Negotiations, which have recently been concluded, did not lead to the elimination, or even limitation in the use of such protectionist measures.

## Conclusions

Official bilateral and multilateral financial flows to Latin America have not kept pace, in recent years, with the increasing magnitude of current account disequilibria, which have had to be financed by having recourse to international private capital markets. This, in turn, has brought about a deterioration in the terms and conditions of external financing available to the region, leading to increasing debt problems which, in some cases, are of the utmost gravity.

As a result, the following points may be considered for further discussion:

a. As long as large disequilibria are maintained on a world level, some countries are bound to become chronic debtors, at the same time as others develop into a position of chronic creditors. This world perspective should not be overlooked while examining the debt problems of Latin American countries;

b. the increasing reliance on international private bank loans has brought about a new preoccupation, whose features are just beginning to come to the surface, about the concept of credit-worthiness referred to international private banks. One wonders what social, economic and political criteria are being employed in this respect;

c. the overall figures for 1980 show a balance of payments deficit of US$2.5 billion for Latin America as a whole (including petroleum exporting countries), down from a surplus of US$7 billion in 1979. One wonders if this sudden change is in any way connected with new difficulties encountered on international private capital markets;

d. in view of what has been mentioned under point (a) above, individual efforts to restore balance of payments equilibria cannot be traded off against the search for global solutions;

e. in this respect, a few points can be mentioned. Short of being able to scrutinize more closely the operations of international private banks, efforts could be made to improve the recycling of capital surpluses. More concretely, the surpluses of petroleum-exporting countries could be transformed directly into credits linked to specific development plans of developing countries;

f. important steps taken in this direction may be considered:

— the agreement between the governments of Mexico and Venezuela for the supply of petroleum to Central America and Caribbean countries. Under the terms of this agreement, 160,000 barrels per day of petroleum are to be supplied to the countries involved, while concessional credit lines will be opened for the financing of 30 per cent of the payment.

— the operations of the OPEC Special Fund and of other financial institutions which have been active in the field of direct re-cycling of petroleum surpluses.

# EUROPE, HUMAN RIGHTS AND LATIN AMERICA

*Tino Thun*

### Plenty of Economic Policy But Little Common Foreign Policy

An examination of the human rights policy of the European Economic Community (EEC) towards other countries means looking first at the extent to which the EEC pursues a common or co-ordinated foreign policy at all. After the Second World War three European bodies, independent of one another, were created: the European Coal and Steel Community (ECSC) in 1951, the European Economic Community (EEC) in 1957 and, in the same year, the European Atomic Energy Community (Euratom). Also in 1957 the European Assembly, Court of Justice and Economic and Social Committees were established. It was only in 1967, through an agreement to amalgamate the three communities (ECSC, EEC and Euratom) that a common Council and Commission of the European Communities were set up.

The scope of these bodies reflected the purpose of the original Communities. They were predominantly concerned with economic considerations, not only between member states but also towards third states, above all with commercial agreements, investment schemes, customs issues and similar matters. Today the institutions of the second strongest economic power in the world exercise a decisive influence on the external relations of its ten member states, yet they lack clear authority concerning general foreign policy questions. Nevertheless, during important economic negotiations with third states, foreign policy interests of the EEC and its member states are introduced and resolutions on current international questions are passed. However, this mostly happens on an *ad hoc* basis as a result of the specific interests of member states in a particular situation; to a large

# The Institutions of the European Community

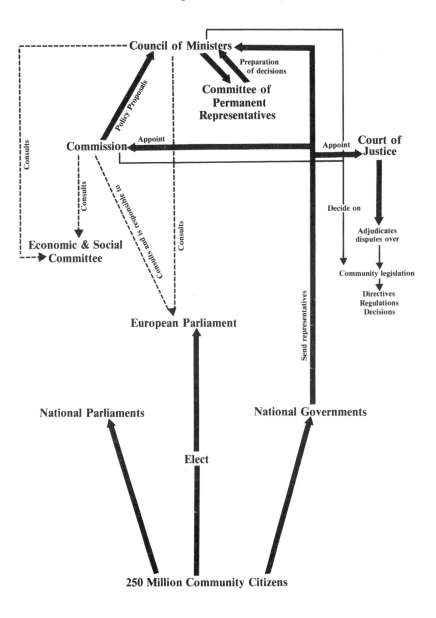

extent no foreign policy global vision exists in the EEC.

Official responsibility for the treatment of foreign policy questions by the Community lies with the EEC Council which meets regularly as a council comprised either of heads of government or of foreign or other cabinet ministers, and which lays down the guidelines for the policies of the Commission. At the 1969 Hague summit, the European Political Co-operation (EPC) was established as an instrument to improve the co-ordination of national foreign policies. The EPC, although it is strictly speaking outside the institutions of the EEC, consists of the same personnel as the Council of Foreign Ministers, and usually meets immediately after formal summits of the Council. Co-operation between the foreign ministers of the member states in the EPC represents an attempt to fill the void in foreign policy responsibility which resulted from the narrow economic focus of the Treaty of Rome.

The work of the EPC is organized according to proposals made by the Davignon and Vedel Reports of 1970 and 1973 respectively. The purpose of these proposals was to reach a 'co-ordination of the position of the member states concerning foreign policy questions and to reach as far as possible some form of concerted action'; Europe should be able 'to speak with one voice'. Nevertheless the institutions of the EEC to a large extent lack the 'instruments' for executing a common foreign policy; EEC embassies, for example, exist only in New York, Geneva, Vienna, Washington, Ottawa, Caracas, Bangkok and Tokyo, and the EEC totally lacks any foreign policy bureaucratic apparatus of its own.

The foreign ministers at first met twice yearly and subsequently four times a year; additional meetings are called on important matters of current concern. The ambassadors of the governments meet at irregular intervals in member states as well as in other countries to try and co-ordinate their common political interests. If at all, progress at a multilateral level has been made through such co-ordination. For example, in the United Nations or at international conferences the member states of the EEC attempt to co-ordinate their actions on questions of human rights, make common declarations, and also attempt to come to some voting agreement. During the Helsinki Conference on Security and Co-operation in Europe in 1975, complete agreement was achieved between the then nine member states concerning their activities.

Until recently, though, the particular political interests of the individual member states of the EEC were always dominant, which complicated the making of common foreign policy decisions. For example, there were difficulties in arriving at a common stance during the Afghanistan crisis in 1979, on Iran in 1980, on Poland during

1981/82 and in the policies towards El Salvador.

In the light of this predominance of economic over political concerns in the institutions of the EEC, how important then are human rights considerations in the EEC's policies towards other countries?

## The Treatment of Human Rights Questions

In a joint declaration the European Parliament, the Council, and the Commission committed themselves in April 1977 to promote human rights, both within member states and internationally. This commitment is based in the first place on the founding treaties of the European Communities and the constitutions of member states. In addition, all member states of the EEC are signatories to the European Convention on Human Rights which was signed in Rome in 1950. Also, as members of the United Nations, they are committed to the Charter and to the Universal Declaration on Human Rights of 1948.

## Human Rights in EEC Member States

One important precondition for any credible human rights policy towards other countries is strict observance of human rights in one's own country. Despite a well developed system for the protection of human rights in Europe, Latin American dictators have frequently been able to reject criticism of human rights violations in their own countries by reciprocating with references to violations of human rights in the member states of the EEC, thus lessening the effect of EEC criticisms. This fundamental prerequisite was the subject of heated debate in the European Parliament in March 1980 when the leader of the French Communist Party, Georges Marchais, demanded that an *ad hoc* committee be set up to investigate human rights violations by the member states of the EEC. Marchais pointed out that within a period of eight months 89 resolutions on the subject of human rights had been introduced in the European Parliament of which 88 concerned countries outside the EEC. It was hypocritical, Marchais said, that the European Parliament discussed neither the 4,000 West German citizens who were banned from employment in the civil service because of their alleged political views, nor the British government's responsibility for torture in Northern Ireland.

In spite of the ulterior political motives there may have been behind Marchais's remarks, this criticism cannot be dismissed on the grounds that in European countries legal systems exist through which a citizen who feels their human rights have been violated may readily seek redress. Such a justification ignores the fact that human rights violations cannot be dealt with in a purely legalistic way but also require a political discussion of the underlying causes and structures leading to these violations. Neither is the reply given by some European politicians that human rights violations in their own countries are far less serious than, for example, those in Latin America, a valid one. The classification of violations of the fundamental rights of human beings into more or less serious cases is at odds with the essential equality of all human rights and paves the way for the arbitrary interpretation of these rights. The point is not to compare different situations but to be concerned about *all* violations of human rights wherever they occur in the world and particularly, of course, in one's own area of responsibility.

Finally, it should be noted that a human rights policy is not a one-way street. Among equal partners, demands for the observation of human rights should never be made one-sidedly by the politically and economically stronger against the weaker. Today, nation states have, through the United Nations and other institutions, turned human rights from a sovereign matter into an international issue. Thus every state ought to be prepared to accept justified criticism from other countries and should not reject this as an interference in their internal affairs. This applies as much to the member states of the EEC as it does to the Latin American countries.


## Treaties of Co-operation and Human Rights

The human rights policy of the EEC encompasses the defence of civic and political liberties. In general, however, the question of the realization of economic, social and cultural rights is not dealt with within the framework of a human rights policy. For example, in discussions on the problem of world hunger in the European Parliament and by the Commission, the term 'human rights' does not occur. Owing to the concentration in the EEC on the regulation of foreign trade relations, the question of human rights in third states such as in Latin America was not dealt with in the past. Only recently has there been any discussion on how far the inclusion of a human rights clause in agreements of an economic nature might be an effective means of combatting violations of human rights.

One attempt to include such a clause was made in the negotiations between the EEC and the ACP countries (58 states in Africa, the Caribbean and the Pacific) on the Lomé II Convention. The ACP states objected caustically and successfully to the inclusion of such a human rights clause in the agreement, accusing the EEC of attempted intervention and of undue interference in their economic and political affairs. It must indeed be considered questionable for the rich EEC countries to refuse to open customs barriers to the generally poorer countries or to permit them to sell their export products to the EEC as a punishment for the violation of human rights. When signing the Lomé II agreement, the speaker on behalf of the ACP countries, the Deputy Prime Minister of Barbados, Bernard St John, emphasized the intention of these states to observe human rights:

We too are militants for human rights . . . Our concern for human rights is not less than yours. All of us subscribe to the Charter of the United Nations and to the resolutions which have been passed in a forum which has the necessary legal competence.

At the signing ceremony in October 1979, the officiating EEC Council president also underlined the political significance that the Community countries placed on the realization of human rights.

In 1980, just as in the 1975 co-operation treaty with Mexico, in the new skeleton agreement on co-operation between the EEC and Brazil it was declared that the agreement would serve to promote 'more rapid political progress'. In its statement on this agreement the Committee on Development and Co-operation of the European Parliament emphasized that such an agreement would contribute to a further improvement in the human rights situation, which, it said, was 'a very important aim of the European Parliament'. However general and non-committal such declarations by the contracting parties are, the Committee on Development and Co-operation, in the same statement on the agreement with Brazil, was clearly critical 'that until now the Community has not had a genuine policy of co-operation with Latin America'. The Committee demanded that the Commission 'outlines a global policy for Latin America'.

In May 1980 the foreign ministers of the EEC member states and of the Andean Pact countries (Bolivia, Colombia, Ecuador, Peru, Venezuela) met for the first time at a conference in Brussels. In a concluding statement the foreign ministers expressed their agreement on 'the rejection of violence and the threat of violence and of intervention in the affairs of third states as well as the upholding of human rights and liberal democracy'. A few weeks later it was asked to ratify a co-operation treaty between the EEC and the Andean Pact countries. Soon afterwards, in July 1980, there was a military coup in Bolivia accompanied by serious violations of human rights. As a result of differences between them regarding the formulation of external economic relations, the governments of the Andean Pact countries no longer found themselves in accord on the signing of the agreement with the EEC, while European politicians indicated that this agreement should be placed in 'cold storage' because of the violations of human rights in Bolivia; to this day the agreement remains unsigned.

## The Parliament of Fine Words

The European Parliament, whose political status was enhanced as a result of the first direct elections in 1979, has been concerned for a long time with issues of human rights in the world. In 1977 its Political Affairs Committee, which is responsible for human rights questions, reiterated these concerns and demanded that all the EEC countries work together internationally for human rights.

In March 1980 the then president of the European Parliament, Simone Veil, in a speech in Athens to mark the occasion of Greece's entry to the EEC, confirmed this commitment in an apparent reference to Greece's recent past under military rule. Alongside resolutions on the situation of human rights in the Soviet Union, Czechoslovakia, the German Democratic Republic, Afghanistan and Iran, resolutions on the situation of human rights in Latin America were debated.

### a. Interparliamentary co-operation

Since 1974 the European Parliament and the Latin American Parliament have met regularly; in Bogota in 1974, in Luxemburg in 1975, in Mexico City in 1977, in Rome in 1979 and again in Bogota in 1981. It is significant that the representatives of dissolved parliaments also participate in these inter-parliamentary conferences. For example, in 1979 members of the Argentine, Uruguayan and Chilean parliaments and in 1981 of the Bolivian parliament were invited as observers.

Since the third meeting in Mexico, 'human rights' has become one of the main themes of these conferences. However, the much discussed establishment of a permanent joint working group for sharing information and common interventions on violations of human rights — the so-called Granelli suggestions — has still not come about.

At the recent conference in Bogota the military regimes in Uruguay, Chile and Argentina were unmistakeably condemned in a joint declaration in the Final Act 'where dictators are using oppression to maintain their illegitimate power'. Similarly, the diplomatic isolation of the Bolivian regime following the military coup was expressly approved. The conference likewise condemned the military coup in Suriname and the acts of violence in El Salvador. It welcomed the fall of the Somoza dictatorship in Nicaragua and the results of the November 1980 referendum in Uruguay which rejected the draft of an undemocratic constitution. And lastly the inter-parliamentary conference also condemned, in this common declaration, all political or military intervention by third states including the sale of arms.

The fact that the declaration also pointed to the connection between economic and social development on the one hand and the support of human rights and basic liberties on the other (commonly known as political freedom and social rights) was clearly due to the participation of the Latin Americans.

Among the recommendations of this inter-parliamentary conference were demands for the reinstatement of parliaments in those countries where they had been undemocratically dissolved, and for a definite timetable for a return to democratic rule and free institutions. There were also demands for an end to systematic intimidation, the kidnapping and disappearance of people for political reasons, arbitrary arrests and detentions, deportations, exile, torture and murder. In addition, the conference recommended that all states which had not yet done so should ratify the international agreements which guarantee basic liberties and defend human rights. Furthermore, it recommended that the Latin American Parliament and the European Parliament should, within the framework of the inter-parliamentary meeting, condemn violations of human rights and should take common measures and immediate action on humanitarian grounds.

It must, however, be asked where, after the solemn declaration and condemnations in the Final Act, the common measures and immediate action called for are to be found. The human rights initiatives taken by the European Parliament within the framework of the inter-parliamentary conferences, far from mobilizing the other institutions of the EEC to take thoroughgoing human rights initiatives of their own, are in fact deemed by the Commission and the Council to make further specific political steps unnecessary.

## b. Argentina

Following the European Parliament's resolution in July 1976 condemning the annulment of important constitutional rights in Argentina, a further resolution in 1977 criticized the serious violations of human rights known to have taken place since the take-over of power by the military in March 1976. During the build up to the World Cup football championship in Argentina in June 1978, numerous solidarity groups all over the world and Amnesty International called for moves to rectify human rights violations. These activities resulted in specific initiatives by the European Parliament. In a resolution in June 1978 it was noted that, according to Amnesty International, among the ten thousand political prisoners in Argentina there were 100 persons from EEC countries, including two French nuns. The Commission, the

Council and the governments of the member states were called upon 'to take all appropriate measures to bring about an improvement in the situation as regards human rights and the respect of democratic freedoms in Argentina'. The Political Affairs Committee of the European Parliament recommended the holding of public hearings on the situation of human rights in Argentina; this led to an open argument between the Socialists and Christian Democrats who boycotted the hearings. Consequently the Socialists held the recommended hearings by themselves in Brussels in May 1978. Representatives of Amnesty International and the International Commission of Jurists, Latin American politicians, relatives of prisoners from the European member states, and former prisoners all gave dramatic evidence of brutal violations of human rights in the form of arrests, kidnappings, torture and murder.

These hearings met with a wide response in the European and Latin American press and led in July 1978 to a further resolution of the European Parliament on the situation in Argentina in which the member states of the Council and the Commission were once again expressly called upon to act. The significance of the impact that further public hearings on the issue of human rights violations could have on world opinion was emphasized in this same resolution. However, to date there have been no further hearings.

A year later, in September 1979, a resolution was put forward which was this time as hard-hitting in its tone as in its actual demands. It explicitly condemned 'the dictatorship of General Videla, terrorism by the state, and the massacre of opponents of the regime'. It further called for the abolition of the law of September 1979 legitimizing the deaths of thousands of 'disappeared' opponents of the regime and for the recall of member states' ambassadors in Argentina.

The continuation of human rights violations in Argentina, above all the kidnapping of Argentinian refugees in Peru in June 1980 and the repeated attempts by the Argentine secret service to intimidate refugees in Europe, eventually led in 1980 to a resolution by the European Parliament which called upon the Commission and the Council to appraise critically economic and trade relations between the EEC and Argentina. The foreign ministers who met together within the EPC were again called upon to take action on behalf of political prisoners and disappeared persons at both bilateral and multilateral levels.

These relatively broad activities of the European Parliament to protect human rights in Argentina had little or no influence on the policies of the Commission, the Council or the member states towards Argentina. In 1978 the Danish foreign minister on behalf of all the foreign ministers working co-operatively within the EPC, conveyed verbally to the Argentine government a demand for the clarification of the fate of the missing European citizens. This move received no coverage in the European press, neither was any clarification of the cases forthcoming. In September 1979 the EEC signed an agreement on the textile trade with Argentina; the 1972 trade agreement between the EEC and Argentina had already been extended annually from 1975. It is not known whether the Commission or the Council raised the question of human rights in connection with these agreements.

It appears that Argentina's European business partners were even less inclined to ask themselves whether the considerable expansion of economic relations with Argentina in the form of trade, investments and international credits had led to any improvement in the economic and social situation of that country and thus made a contribution to securing political liberties. Conversely, the Argentine military had no need to worry about its political relations with the EEC governments. Argentina's political and economic significance led European politicians of all parties time and again to point to their desire for friendly relations with Argentina. To date there has been no clarification of the fate of the disappeared persons nor any fundamental improvement in the situation of human rights in Argentina.

## c. Uruguay

Since 1973 Uruguay has been ruled by generals who have violated human rights on a massive scale. In 1975-76 non-governmental organizations launched a broad campaign against human rights violations in Uruguay. The institutions of the EEC received extensive documentary evidence together with the demand that they should work for the observance of human rights in Uruguay.

In December 1975 the former president of the Uruguayan parliament, Hector Gutierrez Ruiz, gave a report to the European Parliament in Luxemburg on the situation in his country. Six months later Gutierrez Ruiz was himself the victim of a death squad in Argentina.

After moves by several Socialist MEPs, a debate took place in the European Parliament in May 1976 on Uruguay's repressive regime. In an answer to Amnesty International, Lord Thomson, a member of the Commission, explained that the trade agreement which had been signed with Uruguay in 1974 for a period of three years could not be terminated, although 'there is no question of offering any new advantages to Uruguay'. The representatives of the EEC Commission justified this decision on the basis of the undemocratic situation prevailing in Uruguay.

In February 1977 a renewed debate took place in the European Parliament on the deteriorating situation of human rights in Uruguay. The Belgian Socialist MEP Ernest Glinne noted amongst other things that the Uruguayan government had rejected a request by the Red Cross and Amnesty International to investigate the situation of political prisoners. Glinne also pointed out that in 1976 the US Congress had decided to refuse all further military aid to Uruguay. Glinne asked the Commission about the future of the 1974 trade agreement between the EEC and Uruguay which would be renewed annually after the initial three year period unless it was cancelled by one of the two contracting parties.

In reply, the vice-president of the Commission, Willem Haferkamp, confirmed before the European Parliament that the EEC had given Uruguay absolutely no preferential treatment. 'For obvious reasons', he said, 'a comparison between the cancellation of military aid and the attitude of the EEC towards Uruguay was not possible'. How unclear these reasons really were became obvious in 1981 when the European Parliament put forward a resolution in which the member states of the EEC were called upon 'to stop all arms deliveries to the Uruguayan regime immediately'. Belgium had, for example, decided to deliver tanks to Uruguay in 1979.

In the debate Haferkamp shared the concern of the MEPs about the violations of human rights in Uruguay. However, he was unable to announce any concrete plans about future EEC policy towards the regime on the grounds that there was 'no blueprint for a human rights policy'.

In December 1977 a common initiative was taken by the EEC ambassadors in Montevideo when they condemned the current human rights violations in Uruguay. In August 1978 the trade agreement was renewed, just as it had been in 1977.

At the beginning of 1979 the European Parliament, after moves by some MEPs, called for a report by the Committee on External Economic Relations on the annual renewal of the trade agreement so that the Parliament would have time to comment upon any further renewal.

In this report to the Parliament, which was submitted in April 1979, the Committee also emphasized its concern about the serious violations of human rights in Uruguay in the form of detentions without trial, torture, the disappearance of people and deportations. The Committee nevertheless recommended a renewal of the trade agreement for a further year, on the grounds that otherwise it would be the people of Uruguay who would suffer most. However, the report at least declared that on no account should Uruguay be given preferential treatment until there was an improvement in the human rights situation.

Although persistent violations of human rights were time and again confirmed and condemned by the European Parliament, in January

168

1980, as part of the international Multi-Fibre Agreement, a new agreement on trade and textiles between the EEC and Uruguay was signed. Contrary to earlier declarations, preferential treatment was extended. Although due to expire at the end of 1982, this agreement too is renewable.

The example of Uruguay is remarkable in that it came to a discussion at all between the Parliament and the Commission on the question of human rights. One thing, however, is certain: in the final analysis, these discussions had hardly any influence on the EEC's economic co-operation with Uruguay. This discussion also made apparent the lack of political definition with which the question of human rights was tackled. Within the context of economic relations, an economic partner will always be able to claim that reducing co-operation will harm the population in general, whether this is true or not.

### d. El Salvador

In 1981, against the background of the serious violations of human rights in El Salvador, the European Parliament made further progress in its position on human rights. The Socialists and Christian Democrats decided to send an inter-parliamentary delegation to El Salvador in order to gain a first-hand picture of the situation. The existence of such an inter-parliamentary delegation was something of a political peculiarity considering the disagreement over El Salvador between the Christian Democrat parties in Europe and the Socialist International. However, such co-operation was possible within the framework of the EEC since, in the case of El Salvador, the Dutch and Italian Christian Democrat parties were less definite in their support for the head of the junta, Jose Napoleon Duarte, than were the West German Christian Democrats, who supported him unreservedly. The visit of the European parliamentarians generated widespread public interest both in Latin America and in Europe. The SPD MEP Heidi Wieczorek-Zeul, in a report following the trip, stressed that it was above all the tangible and obvious violence which had impressed itself on her very deeply; she added that it was precisely this aspect which delegations did not normally experience. El Salvador was an instance where 'the state no longer guarantees human and civil rights but has instead itself become the terrorist'.

After some difficulty, two of the MEPs were allowed into the Santa Tecla prison. They were led into a courtyard through a cordon of prisoners who broke out into applause which lasted several minutes. The prisoners themselves had requested a visit from the European members of parliament: 'We want you to report everywhere the truth of what is happening to us and to our families in El Salvador'.

In the first six months of 1981 over 7,000 people had been murdered in El Salvador. Only three days after the departure of the delegation the 67-year-old mother of a disappeared person, who had given the delegation a petition, was murdered in her home by plain clothes members of the secret service.

In September 1981 a resolution was passed by the European Parliament in which traditional diplomatic reserve was again dominant. While a resolution put forward by the Socialist MEPs called upon the United States to discontinue military aid and to recognize and negotiate with the FDR/FMLN, the resolution eventually passed stated that the EEC 'should support all efforts to facilitate negotiations between the junta and the government on the one hand and the opposition FDR on the other, and will encourage all efforts to this end'. There was no mention of US military aid and a move to request the Commission and the EEC member states to organize a conference on El Salvador similar to the conference suggested by EEC foreign ministers on Afghanistan, in order to suggest a political solution, was thrown out by the Parliament.

What is certain, however, is that the delegation sent to investigate violations of human rights in El Salvador elicited a greater public response than the numerous resolutions on the question of human rights put forward by the Parliament.

Whilst the political value of publicity has to be recognized, it must nevertheless be asked whether this exhausts the possibilities of an effective human rights policy or whether political and economic approaches are also necessary in order to live up even minimally to the claim to work for the realization of human rights.

## Human Rights Initiatives within the European Political Co-operation (EPC)

The majority of the resolutions on questions of human rights in the European Parliament are most commonly addressed to the foreign ministers of the member states who work together as the EPC when dealing with questions of foreign policy co-ordination not covered by the Treaty of Rome. It is only within this context that the Commission and the Council can be approached since their responsibilities are limited mainly to the regulation of external economic questions.

The EPC, however, lacks a firmly based institutional framework within which to deal with human rights resolutions. Suggestions made by the West German foreign minister, Hans-Dietrich Genscher, on the setting up and institutionalization of a European political union did not even win the unanimous support of the West German cabinet.

Even taking into consideration the positive effect that publicity can have on human rights questions, the many resolutions are reduced to mere lip service when they are not given concrete expression either within the EPC or in the policies of the individual member states or their governments.

The most tangible response still appears to be the attempt to formulate a co-ordinated human rights policy towards third states on a multilateral level by the EPC. For example, there has been co-ordination in international conferences and in common agreements and initiatives by EEC ambassadors, such as those undertaken in Argentina and Uruguay.

However, the governments of the member states of the EEC tend to stall initiatives to protect human rights by pointing out that agreement has first to be reached among the EEC partners. Given the difficulties of establishing a co-ordinated or even common foreign policy within the EPC it is hardly surprising that so many human rights initiatives have withered and died.

## The Council of Europe and Human Rights

The Council of Europe, its executive and its parliamentary assembly have no official connection with the EEC.

As little is known about the frequent differences between the independent institutions, it is worth briefly considering the Council of Europe and its human rights policy. The Council of Europe was founded in 1949 as an organization of European states and at that time encompassed 21 member states. Within the Council of Europe a far-reaching system to protect human rights was established. The basis of this system is formed by the European Convention on Human Rights, which specifies extensive civil and political liberties. Their maintenance is the concern of the European Commission for Human Rights, the European Court of Justice and the Council of Europe's executive. It is particularly significant that the citizens of member states of the Council of Europe who feel that their basic rights have been violated in some way and who have exhausted the process of law in their own countries can turn to the Committee of the Council of Europe with their individual complaints.

As it did with the military government in Greece, the Council of Europe is today encountering particular difficulties with another member state, Turkey, where, under a military government, human rights are seriously being violated. It is also difficult for the Council of Europe to reach agreement on a common human rights policy. As the economic, social and cultural rights are laid down in a somewhat general form in the European Social Charter of 1981, so have demands been growing in recent years to include economic, social and cultural rights within the European Convention on Human Rights.

The Council of Europe is also committed to promoting the observance of human rights in third states. Especially since the entry of Spain and Portugal in the late 1970s, the Council of Europe has strengthened its relations with Latin America. At the parliamentary assembly of the Council of Europe, the Spanish socialist Luis Yarnez-Barnuevo submitted a comprehensive report on the widespread violation of human rights in Latin America. In this report abduction, torture and murder are documented country by country.

In October 1981 in Madrid, well-known politicians and human rights experts from Europe and Latin America participated in a meeting on the situation of human rights in Latin America organized by the Council of Europe. The meeting did not mince its words when it held 'the unjust capitalist system and the national oligarchies in close connection with the interests of the superpowers and multinationals' responsible for the violation of human rights.

Nevertheless, in spite of the fact that all member states of the EEC are also members of the Council of Europe, and that the European Parliament and the Council of Europe regularly meet in the same place in Strasbourg, the human rights work of these two institutions proceeds completely independently of one another.

## Human Rights and the New International Economic Order

A substantial obstacle in the formulation of an effective policy by the EEC on human rights resides in the indisputable fact that the EEC member states have not once been able to produce a common understanding of what constitutes human rights. In a memorandum in 1979 the EEC Commission stated publicly that the compilation of a basic human rights catalogue representing the requirements of the Community had been impossible due to the differences of opinion among the member states of what constitutes economic and social rights.

Despite their solemn declarations most member states of the EEC do not in practice recognize the equal nature of all human rights. The final communique of the 1981 inter-parliamentary conference in Bogota is grammatically incorrect when it talks of 'most elementary' or 'most fundamental' human rights since no superlative of 'elementary' or 'fundamental' can exist. Protection against torture, for example, should not be weighed against the right to food — human rights are elementary rights which cannot be arranged in order of priority.

172

The equal nature of all human rights is reflected in the reciprocal relationship that exists between different human rights. The realization of civil and political liberties is not possible without the simultaneous realization of economic, social and cultural rights, just as the realization of economic, social and cultural rights is not possible without the participation and creativity of men and women who are guaranteed their civil and political freedoms. In this respect the General Assembly of the United Nations in 1977 saw the demand for a New International Economic Order as a particularly important prerequisite for the realization of all human rights.

Two years later, in 1979, the UN General Assembly passed a resolution by a large majority (some western industrialized nations abstained) in which the right to development was recognized as a human right. This right to development was not a new right but rather a synthesis of existing human rights and had a dual nature: it was both a right of the individual and of the people or state.

The commitment to international co-operation (which is also based on Articles 55 and 56 of the Charter of the United Nations) does not remove from individual states the obligations to create the necessary internal conditions for the realization of the right to development for their citizens and to guarantee human rights.

The injustices of the present world economic system cannot, however, be denied. The rich industrialized nations (which, besides the United States and Japan, are principally the EEC states) are confronted with degrading and humiliating poverty in the developing countries. Between 500 million and 1.3 billion people do not have enough to eat; over half these starving people are children; 250,000 children become blind every year through Vitamin A deficiency; and one-third of all children born in developing countries die before they reach the age of five as a result of malnutrition and related illnesses.

In 1980 the European Parliament, in public hearings and in a report, dealt with the problem of world hunger. The fact that the concept of human rights was not used by the European Community in its contribution to the report shows how little Western European politicians considered economic and social rights to be equal to political and civil rights.

In this context one of the few exceptions in the human rights work of the EEC is to be found in the discussion of the violations of human rights in Chile. A report by the Political Affairs Committee of the European Parliament points expressly to the 'closed circle of cause and effect', as evidenced in the case of Chile and the foreign economic aid it receives, between worsening economic and social conditions and resulting violations of human rights.

In addition, the final communique of the 1981 inter-parliamentary conference in Bogota mentions the 'connection that exists between economic and social development on the one hand and on the other hand the demand for basic liberties and human rights, especially in Latin America'.

In recent years Latin American human rights organizations have pointed to the connection between a just economic world order and realization of human rights. When the Latin American Organization for the Defence of Human Rights was founded in August 1980, the Argentine, Jorge A. Llampart, demanded that it should not stop merely at helping political victims but also tackle the structural causes of repression which are based on the unjust world economic order.

The member states of the EEC have yet to respond to the resolution by the 1981 conference of Latin American and European MPs in Bogota which condemned the arms trade. As the United States reduced its exports of arms to some dictatorships in the 1970s because of violations of human rights, Western European governments and industries filled the gap. From 1977 to 1980 West Germany was the biggest exporter of arms to Argentina, Great Britain to Brazil, and France to Chile (see pages 176-216).

The EEC, as the second strongest economic power in the world, must recognize, if it is to have a credible human rights policy towards Latin America, its joint responsibility for the grave human rights violations which are too often the result of an unjust economic order which is maintained by the USA and the European Community.

In relation to the issue of human rights, the important thing is not so much to discuss whether or not to extend economic co-operation but more to consider the question of what kind of economic co-operation contributes to development and thus to the securing of human rights. A policy of economic sanctions should be seen only as a last resort. As was accurately stated in the human rights debate in the European Parliament, such a policy would hit the 'weak strongly and the strong weakly'.

The need for an effective human rights policy by the European Community towards Latin America is made even more urgent by the Reagan administration's support for dictatorships. It is time that the fine words of the Europeans are translated into deeds.


## Suggestions for Action by Solidary Groups

### Long-term

1. To demonstrate to the European public and convince it of the equal nature and mutual interdependence of *all* human rights.
2. To demand the establishment of a New International Economic

Order as a human right.

3. To demand a common foreign policy within the EEC under democratic control.

## *Short-term*

1. To acquaint a wider public with the available material produced by the European Parliament on the situation of human rights in Latin America.
2. To submit appropriate demands by the European Parliament to national parliaments and governments with the request that they take a stand.
3. To introduce the suggestion that resolutions of the European Parliament are fed back automatically to national parliaments for their comments.
4. To supply MEPs with information about specific issues on appropriate occasions and to suggest questions to be put before parliament (a list of all MEPs names and addresses can be requested from the Press Office of the European Parliament in Strasbourg).
5. To suggest hearings on human rights questions.
6. To suggest sending delegations from the European Parliament to countries where human rights are violated.
7. To carry out a campaign in all EEC member states against the sale of arms and the training of military personnel from countries where human rights are violated.
8. To publicize, through giving concrete examples, the economic policies of the EEC, European multinational corporations, and international financial institutions towards Latin America insofar as such policies deny human rights.

# EUROPE, LATIN AMERICA AND THE ARMS TRADE

*Simon Barrow*

The purpose of this article is to explore the growing web of military links between Latin America and Western Europe. In particular, we shall examine the perceived needs of the Latin American governments which continue to import military goods in enormous quantities; the economic, social and political consequences of arms procurements for Latin America as a whole; the principal European suppliers; the growth of arms exports *from* South America, and the issue of nuclear weapons and the arms trade as it affects the region. Some of the proposals to limit this militarization process will be outlined briefly in the conclusion.

## The Extent of Military Spending in Latin America

In 1980 Latin America spent an estimated US$8.2 billion on military equipment, personnel and services, according to the authoritative Stockholm International Peace Research Institute (SIPRI). This amounts to 1.8 per cent of global expenditure on such facilities, which stood at US$455.3 billion for the same period.

Between 1972 and 1980 total Latin American military spending increased 1.69 times, measured at constant 1978 prices. This is a faster rate of expansion than has been achieved by either NATO or the Warsaw Pact. More significantly, Latin American military expenditure grew throughout the seventies at a rate exceeding that of Africa (1.62 times), non-aligned Europe (1.26 times), Oceania (1.20 times), the People's Republic of China (1.20 times at a rough estimate), and South Asia (1.14 times). Only the Far East (1.80 times) and the Middle East (3.01 times) have been expanding faster. Total world military expenditure grew by 1.18 times in the same period.

Much the same pattern emerges from a comparison of regional military spending per capita. According to *World Military and Social Expenditure 1981* (WMSE), Latin America spent an average of US$60.8 per person in 1978, compared with US$45.3 for Africa, US$26.0 for the People's Republic of China, and US$4.18 for South Asia. In the Third World only the Middle East (US$417.8 per capita), the Far East (US$96.14) and Oceania (US$80.2) exceeded the Latin American aggregate.

The level of militarization throughout Latin America is far higher than the bold statistics suggest, since a large proportion of the spending is on cheaper equipment and personnel appropriate to counter-insurgency activities within each country. This is because internal dissent, rather than disputes between states, has been the major problem faced by most regimes in Latin America.

As a result, the pressures leading to increased military spending have produced a markedly different pattern of expenditure distribution than that which prevails, for example, in the Middle East. Furthermore military spending throughout the region as a whole is still growing faster than Gross Domestic Product (GDP).

On the national (as opposed to regional) level, the pattern becomes more variable. Brazil, where arms expenditure has been falling off from its peak of US$2.1 billion in 1975 to US$1.7 billion in 1979, Argentina (US$1.5 billion in 1980), Cuba (US$1.0 billion) and Chile (US$984 million) dominate the picture. Together they make up half of all Latin American military spending. At the other end of the scale are countries such as Trinidad and Tobago, Panama and Haiti which all spend less than US$20 million per annum.

Calculating military expenditure as a proportion of GDP, the six highest regional spenders in 1979 were: Chile (9.4 per cent), Cuba (8.5 per cent approx.), Peru (4.0 per cent), Dominican Republic (3.2 per cent), Argentina (2.3 per cent) and Bolivia and Ecuador (both with 2.0 per cent). It should be stressed however that none of these figures can be taken as an accurate guide to military strength and influence, because they do not include foreign subsidies through licensing arrangements for the production of weapons systems, nor do they reflect military aid — such as that sent from the United States to El Salvador, or the Soviet Union to Cuba.

## Arms Transfers: Latin America in context

The 'arms trade' is effectively an umbrella term which covers both commercial arms dealings and military aid. About half the trade is in major weapons systems — aircraft, missiles, armoured vehicles, and warships. The rest consists of small arms, 'non-lethal technology' (computer and radar systems), spares and components, military-related infrastructure, and 'repressive technology' such as counter-insurgency weapons and torture equipment. Partly because so much of the trade is secret or illegal, and partly because it is so difficult to define and monitor, statistics are notoriously unreliable. For this reason the figures used throughout this article (largely derived from SIPRI) cover only the trade in major weapons systems, unless otherwise specified.

Throughout the past decade 75 per cent of the international trade in arms consisted of weapons supplied by the industrialized nations (especially the members of NATO and the Warsaw Pact) to the Third World. The rest has been made up of imports and exchanges within the industrialized world and the small but growing number of weapons being exported from the Third World. Excluding Vietnam until after 1975, the total value of major weapons imports by Third World countries from 1970 to 1979 was US$63 billion. Of this total, Latin America accounted for US$6.2 billion, or just over 10 per cent. Only the Far East (17 per cent) and the Middle East (48 per cent) were higher — though substantially so — in regional terms. In 1980 SIPRI estimated that Latin American imports were running at US$918 million.

The four largest importers (over the period 1977-1980) were Peru (an average of US$248.7 million), Argentina (US$160.5 million), Brazil (US$160.2 million) and Chile (US$120.5 million). Again working from averages, these four countries alone purchased 17.75 per cent of the arms imported by the region each year.

In terms of total military expenditure, arms imports account for approximately 11 per cent of Latin American military spending. However, this underestimates the extent and importance of the arms trade as a factor in overall militarization for a variety of reasons.

Firstly, as we have already noted, the figures for arms sales, based as they are solely on major weapons systems, only account for a proportion (probably around 50 per cent) of the real size of the trade. Secondly, the proportion of imports to actual expenditure is bound to be lower in Argentina and Brazil because those countries have fast-developing indigenous arms industries albeit heavily dependent on western technology. Thirdly, a great deal of money is also needed to operate, service and maintain weapons systems once they have been imported. This does not show up on the arms sales figures.

The existence of domestic arms industries cannot be equated with military self-sufficiency, which is only achieved when *all* major weapons, spares, components, research and development facilities and infrastructural requirements are possessed indigenously. At the moment only a handful of major industrial powers — the United States, the Soviet Union, France, the United Kingdom and Sweden — can claim to be near this supposedly desirable situation. As far as Latin America is concerned, it is still heavily dependent on a small number of major companies in aerospace (such as Dassault-Breguet in France, and Messerschmitt-Bolkow-Blohm in West Germany) and military electronics (like Plessey in Britain).

At one time the US dominated the Latin American arms market, and during this period, up to 1970, procurement patterns slowly edged away from 'strategic' systems based on the US originated perception of 'hemispheric' defence towards the purchase of counter-insurgency weapons for the control of internal dissent. In the last decade European suppliers have assumed pre-eminence in overall terms, partly because the political 'ties' involved are not liable to be so restrictive as those accompanying US exports, but also because the gradual shift from arms 'aid' to arms 'trade' during the 1950s and 1960s had increased export competition. This, combined with the drain of the Vietnam war on US resources and priorities, the global boom in the arms market following the 1973/74 oil price explosion, and the US refusal to sell sophisticated major weapons systems to the region in the 1970s, boosted the commercial and political attractiveness of Europe as an arms supplying area.

## Latin American Arms Imports: The Rationale for Growth

Various factors can be identified to explain Latin America's military development and its need for arms imports.

The first, at least in order of historical precedence, is US foreign policy towards the region, which has largely been mirrored by the governments of European arms suppliers, and which has proved a major force in moulding indigenous military/security ideology.

At the beginning of World War Two US military missions took root in various countries throughout Latin America, initially as part of the war effort, but from 1945 onwards in order to create a 'cold war' bulwark against a supposed Soviet 'hemispheric plot' against the United States. The 1947 Rio Treaty on Interamerican Mutual Assistance consolidated this strategic goal and paved the way for bilateral South American military aid packages from the US during the 1950s. Arms transfers thus formed part of the US plans to create a Latin American zone of resistance against intercontinental attack. Most of the governments throughout the region acquiesced willingly in this strategy, mainly because of their heavy political and economically dependence upon the US.

However, in the face of post-war competition from Western Europe, rising anti-US feelings in Latin America caused by continuing poverty, and the gradual realization that the supposed Soviet external assault was increasingly unlikely, US policy shifted noticeably during the 1960s. The new threat was 'internal subversion', and the new tactic was the promotion of 'security and development' through the Alliance for Progress and, in the words of Robert McNamara, US Defence Secretary during the Kennedy administration, the consolidation of the Latin American military as a 'stabilizing force'.

This perception continued to mould the pattern of US (and, to an extent, European) arms supplies to the region throughout the 1970s, tempered only by the impact of the Carter 'human rights' policy and the growing political independence of certain Latin American states such as Brazil, Mexico and Venezuela.

On the evidence so far, the Reagan administration is following the same basic line, although the expanding involvement in El Salvador, a hardline attitude towards Nicaragua under the Sandinista government, and the strident anti-communist tone of recent administration statements suggests that arms transfers will be stepped up in the face of internal opposition. Whatever happens over the next few years, it is clear that in spite of a declining portion of the Latin American arms market, US attitudes and influence will continue to be a major determinant of regional military expenditure — whether the people of the region like it or not. US economic and political interests are too pronounced for it to be otherwise.

Secondly, Latin American governments themselves perceive military expenditure and arms imports as necessary for internal security and the suppression of dissent through the fear induced in civilian populations by a noticeable military presence. It is therefore unsurprising that those countries which number amongst the largest regional arms spenders (including Argentina, Chile and Brazil) have strongly militarized governments and also face wide-ranging internal opposition to their political, economic and social policies.

Moreover, counter-insurgency weapons are still estimated to account for 60-65 per cent of total US arms sales to Latin America, and the region's second major supplier (the UK) is calculated to be the world's second largest exporter of 'repressive technology' — military equipment with potential for use against civilian populations.

In addition there is a continuing demand for funds or facilities relating to military training, much of which is obviously relevant to counter-insurgency techniques. In 1979 Latin American requests for military education under the US International Military Education and Training Programme (IMET) were 14.7 per cent higher than for the previous year, in spite of a parallel reduction in some other areas of military assistance; and in 1980/81 the British armed forces received military personnel from Argentina, Belize, Brazil, Peru, Guyana and Venezuela for training purposes, according to information released last year in the House of Commons.

Thirdly, there is a growing perceived need for territorial protection. In this context the continuing Guatemala-Belize dispute is significant, and it should be remembered that in 1980 the disagreement between Argentina and Chile over the Beagle Canal almost resulted in armed conflict.

There are also territorial disputes between Bolivia and Chile and Peru over Bolivia's access to the Pacific; between Colombia and Venezuela over the marine boundary in the Gulf of Venezuela; between Ecuador and Peru over their border which escalated into a brief five day war in January 1981; between Venezuela and Guyana over the area west of the Essequibo river and between Nicaragua and Colombia over Colombian-held Caribbean islands. In April 1982 the dispute between Argentina and Britain over sovereignty of the Falkland Islands resulted in the Argentine invasion of those islands.

The pattern of arms procurement over the 1970s tends to betray the fact that the effective autonomy of Latin American states in determining their own national security precepts has resulted in the equation of 'independence' with the acquisition of sophisticated weapons. This has been strengthened by the ambitions of already entrenched military hierarchies as a major influence on governmental decision-making, together with increased co-ordination amongst national armed forces.

The extension of territorial waters to 12 nautical miles, and the international recognition of a 188 nautical mile exclusive economic zone beyond this limit has probably also assisted the demand for military items such as warships and smaller naval vessels.

The fourth factor connected with increased arms imports is the question of prestige through military expansion. This has always been an important influence on Third World countries in their purchase of sophisticated weapons systems. In a continent dominated by capitalism as is Latin America, there is a strong tendency to perceive military muscle as a direct measure of 'development'. Throughout the region the 'psychology of militarism' must be seen to play an important part in fuelling arms purchases.

Finally there is a strong feeling, inherited from the politico-economic philosophy of the 'developed' world, that military expenditure actually enhances industrialization and accelerates economic modernization. Behind this belief lies the fact that much Western technology is seen at its most impressive (and horrifying) in the form of modern weapons systems. Thus technological capability and know-how is frequently imported under a military guise.

## The Impact of Increased Arms Purchases and Military Expenditure

The effects of this militarization on the Latin American region can best be appreciated by looking at three separate, but interconnected areas: the potential for conflict, economic and social repercussions, and the question of internal repression.

As far as inter-state conflict is concerned Latin America is in a very different situation to other Third World continents, since no major international conflagrations have been waged within the region. Nonetheless Latin America is a very violent area. Twenty civil wars took place between 1947 and 1970, according to the classification of Hungarian expert Istvan Kende.

It is difficult to say whether or not arms purchases and military expenditure were a causal factor in the smaller conflicts such as that between El Salvador and Honduras in 1969. Clearly wars cannot take place without weapons, and, especially in the 1950s and 1960s, Latin American states were overwhelmingly dependent on external supplies. Although hostilities originate from political conflicts, nonetheless it is valid to point out (as John Kenneth-Galbraith once did in relation to the 1965 Indo-Pakistan conflict) that the presence of major weapons systems substantially contributes towards regional tension. By strengthening the hand of the military, their presence also pre-empts the peaceful solution of disputes. Where armed superiority exists, or is deemed to exist, the military path may be embarked upon before all the political and diplomatic avenues of activity have been exhausted. Moreover, the existence of large quantities of arms certainly enhances the level and extent of destruction once a war has broken out.

Thus the pouring of ever-more-sophisticated weapons into the region is bound to heighten suspicion amongst rival states, to confirm the stranglehold of militaristic attitudes, and to provide over-anxious generals with both the means and excuse for using the equipment they have so zealously acquired. In a politically volatile continent militarization could yet be the spark that sets off the powder keg. Already Peru and Venezuela have been arming themselves through fear of a powerful, potentially expansionist, Brazil.

Economically and socially the consequences of arms procurement are even more significant. Firstly, military expenditure has been outstripping GNP growth throughout the region, increasing the overall burden of the arms sector as a proportion of the total economic base. According to IMF and OECD statistics this has been an overall trend throughout the Third World.

Of course for the larger economies (Argentina, Brazil, Mexico and Venezuela) the overall impact may not be that great, especially for the rich. The poor, however, do suffer, since it is far more likely in countries such as Brazil and Chile that money will be diverted away from public programmes to alleviate or eradicate the appalling poverty that exists there, and into military expenditure.

Moreover for smaller countries the burden of arms procurement in relation to GNP is comparatively larger. Peru, for example, spends twice as much on the military per capita than Argentina: the figure being 5.4 and 2.7 per cent of GNP respectively. The drain on foreign exchange is also more significant, and this is especially pronounced in relation to the purchase of capital-intensive modern weaponry.

National balance of payments accounts may also be adversely affected. In mid-1980 the annual overall deficit in Brazil was running at over US$6.6 billion, whilst at the same time around US$2 billion was being spent on arms, not accounting for debts with international banks incurred partly through this burden. Furthermore, precious resources and skills were being invested in an entirely non-productive sector.

In terms of employment arms expenditure also has a deleterious effect. Because major weapons systems are becoming increasingly sophisticated and complex, small groups of technically highly-skilled workers are being siphoned away from work on development projects and into the military sector. Meanwhile the residual pool of semi-skilled or unskilled unemployed are left with nothing to do.

There is, additionally, considerable evidence that arms spending is inflationary — and this problem is particularly apposite to Argentina and Brazil, along with many other non-oil exporting 'developing' countries. Firstly, military expenditure can help to overheat the domestic economy by generating more disposable income than goods and services to absorb it. Secondly, it can result in competition between civilian and military industries for scarce resources, pushing up prices of raw materials and energy. Thirdly, increased costs on the part of the supplier (mainly the industrialized world) are passed on to the consumer.

However it is in the area of social priorities that the economic impact of the arms trade and military expenditure is most noticeable — in that it hits the poorest and most vulnerable members of Latin American society. On the one hand US$8.2 billion was spent on arms in 1980; on the other, there were 43 million illiterate adults and more than one million infant deaths throughout the region. A small fraction of the military budget could largely remove these problems. Yet of the 24 countries that make up Latin America, 13 spend more per head on arms than on either (or both) education or health care, according to WMSE rank indicators for the year 1978. Peru spends 45 per cent more per capita on the military than health and education combined;

Uruguay spends twice as much on arms as on health; with Paraguay the ratio is 13:3 (US$), Argentina 55:11; Bolivia 18:8; Chile 73:34; Ecuador 29:9; El Salvador 13:9 and so on.

It would of course be simplistic to suggest that money not spent on arms would automatically benefit the poor and underprivileged; that would depend on the political will for change, and a more equal distribution of wealth. Even so, it is clear that resources, people and capital are being diverted away from social/economic development and into the abyss of modern weaponry.

Thirdly, and following on from earlier observations, there is the highly significant area of repression and human rights violations. Since counter-insurgency weapons are high on the list of military priorities throughout the region, and because (as we have seen) the need to control internal dissent is a prime motivating factor behind arms spending, it is fair to point out that repression has been both facilitated and exacerbated by Latin American militarization. Almost all weapons increase the capacity of governments to imprison, torture, harass and kill their opponents — be it police equipment, rubber or plastic bullets, tear gas, electric shock devices, computer information systems, surveillance equipment, armoured personnel carriers, small arms, or tracker aircraft/patrol boats. In 1973/4 the Chilean navy even used a British-made military training ship, the *Esmeralda* as a torture centre for detainees.

The 1981 Amnesty International (British Section) revised briefing paper on *The Repression Trade* specifically acknowledged the contribution of the arms trade to global violations of human rights, making direct reference to the police forces of Argentina, Chile, Uruguay and Brazil.

## The Major Weapons Suppliers

The international market in major weapons systems is effectively cornered by the two superpowers, responsible between them for 70.7 per cent of total global arms sales, and a sub-group of leading European suppliers who account for 21.5 per cent. This means that just six countries supplied 92.2 per cent of the arms sold around the world, during the period 1977-1980 inclusive.

The largest exporter (on the basis of 1977-1980 aggregates) is the USA (US$24.9 billion; 43.3 per cent of the world market), followed by the Soviet Union (US$15.7 billion; 27.4 per cent). France (US$6.2 billion; 10.8 per cent); Italy (US$2.3 billion; 4.0 per cent), the United Kingdom (US$2.1 billion; 3.7 per cent) and West Germany (US$1.7 billion; 3.0 per cent).

Calculating the percentages of total arms exports to the Third World, the rank order is as follows: USA (US$15.1 billion), Soviet Union (US$12.5 billion), France (US$4.7 billion), United Kingdom (US$1.75 billion), Italy (US$1.74 billion), West Germany (US$643 million) and Netherlands (US$466 million). Of all arms exported between 1977 and 1980. 68.7 per cent (or US$39.5 billion) went to the nations of the Third World. These seven leading sellers contributed US$35.3 billion or around 89 per cent of that total.

As far as sales to Latin America are concerned the 'big six' plus Netherlands and Israel are the principal suppliers. The Soviet Union dominates the Central American and Caribbean market solely on account of its relationship to Cuba. Suppliers to Central America and the Caribbean from 1975 to 1979 were the Soviet Union (45 per cent), United Kingdom (21 per cent), USA (8 per cent) and France (3 per cent).

The main suppliers to South America (which imported 94 per cent of all major weapons sold to the Latin American region between 1979-1980 are: the USA (21 per cent of the market), United Kingdom (18 per cent), France (11 per cent), Italy (11 per cent), and West Germany (8 per cent approx). The four main Western European suppliers thus account for just under half of all South American arms imports.

With regard to the distribution of arms exports to Latin America as a whole, there have been some notable changes during the 1970s. In Central America and the Caribbean the Soviet proportion of sales has dropped from 66 per cent (1970-1974) to 45 per cent (1975-1979). Meanwhile the US contribution has also fallen from 19 to 8 per cent, whilst the United Kingdom share tripled in percentage value from 7 to 21 per cent. In South America there has been a steady erosion in US supplies over the same period (from 24 to 21 per cent), while the European share has increased in real terms, although the 'big four' European suppliers have all suffered at the hands of smaller competitors such as Netherlands, Switzerland and Austria. The overall trend is towards diversification, with European arms sellers retaining the largest proportion of the market.


## The Incentive to Sell: France, Italy, West Germany and Austria

In this section we shall look at the general arguments for participation in the international arms market, and refer specifically to France, Italy and West Germany — three important South American suppliers. Mention will also be made of Austria, a growing arms supplier whose markets now include Latin America.

There are four arguments given for the European commitment to maintain significant levels of arms sales. The first is political. Military exports form an important part of any government's foreign policy. Not only are they a means of consolidating allies and undermining foes, but they are also a lever that can be used to influence Third World governments. It is not without significance that European suppliers have tended to favour these states to which their own trans-national business organisations are most heavily committed, for example. Moreover, military exports have often been a principal means of retaining the loyalty of newly-independent developing countries, at least in theory, though in practice it has not always worked out that way.

Secondly, there is the question of reducing unit costs in the production of military equipment by producing for export. The technical advances made in the fields of engineering, electronics and computing since World War Two have been quite phenomenal. As a result capital and research and development costs have soared. According to WMSE, military research budgets in the US and Western Europe increased by 75 per cent between 1970 and 1978. A World War Two tank would have cost around £25,000; a modern XMI tank costs £750,000 at 1980 prices. This is a 3000 per cent increase in actual terms, or 500 per cent allowing for inflation. Arms manufacturers therefore have sought to relieve the crippling costs by extending production runs and exporting the resulting surplus equipment. The idea has been to achieve economies of scale, and to fill troughs in demand. In addition it has been necessary to seek government underwriting of research costs, to amalgamate arms industries in order to alleviate competition, to collaborate on major projects (such as the Tornado multi-role combat aircraft), and, where possible, to form cost-plus contracts with the government whereby the total cost of production plus an agreed profit margin is paid for through state funding.

Thirdly, there are various economic justifications. Arms production and exports are believed to provide employment (especially in a time of recession) and to contribute favourably towards the balance of payments. Technological spin-offs resulting from military research are also meant to provide a bonus to civilian industry.

Fourthly, arms deals may be very beneficial to individual companies and specific sectors. The share of exports as a proportion of total production in the French naval industry increased fivefold from 1970-1974, and with heavy government support, these exports can be very profitable. This does not necessarily imply, however, that what is good for the manufacturer is beneficial for the economy as a whole.

Looking at France, Italy, West Germany and Austria, these processes can be seen at work. French expansion in the arms market (resulting in the country's current position as Europe's largest exporter) dates back to the Gaullist days, and for many years has been sustained partly through the commercial success of the Dassault produced Mirage aircraft. Ironically, the spiralling increase in military deals occurred at roughly the same time as the Council of Ministers stated that an international agreement on restraining arms sales would represent a realistic approach to disarmament. That was on 24 July 1968. Three years later President Pompidou urged weapons manufacturers to give special emphasis to producing simpler, less costly and more exportable military equipment.

Between 1974 and 1977 the French trade in arms virtually doubled, and between 1978/79 and 1979/80 both deliveries and orders were up by around 20 per cent — considerably ahead of inflation. Today there are reckoned to be 75,000 workers employed directly in export production, roughly a quarter of all those presently working on arms manufacture.

Export sales have shifted away from aerospace and into other areas. In 1980 naval vessels accounted for 41 per cent of the 37,400 million franc total trade value, aircraft for 30 per cent and land force equipment for 20 per cent. 78 per cent of all weapons sales are directed towards the Middle East and North Africa. After Western Europe and the US (7.4 per cent), Latin America takes the next largest portion, 7.0 per cent, against 2.8 per cent for sub-Saharan Africa, 2.8 per cent for the Far East, and 1.2 per cent for all others.

The advantages of this trade to France are seen as the generation of employment, the maintenance of indigenous research facilities upon which the country's independent military strategy is held to be dependent, and export earnings to offset the effects of the oil crisis. Prime Minister Jacques Chirac (1974-1976) also emphasized the fact that large scale arm sales enabled France to challenge superpower hegemony in the military field, and to reassert the nation's role as a major nuclear power.

All this, together with the world-wide reputation of the French as comparatively ruthless "arms pushers" presents a tricky problem for socialist President Francois Mitterrand, who, as a former critic of 'indiscriminate sales', has already endorsed record weapons exports between April and August 1981, though it should be pointed out that these deals (including the supply of two frigates to Argentina) were signed well before he came into office.

Socialist (and Communist) party policy towards arms sales has always reflected a dissatisfaction with the role of the Inter-Ministerial Committee for the Study and Export of War Materials, which is seen as legitimizing the role of the trade rather than challenging it. Instead, the Socialist manifesto advocated obligatory information on weapons exports to be provided for government committees, a ban on sales to colonialist, racist or fascist regimes; international negotiations, and regional supplier-recipient conferences on arms trade restraint. There is also a stated intention to 're-orientate' undesirable sales elsewhere.

If implemented rigorously, these policies could go some way towards reducing French weapons exports, but several major problems might thwart this process.

Firstly, if the prohibition of sales to racist or fascist countries is implemented, the question arises as to *whom* the arms will be sold. The great majority of the trade is currently with the Third World, and the European market is likely to prove too competitive and unresponsive to absorb extra French exports.

Secondly, Mitterrand is firmly committed to the modernization of the country's armed forces and independent nuclear strategy, and national research and development. Without changes in these policies arms sales restrictions are likely to have little impact. Thirdly, there will be a substantial lobby from arms manufacturers in favour of continued exports. The French aerospace industry, for example, is said to be dependent on foreign sales for 40 per cent of its activity. Without a firmly backed policy of restructuring and alternative (non-military) production, reduced French military exports look unlikely.

For West Germany the starting point is slightly different. In 1971 the Federal Republic banned exports to 'areas of tension', and this reflected a fairly strict export policy. As a consequence, the proportion of West German arms sales directed towards the Third World has been lower than for any other major European supplier. Also, in 1977, the government emphasized that it did not want exports to increase substantially.

However, in spite of the restrictions and good intentions, West German arms exports have continued to grow. Between 1971-73 and 1974-76 such exports grew by 450 per cent, and 1978 sales were US$1 billion up on the previous year. According to SIPRI, West Germany sold US$1.7 billion worth of major weapons between 1977 and 1980, of which 37.6 per cent went to the Third World.

Moreover, the early 1980s have seen controversial changes in arms trade policies concomitant with its continued growth. In 1980 it was made known that the foreign ministry would no longer define restrictive 'areas of tension', and that commercial considerations would come to the fore in weapons sales decision-making. This is far more likely to affect the Middle East market than Latin America, but it is nonetheless an alarming development.

Why has this change in emphasis taken place? The main reason is that the domestic defence budget has been spiralling as a result of the excessive costs in developing and acquiring high-technology weapons systems, in spite of European collaboration especially in the field of aerospace. For example, the 1981 cost of the Tornado multi-role combat aircraft is 400 per cent higher than previously estimated. Not only has the proposed Franco-German TKF-90 main battletank project been cancelled as a result of this kind of escalating cost, but defence minister Hans Apel stated in mid-1981 that Bonn's defence expenditure between 1982 and 1984 inclusive will have to rise by DM1 billion over the figure originally anticipated. Thus arms sales are seen as crucial if overall unit costs are to be reduced. Despite a more enthusiastic West German export policy, its proportion of arms supplies to Latin America should continue to decline, because the emphasis on underwriting domestic defence costs could price West Germany out of the market for cheaper equipment.

In Italy there have also been significant increases in arms sales since the latter half of the 1970s. Almost 97 per cent of the US$2.3 billion worth of weapons exported between 1977 and 1980 were destined for the Third World, with Latin America (especially Peru, Argentina and Brazil) proving a particularly lucrative market. Venezuela has been a big customer for Lupo class frigates and ship-to-ship/air missiles. Italy has helped finance its domestic naval development through such overseas sales.

Amongst the smaller suppliers, Austria is particularly interesting. In 1981 a significant order for light tanks from Chile (worth £70 million) was lost as a result of a public outcry which caused severe embarrassment to the socialist government. However, Austrian sales to Latin America have been increasing rapidly, with large orders for Argentina and Uruguay in the pipeline.

Twenty-five to thirty companies are involved in the manufacture of arms in Austria, including Voest-Alpine (iron and steel) and Steyr-Daimler-Puch (vehicles). In the case of the latter, armoured vehicles are said to account for 25 per cent of gross turnover. According to the director-general of the nationalized Kreditanstalt Bankverein around 40,000 jobs are dependent on the arms industry. Other factors have also encouraged the promotion of arms exports: the fluctuation in markets for certain consumer products (such as mopeds); a series of commercially attractive deals with Middle Eastern and other Third World countries; and a trade deficit of US$3.4 billion at the end of 1981, largely as a result of escalating energy costs.

Some analysts would like to believe that the enlarged Austrian participation in the international arms market will be a temporary development, to offset the effects of the recession occurring throughout the industrialized world. This, however, seems somewhat optimistic. On past evidence there is little doubt that small suppliers who use arms sales as an economic tool end up fully integrated into the world arms market.

## Britain as an Arms Supplier

Between 1977 and 1980 Britain was the world's fifth largest arms exporter. According to figures released by the former head of the Defence Sales Organisation (DSO), Sir Ronald Ellis, arms sales in 1980 amounted to £1.2 billion. The DSO (the arms exporting branch of the Ministry of Defence) estimates the 1981 figure at £1.5 billion, and predicts £1.7 billion worth of sales in 1982. Analysing these total sales into categories, the most important are ships (34 per cent between 1977-1980) and aircraft (33 per cent), followed by armoured vehicles (19 per cent) and missiles (14 per cent). Military electronics, not differentiated in these statistics, are also of major importance. Moreover, a large part of the DSO figures, which differe substantially from defence white paper estimates, are accounted for by infrastructural projects.

In terms of the general UK defence industry, exports amount to about 25-35 per cent of total activity, and two-thirds of these arms sales (including 80 per cent of major weapons systems) go to the Third World.

So why does Britain retain this deep commitment to the trade in military equipment? There are three principal reasons.

Firstly, political motivations. Arms sales are seen as a way of consolidating friends, and defending the interests of NATO. Perhaps more significantly, they create the illusion that a country which has lost much of its direct influence overseas can still mould world events by the back door.

However, in terms of real, as opposed to psychological security, none of these arguments can be given much credibility. The collapse of the Shah in Iran (a major UK client) considerably shook the faith of the defence establishment which saw arms exports as an easy road to 'security' in the Gulf and elsewhere. Ultimately the whole sophisticated arsenal of modern weaponry that the Shah had amassed could not prevent his demise. Furthermore, it is widely recognized that the supplier country has little control over where arms end up. Thus weapons sold to Allende in Chile have ended up in the hands of the Pinochet junta; Centurion tanks sold to Jordan have been passed on to South Africa, and American equipment in Vietnam has come into the hands of the anti-US Heng Samrin regime.

As far as non-superpower suppliers are concerned the real political leverage afforded by arms sales is fairly limited, although there may be some tactical advantages. For instance the present Conservative administration in Britain, committed to the acquisition of the US Trident nuclear weapons system, seems to see its arms exports as a way of appeasing Reagan's foreign policy. Thus the end of the military embargo on Chile, and the refusal to prohibit sales to El Salvador gain greater diplomatic significance than their actual effects merit.

Secondly, there are a range of national economic justifications for British arms sales. These have gained increasing importance as the collapse of the 'grander strategic arguments' (Lawrence Freedman) have been recognized.

In a climate of rising unemployment (3 to 4 million, depending on the method of calculation) jobs are a big issue, and politicians make frequent recourse to the argument that military exports sustain employment. Of the 500,000 people who work in the UK defence industry (around 50 per cent on direct Ministry of Defence projects, the rest indirectly) some 75-80,000 are calculated to be directly involved in export manufacture, with perhaps another 90,000 peripherally involved. These jobs, it is maintained, are preserved by Britain's overseas sales.

But this ignores the fact that the arms industry is capital intensive. This means that, increasingly, labour is being displaced by technological innovations in electronics and in computer-aided design. The introduction of micro-processors will certainly compound these developments.

Thus as a result of the pace of technological change it has been estimated that 100,000 jobs were lost in the aerospace industry between the mid-1960s and the mid-1970s, and the continuing process of amalgamation within the arms sector has led to a spate of redundancies in British Shipbuilders and the Royal Ordinance Factories amongst others.

Instability in recipient nations has also an effect on employment in the arms industry. In 1979 Britain lost £1.7 billion worth of orders from Iran, plus £500 million through the collapse of the Arab Organisation for Industrialization. Many jobs were shed as a result. Moreover, a number of recent investigations including studies by the International Association of Machinists and Aerospace Workers Union, and by the US Bureau of Labor Statistics, have demonstrated that far more employment can be generated by investment in areas such as industrial machinery, construction, transportation, consumer goods, health and education. Some estimates suggest up to 2.5 times as many jobs as investment in defence industries.

In Britain concrete alternatives to arms manufacture developed in the 1976 Alternative Corporate Plan of the Lucas Aerospace Combine Shop Stewards Committee include a mix of socially useful and economically viable projects ranging from heat pumps to telechiric remote handling devices, transportation systems, oceanic vehicles, braking systems and medical equipment. Such plans could form the basis of a large scale redeployment of resources away from military production.

The British government has also maintained that arms exports benefit the economy by generating foreign exchange and assisting the balance of payments. Yet in 1979 it was noted that whilst the UK arms industry absorbed 20 per cent of the UK's total research and development effort, military sales account for only 2.5 to 3.5 per cent of all exports.

Nor are general commercial prospects that bright. In 1977 the House of Commons Public Accounts Committee estimated that of the £206 million land forces sales made in the previous fiscal year, only £58 million covered costs, and a mere £19 million yielded a profit. Even allowing for the spread of capital costs relating to modernization in the Royal Ordinance Factories, these were startling figures. Recovery since that time has not been substantial, in view of the need to lower prices in the face of US and European competition.

The final economic rationale is that there are numerous civilian spin-offs from military research. The hovercraft, for example, was originally developed out of military research. But it seems significant to note that the greatest industrial advances have often occurred in low military-spending countries, such as Japan and West Germany, whilst the Soviet Union, which spends 12-15 per cent of its GDP on defence is substantially behind the West in microelectronics, data processing and aero-engine technology. In the UK a major study of the arms industry carried out on behalf of the Royal Institute for International Affairs concluded that the return from military research to the civilian sector was very small.

Thirdly, there is the question of arms exports as a response to escalating defence expenditure through the reduction of unit costs on domestically required military equipment. Here there are a number of points to be made.

The first is that this argument is not supported by a study of the relationship between official research spending and British defence exports. Rather, looking at the years 1975/6 to 1979/80, the sector which absorbed the largest research budget (aircraft, 55.4 per cent) accounted for least exports (16.8 per cent of total arms sales). Conversely, the largest selling item (land forces equipment, 55.3 per cent of total sales) accounted for the least research expenditure (11.7 per cent), all according to the government's own figures.

Neither should it be assumed that current export categories match the services' defence equipment requirements. In 1980 Prime Minister

Thatcher called upon military industries to start making cheaper and simpler weapons in order to boost exports. This presupposed a distinction, instead of a correlation, between foreign sales and domestic needs, given existing procurement patterns.

Moreover, there is a good deal of evidence to suggest that exports have a tendency to direct national defence priorities, rather than the other way round. For example, the value of both the Tornado multirole combat aircraft and Hawk fighter/trainer aircraft have been questioned by sections of the military establishment. Yet the lobby for production was very much influenced by considerations of export potential. This is perhaps not surprising, since the DSO has a seat on the Defence Procurement Executive of the Ministry of Defence and, despite protestations to the contrary, is held to exercise considerable pressure within this decisive forum.

Arms sales may also help to spread the fixed costs of production lines over a longer run, keeping them open until the British forces are ready to procure. This argument presupposes the existence of a widespread relationship between export and domestic defence requirements which is rather difficult to identify. The supporting evidence lies mainly in the findings of a study (undertaken by the US Congressional Budget Office). This is exceptionally difficult to apply in a British context, since it assumes that a much larger peace-time production base will need to be maintained (with or without exports) than is the case for the UK, and its findings also hinge mainly on savings achieved through tank production and export — although in Britain the experience of tank sales has been somewhat less than beneficial. Even in the US such exports represent only 37 per cent of the arms trade examined, as against 67 per cent of military production.

Thus none of the conventional military or economic grounds for British arms sales can be deemed to be totally convincing, and nor can the political motives — aside from delusions of grandeur! Where, then, does the other pressure come from to maintain this trade?

The answer to this question lies most obviously in vested business interests. A glance at the performance and profits of the UK's top arms companies, the number of cost-plus deals, and the distribution of government funding will confirm the truth in this assertion. Even at a time of industrial recession there are huge profits to be made from the export of military hardware, especially when the government is prepared to reimburse production costs, plus a margin of profit on domestic equipment, at the taxpayers' expense. Once a weapons system has been developed, the producing company is in an excellent position to cash in on excess export sales, with the taxpayer receiving little of the proceeds. According to the Centre for Alternative Industrial and Technological Systems (CAITS) at the North-East London Polytechnic, the government levy on commercial sales of military equipment developed wholly or substantially through government funding amounted (in 1980) to only £9 million for an initial outlay of £1.5 billion.

In addition, there are numerous other incentives for the arms producers. As well as marketing and promotion facilities offered by the DSO, established in 1966 under the then Labour Government, military exporters receive further state assistance through the Department of Trade's British Overseas Trade Board, through the biennial Royal Naval Equipment Exhibition at Portsmouth, the British Army Equipment Exhibition at Aldershot, the Farnborough Air Show, the Defence Manufacturers Association exhibitions and various other military trade fairs. One of the most noticeable features of all these arrangements is the close collaboration between business interests and the military. This is the key to government encouragement of defence exports, not just in Britain but throughout Western Europe, where most of the arguments outlined above apply, in different degrees and in differing circumstances.

## Indigenous Arms Industries and Nuclear Proliferation

Finally, there are two other important matters relating to Latin America and the arms trade which bear mentioning, largely because they will be of increasing importance in the future. These are the expansion of South American defence export industries, and the link between conventional military sales and nuclear power weapons proliferation.

Both Brazil and Argentina rank amongst the largest Third World producers and exports of arms. In both cases the developing industries are licensed producers, with the US and Western European countries granting the licenses. In Brazil's case, France has made provision for the local production of 230 military and civilian helicopters, West Germany for army helicopters and anti-tank missiles, and Italy for counter-insurgency fighter and trainer aircraft. Brazilian arms exports include the EE-9 Cascavel and Engesa armoured cars; and the Xavante anti-guerrilla aircraft. According to SIPRI, Brazil was responsible for 21 per cent of all Third World arms exports between 1970 and 1979. Between 1977 and 1980 this had risen to 33.1 per cent, or US$421 million. Almost all of this trade was with other 'developing' countries, the biggest client being Chile. Another important development is the co-production of the AMX Close Air Support aircraft (for domestic and export use) with the Italian companies

Aeritalia and Macchi. The Brazilian firm involved is Embraer. Argentina's defence industry has continued to expand in accordance with the Europa Plan of 1967. Shipbuilding (destroyers, corvettes, survey ships, submarines etc.) is important, and aircraft, helicopters, the TAM tank, and various missiles are also under production or discussion. Amongst the countries which grant licenses are West Germany, the US and Britain. Argentina was the seventh largest Third World exporter (2.8 per cent of the total from 1977-1980, or US$35 million at constant 1975 prices), and again the most important client is Chile.

The significance of these developments in indigenous design, production and export lies not in the fact that Brazil or Argentina are anything like self-sufficient (the Brazilian EE-9 armoured car contains components from Belgium, France, Germany and the US), but that it is yet another spur to the militarization of Latin America.

In relation to nuclear proliferation, the important point to bear in mind is the correlation between two factors: the development of civilian nuclear power facilities, and the availability (through the arms trade, and licensing arrangements) of potential delivery systems for small scale nuclear bombs. Significantly, Argentina, Brazil and Chile (who have not signed the nuclear Non-Proliferation Treaty, and are widely believed to be developing a nuclear weapon capability) all have access to the fuel cycle that both nuclear bombs and power plants share. At the same time they also possess sophisticated aircraft to carry and fire any small weapons that they may wish to produce. Given economic and military tensions, the power-seeking of sections of the armed forces in highly militarized societies, and the necessary capability, the acquisition of small-scale nuclear weapons may be seen as the next logical step for such countries.

## Conclusions

The conclusions to be drawn from the current situation involving Latin America and the arms trade could very easily be pessimistic, bearing in mind the steady increase in militarization throughout the region. In particular, the demand for new weapon systems will continue to exist as long as militaristic governments and inequitable economic systems dictate that this is necessary for their own preservation. On present trends the arms trade will remain the primary source of military expansion and procurement for some time, since the growth of indigenous industries under licence is still far from reaching the threshold of self-sufficiency.

However, one popular misconception surrounding this issue is the notion that 'demand factors' are always of paramount importance. This seriously underestimates the 'supply push' emanating from western countries in particular. As we have seen, the military-industrial complex provides strong commercial and organic motivation for numerous individuals and organizations within the industrialized world's arms industry. Moreover, the political presuppositions behind the perceived need for arms sales cannot really be seen in isolation from the East-West arms race, and the psychology of security through military growth that it breeds. Because of this, it is unlikely that substantial demilitarization (including large reductions in arms trade) will occur in 'developing' countries unless there are further signs of a similar process in the industrialized world. For, since the Second World War the superpowers have not just been exporting military hardware, they have also been exporting their own conflicts by proxy.

Therefore a prime target for organizations concerned about the growth of the arms trade ought to be the major supplying regions, Europe included. Restraints on the commercial and military thrust of arms promotion in the industrialized world, whilst not directly coping with the very real political conflicts of interest that stimulate purchases in Latin America, nevertheless go some way towards reducing the temperature of a market which is being continually overheated by the pace of technological competition. There is a great need for more accurate information on arms transfers. Supplier governments have frequently expressed the opinion that national and international registers, whilst desirable, are not practicable because they would infringe security interests. For major weapon systems, infrastructural projects and arms industry developments, however, it is very difficult to disguise the sales for more than a short time. In the long term more information of this kind, though it may provide some immediate practical problems, could only increase the trust and security amongst nations. As the first step towards an internationally supervised and verified register of arms exports through the United Nations, non-governmental organisations in a number of European countries are pressurizing their governments on the need for national registers and a reduction in the secrecy that surrounds arms deals.

Secondly, a good deal of work has been done on sales to specific countries known for their violation of basic human rights. In 1978, partly due to the pressure of public opinion, a British sale of armoured vehicles to El Salvador was stopped. The Austrian administration has been placed under similar pressure recently concerning arms to Chile, and a number of military exhibitions designed to promote exports have been cancelled or postponed — including those at Anaheim, Wiesbaden and Panama. Further initiatives in this field are much needed.

Thirdly, the practical ideas espoused in the alternative corporate plan at Lucas Aerospace have led to dramatic growth in the conversion movement, which seeks to develop plans and a strategy for encouraging the diversification of individual industries away from arms production and into more socially useful activities. In addition, trade union and academic research has gone some way in recent years towards undermining the narrow economism that underlies many of the structural reasons put forward for reliance on arms exports.

Fourthly there is a growing recognition amongst those non-governmental organizations concerned with disarmament and on the part of trade unionists, of the need for information and a political response to be co-ordinated across national boundaries. This stems from the increasingly transnational and collaborative nature of the arms export industries.

These are just four areas in which work is being done not only to analyse, but also to counteract, the forces involved in the militarization process exemplified by current trends in Latin America. For those concerned about the future of the region they cannot be ignored.

## References

Amnesty International, *The Repression Trade: Revised Briefing Paper*, AI British Section, London, January 1981.

Marion Anderson, *The Impact of Military Spending on the Machinists Union*, Centre for Alternative Industrial and Technological Systems (CAITS), North-East London Polytechnic, London, 1981 (reprint from US edition).

Campaign Against the Arms Trade, *Factsheet No.5: Employment*, CAAT, London, 1976.

Duncan Campbell, 'The bribe machine', *New Statesman*, 17 October 1980.

Centre for Alternative Industrial and Technological Systems, *Arms Conversion*, CAITS, London, July 1981.

Lamri Chirouf, 'The French Debate: Arms Sales', *ADIU Report*, Armament and Disarmament Information Unit, Sussex, July/August 1981.

Committee on Poverty and the Arms Trade, *Bombs for Breakfast: How the Arms Trade Reinforces a Vicious Cycle of Impoverishment, Repression and Militarization in the Third World*, COPAT, London, 1981 (revised edition).

Robin Cook, 'The Tragic Cost of Britain's Arms Trade', *New Statesman*, 30 June 1978.

Rupert Cornwell, 'MPs Rap Defence Ministry over Arms Sales Procedure', *Financial Times*, 16 June 1977.

*The Corporate Plan of the Lucas Aerospace Combine Shop Stewards Committee*, LACSSC, UK, 1976.

Counter-Information Services, *The War Lords*, CIS, London, 1982.

'West Germany Faces Higher Arms Bill', *Financial Times*, 9 March 1981.

'Minister Supports Arms Sales', *Financial Times*, 5 March 1982.

'Increasing Arms Orders Embarrass Socialists', *Financial Times*, 28 January 1982.

Lawrence Freedman, *Arms Production in the United Kingdom: Problems and Prospects*, Royal Institute for International Affairs, London, 1978.

'Arms Drive Aids Exports says Thatcher', *Guardian* (London), 4 September 1980.

*Hansard, Written Answers to Parliamentary Questions*, 19 December 1979, 19 February 1981 and 12 May 1981.

Hugh Herbert, 'Can We Enjoy Both Profits and Peace?', *Guardian* (London), 27 March 1979.

Human Rights Network, *Truncheons and Tanks: the Arms Trade and Human Rights*, HRN/CAAT, London, 1980.

Istvan Kende, quoted in Frank Barnaby, 'Latin America and the Arms Trade', *Britain and Latin America*, Latin America Bureau, London, 1979 edition.

*Le Monde*, 23 and 24 May 1971.

David Manasian, 'A Defence for Arms?', *Engineering Today*, III,5, 5 February 1979.

Newcastle-upon-Tyne Trades Council, TANC, TND, *Jobs for a Change: Alternative Production on Tyneside*, Newcastle Trade Union Studies Information Unit, Newcastle, 1981.

David Patterson, *The Federal Republic of Germany's Arms Industry*, (Unpublished paper for CAAT), London, 24 March 1981.

'Conversion', *Ploughshares Monitor* (USA), 4 February 1978.

Ruth Leger Sivard, *World Military and Social Expenditures 1981*, World Priorities, Leesburg (USA), 1981.

M.H. Spooner, 'Democracies Endangered by Heightening Tension', *Financial Times* (Supplement on Latin America), 29 June 1981.

Stockholm International Peace Research Institute, *The Arms Trade and the Third World*, Penguin, Harmondsworth (UK), 1975.

Stockholm International Peace Research Institute, *World Armaments and Disarmament: SIPRI Yearbook 1981*, Taylor and Francis, London, 1981.

Trevor Taylor, 'Research Note: British Arms Exports and Research and Development Costs', *Survival*, International Institute for

Strategic Studies, London, November-December 1980.

'Higher Defence Exports Urged', *Times*, 4 September 1980.

'Boom in French Arms Sales to Arab Nations', *Times*, 14 October 1981.

UK, *1980 Defence White Paper*, HMSO, London, 1980 (annual).

Augusto Varas, Carlos Portales and Felipe Aguero, *The National and International Dynamics of South American Armamentism*, FLACSO, Santiago de Chile, 1980.

W Wilson, 'Arms Sales: Policy Without a Profit', *Observer*, 30 July 1978.

## Useful Addresses

Stockholm International Peace Research Institute (SIPRI), Bergshamra, S-171 73 Solna, Sweden.

Campaign Against the Arms Trade (CAAT), 5 Caledonian Road, London N1 9DX. 01-278 1976.

Centre for Alternative Industrial and Technical Systems (CAITS), North-East London Polytechnic (NELP), Longbridge Road, Dagenham, Essex.

**TABLE 1**

Register of The Arms Trade With Latin America 1980/1981[1]

| Recipient | Supplier | No. ordered | Weapon designation | Weapon description | Year of order | Year of delivery | No. delivered |
|---|---|---|---|---|---|---|---|
| Argentina | Austria | 50 | Cuirassier | SPG ATW | (1979) | 1980 | (50) |
| | | 57 | Cuirassier | SPG ATW | 1981 | 1982* | ... |
| | Belgium | 13 | BDX | APC | (1979) | 1980 | 13 |
| | France | 7 | Mirage-3E | Fighter/Bomber | 1978 | 1980 | 7 |
| | | 12 | SA-315B Lama | Hel | 1978 | | |
| | | 12 | SA-316B | Hel | 1979 | | |
| | | 12 | SA-330J Puma | Hel | 1978 | | |
| | | 3 | SA-330J Puma | Hel | 1980 | | |
| | | 14 | Super Etendard | Fighter/ASW | 1979 | | |
| | | 1000 | HOT | ATM | 1980 | 1980 | (200) |
| | | 1 | A-69 Type | Frigate | 1979 | 1980 | |
| | | 10 | Roland | SAM | 1981 | 1981 | ... |
| | Germany FR | 4 | Meko-360 | Frigate | 1978 | | |
| | | 2 | Type 122 | Frigate | (1978) | | |
| | | 2 | Type 148 | FPB | (1979) | | |
| | | 1 | Type 1700 | Submarine | 1977 | | |
| | Italy | 9 | A-109 Hirundo | Hel | 1977 | | |
| | | 10 | MB-339A | Trainer/Strike | (1980) | 1980 | 3 |
| | Spain | 5 | | FPB | 1979 | | |
| | United Kingdom | 8 | Lynx | Hel | 1979 | | |
| | USA | 3 | CH-47C Chinook | Hel | (1977) | 1980 | 3 |
| | | 2 | KC-130H | Transport | (1978) | | |
| | | 1 | Learjet-35A | Transport | 1980 | (1981) | 1 |
| | | 1 | Metro-2 | Transport | (1979) | | |

| Country | Supplier | No. | Designation | Description | Year of order | Year of delivery | No. delivered |
|---|---|---|---|---|---|---|---|
| **Bolivia** | Austria | 31 | Curassier | | (1978) | (1979) | (15) |
| | | | | | | (1980) | (18) |
| | Brazil | 12 | T-25 Universal | Trainer | (1979) | 1981 | 6 |
| | Brazil | 6 | Gaviao Lama | Hel | 1981 | 1980 | 4 |
| | Netherlands | 6 | F-27 MK-400M | Transport | 1979 | (1980) | |
| | Switzerland | 16 | PC-7 | Trainer | 1977 | 1980 | (16) |
| | USA | 1 | L-100-30 | Transport | 1979 | 1980 | 1 |
| **Brazil** | France | 3 | Mirage-3E | Fighter/Bomber | 1977 | 1980 | 3 |
| | France | 6 | SA-330 Puma | Hel | 1980 | 1980 | 6 |
| | France | | AS-11 | ASM | 1972 | 1974 | (144) |
| | | | | | | 1975 | (144) |
| | | | | | | 1976 | (144) |
| | | | | | | 1977 | (144) |
| | | | | | | 1978 | (144) |
| | | | | | | 1979 | (144) |
| | | | | | | 1980 | (144) |
| | Italy | 12 | | Corvette | 1980 | | .. |
| | S. Korea | 38 | 155mm | SPH | 1981 | 1981 | 4 |
| | S. Korea | 9 | Sauro Class | Submarine | 1980 | 1980 | |
| | United Kingdom | 4 | Wasp | Hel | (1979) | 1980 | 4 |
| **Chile** | Brazil | 6 | EMB-326 Xavante | Trainer/COIN | (1978) | (1980) | |
| | Brazil | 20 | T-25 Universal | Trainer | (1979) | 1980 | |
| | Brazil | 10 | Anchova Class | PB | 1977 | (1980) | (10) |
| | France | 16 | Alpha Jet | Trainer | (1980) | (1980) | (16) |
| | France | 50 | Mirage-50 | Fighter/MRCA | 1979 | (1981) | .. |
| | France | (128) | AMX-30 | MT | 1980 | (1980) | (28) |
| | France | | R-530 | AAM | 1979 | (1980) | .. |

| Recipient | Supplier | No. | Weapon | Description | Year of order | Year(s) of delivery | No. delivered |
|---|---|---|---|---|---|---|---|
| | Germany FR | 2 | Type 209 | Submarine | 1980 | 1982/3* | |
| | Israel | 6 | Reshef Class | FPB | 1979 | (1979) (1980) (1981) | (2) (2) (2) |
| | South Africa | 6 | Cactus | Landmob SAM | (1980) | 1980 | 6 |
| | Spain | ... | C-101 | Trainer/Strike | 1980 | 1980 | |
| | Switzerland | 10 | PC-7 | Trainer | 1979 | 1980 | 10 |
| **Colombia** | Germany FR | 4 | FS-1500 | Frigate | 1980 | 1982* | |
| | | 4 | FV-1500 | Corvette | 1981 | 1980 | |
| | Israel | 3 | IAI-202 Arava | Transport | (1979) | | 3 |
| | USA | (2) | C-130H Hercules | Transport | (1980) | | |
| | | ... | Seasparrow | ShAM/ShShM | (1980) | 1982* | |
| | | 2 | C130H | Transport | 1981 | | |
| **Dominican Republic** | Argentina | ... | 1A-58A Pucara | Trainer/COIN | (1980) | ... | |
| | USA | 3 | A-37B | Striker/COIN (A) | 1981 | ... | |
| | | 2 | UH-1 | SAR Hel (A) | 1981 | ... | |
| | | 1 | PTF-23 | PB (A) | 1981 | ... | |
| **Ecuador** | Canada | 1 | DHC-5D Buffalo | Transport | (1980) | | |
| | France | 16 | Mirage F-1C | Fighter/interceptor | 1977 | 1979 1980 | (4) (12) |
| | | ... | VAB | APC | (1977) | | |
| | | 35 | F-4E Phantom | Fighter | 1979 | 1980 | 35 |

| Country | Supplier | Qty | Designation | Type | Ordered | Delivered | No. |
|---|---|---|---|---|---|---|---|
| | | 550 | M-113-A2 | APC | (1980) | 1980 | (200) |
| | | 550 | M-113-A2 | APC | 1979 | | |
| | | 50 | M-125-A2 | APC | (1979) | | |
| | | 50 | M-548 | Cargo | (1979) | | |
| | | 50 | M-577-A2 | CPC | (1979) | | |
| | | 43 | M-578 | ARV | (1980) | | |
| | | 244 | M-60-A3 | MBT | (1980) | | |
| | | 67 | M-60-A3 | MBT | 1980 | | |
| | | 43 | M-88-A1 | ARV | (1980) | | |
| | | 52 | M-901-TOW | ICV | 1980 | | |
| | | 600 | AGM-65A | ASM | 1980 | 1980 | (75) |
| | | 70 | AIM-7E Sparrow | AAM | 1979 | 1980 | 70 |
| | | 100 | AIM-9E | AAM | 1979 | 1980 | (100) |
| | | 250 | AIM-9P | AAM | 1979 | 1980 | (100) |
| | | . . . | BGM-71ATOW | ATM | 1980 | | |
| | | 36 | MIM-23B Hawk | Landmob SAM | 1979 | 1981 | 12 |
| | | 12 | Spectre Class | FPB | (1979) | | |
| El Salvador | USA | 6 | Model 209 AH-1G | Hel | (1980) | 1981 | (6) |
| | | 3 | | PB | 1976 | | |
| | | 6 | UH-14 | Hel (A) | 1981 | 1981 | |
| Mexico | France | 10 | SA-315B Lama | Hel | 1979 | | |
| | Spain | 6 | F-30 | FPB | 1980 | | |
| | | 6 | | Corvette | 1981 | 1982* | |
| | Switzerland | 38 | PC-7 | Trainer | 1978 | 1979 | (6) |
| | | 26 | PC-7 | | 1980 | 1980 | (6) |
| | United Kingdom | 36 | BN-2A Islander | Transport | 1980 | 1980 | (21) |
| | | | | | (1981) | | (15) |

203

| Recipient | Supplier | No. | Designation | Description | Year of order | Year of delivery | No. delivered |
|---|---|---|---|---|---|---|---|
| | USA | 3 | HU-16A Albatros | ASW/Mar patrol | 1979 | 1980 | 3 |
| | | 1 | Gearing Class | Destroyer | (1980) | | 1 |
| | | 10 | F-5E | Fighter | 1981 | 1982* | |
| **Paraguay** | Argentina | 1 | C-47 | Transport | 1980 | 1980 | 1 |
| | Brazil | 10 | EMB-110 | Transport | 1977 | | |
| | | 9 | EMB-326 Xav | Trainer/COIN | 1979 | | |
| | | (12) | Uirapuru-122A | Trainer/COIN | 1979 | | |
| | Chile | 1 | UH-12E | Hel | (1980) | 1980 | 1 |
| | | 1 | Hiller | Hel (A) | 1980 | 1980 | 1 |
| **Peru** | Australia | 2 | N-22L Nomad | Coast Patrol | (1978) | | |
| | France | (48) | MM-38 Exocet | ShShM | 1977 | 1979 | (16) |
| | | | | | | 1980 | (32) |
| | | 6 | PR-72P Type | FPB | 1976 | 1979 | 2 |
| | Germany FR | 4 | Type 209 | Submarine | 1976 | 1980 | 1 |
| | | 50 | M-48 AS | MT | 1980 | 1982/83* | |
| | | 100 | Shutzenpanzer 12-3 | MICV | 1980 | 1982/83* | |
| | | 150 | M-113 | APC | 1980 | 1982/83* | |
| | Italy | (14) | MB-339A | Trainer/Strike | 1980 | | |
| | | 96 | Aspide/Albatros | ShAM/ShShM | 1975 | 1978 | 48 |
| | | 96 | OTOMAT-1 | ShShM | 1974 | 1978 | 48 |
| | | 14 | MB-339A | Trainer/Strike | 1981 | ... | |
| | | 15 | Type 66-16 | AC | 1981 | ... | |
| | | 10 | Type 66-14 | APC | 1981 | ... | |
| | Netherlands | 1 | Friesland Class | Destroyer | (1978) | 1980 | 1 |
| | | 2 | Friesland Class | Destroyer | 1980 | 1980 | 2 |

| Country | Supplier | No. | Weapon designation | Weapon description | Year of order | Year of delivery | No. delivered |
|---|---|---|---|---|---|---|---|
| | USSR | 18 | T-37B | Trainer | 1980 | | |
| | | 16 | Su-22 Fitter C | Fighter/Bomber | 1980 | 1980 | 2 |
| | | 200 | T-55 | MBT | (1978) | | |
| | | 100 | SA-7 Grail | Port SAM | (1978) | | |
| Trinidad-Tobago | Sweden | 2 | Spica Class | FPB | 1978 | (1980) | 2 |
| | United Kingdom | 1 | Sword Class | FPB | (1978) | | |
| Uruguay | Argentina | 3 | C-45 Expeditor | Transport | 1980 | 1980 | 3 |
| | | 5 | 1A-58APucara | Trainer/COIN | 1980 | 1981 | 5 |
| | | 9 | T-28 | Trainer | 1980 | 1980 | 9 |
| | Austria | ... | Cuirassier | SPG ATW | 1980 | | |
| | Belgium | ... | FN-4RM/62F | AC | 1980 | | |
| | | 15 | Scorpion | LT | 1981 | 1982* | |
| | Brazil | 1 | EMB-110B | Transport | (1979) | 1980 | 1 |
| | France | 3 | Vigilante | PB | 1979 | | |
| | USA | 3 | S-2G | ASW/AF | 1981 | 1981 | 3 |
| Venezuela | Argentina | (24) | 1A-58A Pucara | Trainer/COIN | (1980) | | |
| | Germany FR | 2 | Type 209 | Submarine | 1977 | | |
| | Israel | 3 | IAI-201 Arava | Transport | 1979 | 1980 | 3 |
| | Italy | 8 | A-109 Hirundo | Hel | (1979) | 1979 | 1 |
| | | 10 | AB-212ASW | Hel | (1977) | 1980 | 2 |
| | | 48 | Aspide/Albatros | ShAM/ShShM | 1977 | 1979 | 8 |
| | | | | | | 1980 | 16 |

| USA | 72 | OTOMAT-1 | ShShM | 1975 | 1980 | 12 |
|-----|----|----------|-------|------|------|----|
|     | 2  | Bell-412 | Hel   | 1981 | 1981 | 2  |
|     | 2  | C-130H-30| TA    | 1981 | . .  |    |

**Notes**

1. Includes some aid as indicated.

**Conventions**

| . . | Information not available |
|-----|---------------------------|
| ( ) | Uncertain |
| * | Delivery due date |

**Abbreviations**

| (A) | Aid | COIN | Counter-insurgency |
|-----|-----|------|--------------------|
| AAM | Air-to-air missile | CPC | Command Post Carrier |
| AC | Armoured car | FPB | Fast Patrol Boat |
| AF | Air Force | Hel | Helicopter |
| APC | Armoured Personnel Carrier | ICV | Infantry Combat Vehicle |
| ARV | Armoured Recovery Vehicle | Landmob | Landmobile Missile |
| ASM | Air to Surface Missile | MBT | Main Battle Tank |
| ASW | Anti-Submarine Warfare | MICV | Mechanized Infantry Combat Vehicle |
| ATM | Anti-Tank Missile | MRCA | Multi-role Combat Aircraft |
| ATW | Anti-Tank Weapon | MT | Medium Tank |
| Cargo | Cargo Vehicle | PB | Patrol Boat |
| | | SAM | Surface-to-air Missile |
| | | SAR | Search and Rescue |
| | | ShAM | Ship-to-air Missile |
| | | ShShM | Ship-to-Ship Missile |
| | | SPG | Self-Propelled Gun |
| | | SPH | Self-Propelled Howitzer |
| | | TA | Transport Aircraft |
| | | t | tonne |

*Sources:* Stockholm International Peace Research Institute, *World Armaments and Disarmament, SIPRI Yearbook 1981*, Taylor & Francis, London, 1981, Appendix 7A, pp.202-257; International Institute for Strategic Studies, *The Military Balance 1981-1982*, IISS, London, 1981, Table 5, p.118.

## TABLE 2
### Register of Licensed Production of Major Weapons in Latin America 1980

| Recipient | Licenser | No. ordered | Weapon designation | Weapon description | Year of license | Year of production | No. produced |
|---|---|---|---|---|---|---|---|
| **Argentina** | Germany FR | 220 | TAM | MT | (1976) | 1979 | (50) |
| | | | | | | 1980 | (120) |
| | | 300 | VC1 | MT | 1976 | (1979) | (25) |
| | | | | | | 1980 | (100) |
| | | 6 | Meko-140 | Corvette | 1979 | | |
| | | 2 | Type 1400 | Submarine | 1977 | | |
| | | 3 | Type 1700 | Submarine | 1977 | | |
| | United Kingdom | 1 | Type 42 | Frigate | 1971 | | |
| | USA | ... | Arrow-3 | Trainer | 1977 | 1978 | (10) |
| | | | | | | 1979 | (10) |
| | | | | | | 1980 | (10) |
| | | 120 | Model 500M | Hel | 1972 | 1977 | (12) |
| | | | | | | 1978 | (12) |
| | | | | | | 1979 | (12) |
| | | | | | | 1980 | (12) |
| **Brazil** | France | 200 | AS-350 Esquilo | Hel | 1978 | 1979 | 6 |
| | | | | | | 1980 | (20) |
| | | 30 | SA-315B Lama | Hel | 1978 | 1979 | (3) |
| | | | | | | 1980 | (3) |

| Country | Number | Designation | Description | Order year | Delivery year | Quantity |
|---|---|---|---|---|---|---|
| Germany FR | (34) | SA-330L | Hel | 1980 | | |
| | ... | Cobra 2000 | ATM | 1973 | (1975) | (10) |
| | | | | | (1976) | (100) |
| | | | | | (1977) | (200) |
| | | | | | (1978) | (200) |
| | | | | | (1979) | (200) |
| | | | | | 1980 | (200) |
| Italy | (150) | AMX | Fighter/ground | 1980 | | |
| | 184 | EMB-326 Xavante | Trainer/COIN | 1970 | 1971 | 4 |
| | | | | | 1972 | 24 |
| | | | | | 1973 | 24 |
| | | | | | 1974 | 24 |
| | | | | | 1975 | 24 |
| | | | | | 1976 | 12 |
| | | | | | 1977 | 24 |
| | | | | | 1978 | 12 |
| | | | | | 1979 | (12) |
| | | | | | 1980 | (12) |
| USA | ... | EMB-810C | Lightplane | 1974 | 1975 | 27 |
| | | | | | 1976 | 23 |

| Country | Supplier | No. | Type | | Year | Delivery years | |
|---|---|---|---|---|---|---|---|
| | | | | | | 1 5 (1979) 1980 | (48) (24) |
| Chile | France | 2 | Batral Type | LST | 1979 | | |
| Colombia | USA | | Lightplane | | 1969 | 1973 | 65 |
| | | | | | | 1974 | 93 |
| | | | | | | 1975 | (90) |
| | | | | | | 1976 | (90) |
| | | | | | | 1977 | (90) |
| | | | | | | 1978 | (90) |
| | | | | | | 1979 | (90) |
| | | | | | | 1980 | (92) |
| Peru | Italy | 2 | Lupo Class | Frigate | 1974 | | |

*Source:* Stockholm International Peace Research Institute, *World Armament and Disarmament: SIPRI Yearbook 1981*, Taylor & Francis, London UK, 1981, Appendix 7BII, pp.252-6.

# TABLE 3

### British Military Equipment Supplied to/Ordered by Argentina[1]

| No. ordered | Weapon or Equipment | Supplied[2] | Comment |
|---|---|---|---|
| 1 | 'Colossus' Aircraft Carrier | . . . | Second hand |
| 6 | Coastal minesweeper | . . . | Second hand |
| 8 | Frigate, Type 21 | (1965) | Under licence from Vosper Thorneycroft |
| 1[3] | Frigate, Type 42 | . . . | Under a licence negotiated in 1970 |
| . . . | Seacat ShAM | . . . | Made by Short Bros. Belfast |
| 12 | Sea Dart ShAM | . . . | Made by BAe Dynamics |
| 20 | Tigercat SAM | . . . | Short Bros.: 10 to Marines, 10 to Army |
| 72 | Seawolf Anti-missile Missiles | (1975)[4] | Made by BAe Dynamics |
| 8 | Lynx Hel | 1978[5] | Made by Westland Aircraft Ltd. |
| 100 | Sub Machine guns | (1975) | 5 with silencers. Sterling Armament Co. |
| . . . | Isis sights for (US) Skyhawk | (1976) | Ferranti |
| . . . | Seaspray radar for Lynx Hel | (1977) | Ferranti |
| . . . | Clearscan radar for FPB | (1979) | Decca |
| . . . | HF & VHF radio for PB | (1979) | Redifon |
| . . . | Gear pumps for FRG frigates | (1980) | Vickers |
| . . . | Radio systems for naval stations | (1981) | Rediffusion |
| . . . | Engines for Italian trainer | (1981) | Rolls Royce |
| . . . | 'Morgrip' bolts for naval propellors | (1981) | Doncasters Moorside |
| . . . | ESM[6] | (1981) | Racal/Decca |
| 250 | Mach airspeed COIN indicators | (1981) | Smiths Industries |
| . . . | Pneumatic controls for FPB & corvettes | (1981) | Vosper Thorneycroft |

*Source:* Campaign Against the Arms Trade, *Factsheet 32: British Military Involvement in Argentine,* CAAT, London, 1982, based on reported deals.

**Notes**
1. Indicates production under licence, approx. 1960-81.

2. Brackets indicate date of order.
3. Some reports state two such.
4. Sold.
5. Contact 1977, two delivered 1978.
6. Electronic support measures for eavesdropping on radio and radar.

## TABLE 4

### Largest Exporters of the Four Categories of Major Weapons, 1977-80

(Figures are percentages of total major-weapon exports of each country, based on SIPRI trend indicator values)

| Country | Aircraft | Weapon category Armoured Vehicles | Missiles | Ships |
|---|---|---|---|---|
| 1. USA | 52 | 8 | 39 | 1 |
| 2. USSR | 60 | 13 | 24 | 3 |
| 3. France | 57 | 14 | 20 | 9 |
| 4. Italy | 36 | 17 | 34 | 13 |
| 5. United Kingdom | 33 | 19 | 14 | 34 |
| 6. FR Germany | 11 | 45 | 6 | 38 |
| 7. Third World countries | 34 | 30 | 10 | 26 |
| 8. Norway | — | — | 91 | 9 |
| 9. Netherlands | 43 | — | — | 57 |
| 10. Brazil[a] | 10 | 62 | — | 28 |
| 11. Israel[a] | 37 | — | 18 | 45 |

a. Included also in the Third World group of exporters.

Source: Stockholm International Peace Research Institute, *World Armaments and Disarmament: SIPRI Yearbook 1971*, Taylor & Francis, London 1981, Table 7.4, p.188.

Note: The British Defence White Paper estimate of arms trade categories are very different from those of SIPRI. Part of the reason for this is that SIPRI data relates mainly to values constructed on the basis of observed transactions. The Defence White Paper also includes military hardware not covered by SIPRI (i.e. non-major weapons systems), plus goods otherwise disguised in official trade statistics. As a rule, SIPRI figures are most applicable to evaluating trends. In relation to unit costs it is obviously necessary to use government figures.

211

## TABLE 5

### Rank Order of the 20 Largest Major-Weapon Exporting Countries of the World, 1977-80[a]

Figures are SIPRI trend indicator values, as expressed in US million dollars at constant (1975) prices

| Exporting country | Total value | Percentage of total exports | Percentage of total value to Third World | Largest importer per exporter |
|---|---|---|---|---|
| 1. USA | 24,893 | 43.3 | 60.8 | Iran |
| 2. USSR | 15,755 | 27.4 | 79.5 | Syria |
| 3. France | 6,213 | 10.8 | 76.5 | Morocco |
| 4. Italy | 2,273 | 4.0 | 76.6 | South Africa |
| 5. United Kingdom | 2,141 | 3.7 | 81.7 | India |
| 6. FR Germany | 1,712 | 3.0 | 37.6 | Italy |
| 7. Third World | 1,271 | 2.2 | 98.0 | — |
| 8. Norway | 724 | 1.3 | — | Sweden |
| 9. Netherlands | 536 | 0.9 | 87.0 | Peru |
| 10. Brazil[b] | 421 | 0.7 | 97.2 | Chile |
| 11. Israel[b] | 367 | 0.6 | 100.0 | South Africa |
| 12. Australia | 361 | 0.6 | 63.7 | Philippines |
| 13. China | 333 | 0.6 | 95.0 | Pakistan |
| 14. Sweden | 277 | 0.5 | 50.9 | United Kingdom |
| 15. Switzerland | 240 | 0.4 | 27.1 | Canada |
| 16. Canada | 177 | 0.3 | 98.3 | Ivory Coast |
| 17. South Africa[b] | 116 | 0.2 | 100.0 | Zimbabwe |
| 18. Finland | 112 | 0.2 | — | USSR |
| 19. Czechoslovakia | 107 | 0.2 | 43.9 | Bulgaria |
| 20. Libya[b, c] | 98 | 0.2 | 96.0 | Syria |
| Others | 334 | 0.6 | 80.8 | — |
| World total | 57,459 | 100.0 | 68.7 | |

a. The values include licences sold for the production of major weapons.
b. Included also in the Third World group of exporters.
c. Figures for Libya are not representative of a trend, due to the resale of aircraft and armoured vehicles in 1979.

# TABLE 6

## EEC Arms Exports (Declared Trade)[1] 1980
### In '000 European Units of Account (EUA)[2]

| Supplier | Value | % value of total exports |
|---|---|---|
| Italy | 113,557 | 0.20 |
| Netherlands | 76,602 | 0.14 |
| Denmark | 12,692 | 0.10 |
| FR Germany | 98,725 | 0.07 |
| France | 38,757 | 0.04 |
| Belgium/Luxembourg | 20,476 | 0.04 |
| United Kingdom | 30,221 | 0.03 |
| Ireland | 18 | 0.00 |
| The Nine | 391,039 | 0.08 (av.) |

Source: *European Report 818;* European Commission reply to question from Andre Damseaux MEP, 3 November 1981.

1. Not transactions considered confidential. This chart represents only those arms exports contained within the official national export statistics. As such its purpose is to indicate the level of secrecy that surrounds the trade compared with SIPRI values (Table 5).
2. Conversion Scale 1 EUA = £0.56p (18 January 1982).

# TABLE 7

## Military Manpower Comparisons: Latin America[1] 1975-1981

| Country | Numbers in Armed Forces '000 | | | Growth[2] % |
|---|---|---|---|---|
| | 1975 | 1980 | 1981 | |
| Argentina | 133.5 | 139.5 | 185.5 | 39.0 |
| Brazil | 245.5 | 272.6 | 272.6 | 11.0 |
| Colombia | 64.3 | 65.8 | 70.0 | 8.9 |
| Cuba | 117.0 | 206.0 | 227.0 | 94.0 |
| Mexico | 332.5 | 357.0 | 369.5 | 11.1 |
| Peru | 56.0 | 95.5 | 130.0 | 132.1 |
| Venezuela | 44.0 | 40.5 | 40.8 | 7.3 |

1. Selected countries.
2. 1975 to 1981 total.

Source: International Institute for Strategic Studies, *The Military Balance 1981-1982*, IISS, London, 1981, Table 4, pp.112-113.

## TABLE 8

### Latin American Military Expenditure to 1980

US$ million, 1978 prices and exchange rates; constant figures. Totals may not add up due to the effect of rounding

**Central America and the Caribbean**

| | 1971 | 1972 | 1973 | 1974 | 1975 | 1976 | 1977 | 1978 | 1979 | 1980 |
|---|---|---|---|---|---|---|---|---|---|---|
| Costa Rica | 9.8 | 9.9 | 10.9 | 11.2 | 13.5 | 17.7 | 19.5 | 22.1 | 19.2* | 19.2 |
| Cuba[a, c] | 367 | 338 | 342 | 357 | 413 | .. | 886 | 992 | 1,065 | 1,026* |
| Dominican Republic | 64.6 | 64.6 | 59.7 | 68.6 | 72.1 | 78.8 | 78.5 | 87.1 | 145 | .. |
| El Salvador[c] | 24.4 | 25.1 | 38.8 | 42.1 | 37.8 | 48.0 | 56.8 | 59.0 | (58.7) | .. |
| Guatemala | 37.5* | 45.4 | 38.1 | 41.7 | 57.7 | 60.3 | 83.9 | 73.2 | 64.4* | .. |
| Haiti | 3.7 | 3.8 | 3.2 | 2.9 | 3.0 | 3.2 | 3.5 | .. | .. | .. |
| Honduras | 18.3 | 23.5 | 23.2 | 21.7 | 25.8 | 27.2 | 26.8 | 31.4 | .. | .. |
| Jamaica | 14.0 | 14.9 | 23.1 | 21.7 | 24.0 | 29.1 | 27.7 | .. | .. | .. |
| Mexico | 361 | 401 | 447 | 477 | 520 | 543 | 531 | 536 | 588 | 563 |
| Nicaragua | 22.3 | 28.1 | 22.7 | 27.2 | 32.5 | 43.5 | 43.2 | .. | .. | .. |
| Panama | 21.8 | 13.9 | 14.9 | 15.5 | 17.7 | 16.7 | .. | .. | .. | .. |
| Trinidad and Tobago | 7.9 | 7.4 | 5.9 | 6.3 | 7.4 | 8.2 | 8.9 | .. | .. | .. |
| **Total** | 953 | 975 | 1,030 | 1,093 | 1,223 | (1,526) | 1,786 | (1,912) | (1,969) | 2,186* |

| Country | | | | | | | | | | |
|---|---|---|---|---|---|---|---|---|---|---|
| Bolivia | | | | | | | | | | |
| Brazil[b] | 1,367 | 1,462 | 1,737 | 1,764 | 1,758 | 2,100 | 1,986 | 2,041 | 1,744 | .. |
| Chile[b] | 199 | 199 | 318 | 554 | 432 | 430 | 500 | 630 | 839* | 984 |
| Colombia | 380 | 200 | 182 | 174 | 193 | 199 | 182 | 168 | (184) | 229 |
| Ecuador | 71.9 | 83.8 | 100 | 115 | 141 | 129 | 215 | 164 | 168 | .. |
| Guyana[c] | 13.6 | 14.4 | 15.2 | 21.9 | 42.0 | 58.5 | 33.0 | (25.5) | .. | .. |
| Paraguay | 30.0 | 29.4 | 28.6 | 26.6 | 33.3 | 34.5 | 37.0 | 38.8 | 35.9 | .. |
| Peru[b] | 300 | 280 | 338 | 359 | 474 | 537 | 780 | 599 | 464 | 469 |
| Uruguay[b] | 121 | 109 | 109 | 131 | 123 | 95 | 100 | 132 | .. | .. |
| Venezuela | 411 | 470 | 452 | 628 | 707 | 482 | 631 | 590 | 568 | 577 |
| **Total** | 3,942 | 3,906 | 4,121 | 4,765 | (5,175) | 5,867 | 5,980 | 5,953 | (5,953) | 6,050* |

..   not available.

( )   SIPRI estimate.

\*   Imputed value, high degree of uncertainity.

a. Current prices and 1978 exchange rates.

b. Inflation uncertainty; prices trebled between 1975 and 1979. Constant values are less reliable in these circumstances. See note in Appendix 6B of *SIPRI Yearbook 1981*, p.174.

c. Includes internal security.

*Source:* Stockholm International Peace Research Institute, *World Armament and Disarmament: SIPRI Yearbook 1981*, Taylor & Francis, London UK, 1981, Appendix 6A part II, pp.160-1.

## TABLE 9

### Value of Latin American Major Weapon Imports 1970-1980
### (including licensed production)
US$ million, 1975 constant prices[1]

| Region | 1970 | 1971 | 1972 | 1973 | 1974 | 1975 | 1976 | 1977 | 1978 | 1979 | 1980 |
|---|---|---|---|---|---|---|---|---|---|---|---|
| South America | 148 | 222 | 310 | 352 | 446 | 630 | 710 | 826 | 808 | 949 | 872[2] |
| Central America and Caribbean | 6 | 47 | 35 | 56 | 87 | 137 | 58 | 60 | 250 | 75 | 46 |
| Total | 154 | 269 | 345 | 408 | 533 | 767 | 768 | 886 | 1,058 | 1,024 | 918[2] |

1. SIPRI trend indicator value.
2. Yearly figures: calculated on the basis of five years moving averages the import statistics continue to show an underlying growth.

*Source:* Stockholm International Peace Research Institute, *World Armaments and Disarmament: SIPRI Yearbook 1981*, Taylor & Francis, London UK, 1981, Table 7.1, pp.184-5.

# STATISTICAL APPENDIX

## Appendix 1 — TRADE

## Appendix 2 — INVESTMENT

217

## Appendix 3 — DEBT and SOURCES OF CREDIT

Appendix 1 — Trade

## TABLE 1

Latin America: Contribution of Major Commodity Exports to Total Value of Merchandise Exports, 1970-72 and 1977-79[a] in Per Cent

| | First Product | 1970-72 | 1977-79 | Second Product | 1970-72 | 1977-79 | Third Product | 1970-72 | 1977-79 | Number of Products | 1970-72 | 1977-79 |
|---|---|---|---|---|---|---|---|---|---|---|---|---|
| Argentina | Beef | 28.1 | 13.1 | Corn | 14.5 | 8.6 | — | — | — | Two | 42.6 | 21.7 |
| Bolivia | Tin | 57.2 | 53.8 | Natural gas | 4.9 | 12.3 | Crude petroleum | 12.0 | 7.5 | Three | 74.1 | 73.6 |
| Brazil | Coffee | 28.0 | 15.4 | Soybeans & products | 4.9 | 13.3 | — | — | — | Two | 32.9 | 28.7 |
| Chile | Copper | 70.0 | 50.1 | — | — | — | — | — | — | One | 70.0 | 50.1 |
| Colombia | Coffee | 56.6 | 62.5 | — | — | — | — | — | — | One | 56.6 | 62.5 |
| Costa Rica | Coffee | 28.5 | 36.2 | Bananas | 29.0 | 17.8 | — | — | — | Two | 57.5 | 54.0 |
| Dominican Republic | Sugar | 49.8 | 26.3 | Coffee | 9.8 | 18.9 | Cocoa | 6.1 | 11.3 | Three | 65.7 | 56.5 |
| Ecuador | Crude petroleum | 7.8 | 40.9 | Coffee | 17.0 | 14.9 | Bananas | 47.7 | 11.6 | Three | 72.5 | 67.4 |
| El Salvador | Coffee | 46.1 | 58.9b | Cotton | 11.6 | 9.1b | — | — | — | Two | 57.7 | 68.0b |
| Guatemala | Coffee | 33.2 | 45.4b | Cotton | 10.2 | 12.9b | — | — | — | Two | 43.4 | 58.3b |
| Haiti | Coffee | 38.3 | 38.4 | Bauxite | 14.4 | 11.4 | — | — | — | Two | 52.7 | 49.8 |
| Honduras | Coffee | 12.9 | 31.3 | Bananas | 44.7 | 25.6 | — | — | — | Two | 57.6 | 56.9 |
| Mexico | Crude petroleum | 2.0 | 33.8 | — | — | — | — | — | — | One | 2.0 | 33.8 |
| Nicaragua | Coffee | 15.3 | 31.1b | Cotton | 22.5 | 23.3b | — | — | — | Two | 37.8 | 54.4b |
| Panama | Bananas | 54.2 | 26.0 | Petroleum products | 19.5 | 25.6 | Shrimp | 10.5 | 13.2 | Three | 84.2 | 64.8 |
| Paraguay | Cotton | 4.0 | 33.1 | Soybeans | 2.2 | 21.1 | — | — | — | Two | 6.2 | 54.2 |
| Peru | Copper | 21.8 | 20.0 | Fishmeal | 27.9 | 8.0 | — | — | — | Two | 49.7 | 28.0 |
| Uruguay | Wool | 29.5 | 17.0 | Beef | 37.7 | 14.9 | — | — | — | Two | 67.2 | 31.9 |
| Venezuela | Crude petroleum | 59.7 | 60.3 | Petroleum products | 29.2 | 34.8 | — | — | — | Two | 88.9 | 95.1 |

a. For each country, products listed are those representing 10 per cent or more of total exports in 1970-72 or 1977-79. Products are listed according to their relative importance in 1977-79.

b. Based on 1977-78 data.

Source: Information from the Inter-American Development Bank, Annual Report 1981.

219

## TABLE 2

### EEC (9 countries) trade with Latin America[1]
### Value: ECU million[2]

| | 1975 | % | 1976 | % | 1977 | % | 1978 | % | 1979 | % |
|---|---|---|---|---|---|---|---|---|---|---|
| *Imports* | | | | | | | | | | |
| Sitc 0[3] | 4783.2 | 56.0 | 5717.5 | 55.5 | 7202.4 | 60.8 | 6590.7 | 57.5 | 7062.8 | 52.1 |
| Sitc 1 | 116.6 | 1.4 | 152.4 | 1.5 | 171.4 | 1.4 | 176.7 | 1.5 | 203.9 | 1.5 |
| Sitc 2 | 1679.6 | 19.7 | 1966.4 | 19.1 | 1993.2 | 16.8 | 1966.3 | 17.2 | 2433.5 | 18.0 |
| Sitc 3 | 650.8 | 7.6 | 672.8 | 6.5 | 410.2 | 3.5 | 492.6 | 4.3 | 871.9 | 6.4 |
| Sitc 4 | 102.7 | 1.2 | 121.8 | 1.2 | 182.4 | 1.5 | 197.0 | 1.7 | 228.0 | 1.7 |
| Sitc 5 | 123.3 | 1.4 | 144.5 | 1.4 | 161.6 | 1.4 | 173.7 | 1.5 | 200.7 | 1.5 |
| Sitc 6 | 822.8 | 9.6 | 1157.8 | 11.2 | 1233.3 | 10.4 | 1233.7 | 10.8 | 1785.4 | 13.2 |
| Sitc 7 | 118.8 | 1.4 | 155.4 | 1.5 | 269.7 | 2.3 | 384.4 | 3.4 | 456.1 | 3.4 |
| Sitc 8 | 100.8 | 1.2 | 152.5 | 1.5 | 181.1 | 1.5 | 191.9 | 1.7 | 248.0 | 1.8 |
| Sitc 9 | 35.7 | .4 | 56.0 | .5 | 34.4 | .3 | 50.1 | .4 | 54.1 | .4 |
| Sitc 0 to 9 | 8534.3 | 100.0 | 10297.0 | 100.0 | 11839.7 | 100.0 | 11457.1 | 100.0 | 13544.4 | 100.0 |
| *Exports* | | | | | | | | | | |
| Sitc 0 | 2210.2 | 22.8 | 2225.2 | 22.9 | 2346.0 | 21.6 | 2334.5 | 21.0 | 2373.3 | 19.1 |
| Sitc 1 | 105.2 | 1.1 | 102.8 | 1.1 | 130.9 | 1.2 | 172.3 | 1.5 | 185.5 | 1.5 |
| Sitc 2 | 69.5 | .7 | 72.1 | .7 | 93.0 | .9 | 88.9 | .8 | 112.7 | .9 |
| Sitc 3 | 40.8 | .4 | 37.3 | .4 | 72.3 | .7 | 88.1 | .8 | 110.9 | .9 |
| Sitc 4 | 23.9 | .2 | 12.7 | .1 | 9.1 | .1 | 11.0 | .1 | 16.5 | .1 |
| Sitc 5 | 1280.4 | 13.2 | 1414.5 | 14.6 | 1533.9 | 14.1 | 1565.4 | 14.1 | 1808.1 | 14.5 |
| Sitc 6 | 1478.8 | 15.3 | 1053.0 | 10.8 | 1235.2 | 11.4 | 1536.0 | 13.8 | 1494.5 | 12.0 |
| Sitc 7 | 4006.6 | 41.3 | 4301.1 | 44.3 | 4766.6 | 43.9 | 4582.6 | 41.2 | 5454.0 | 43.9 |
| Sitc 8 | 309.3 | 3.2 | 347.3 | 3.6 | 410.7 | 3.8 | 512.5 | 4.6 | 619.0 | 5.0 |
| Sitc 9 | 170.8 | 1.8 | 148.4 | 1.5 | 261.5 | 2.4 | 234.0 | 2.1 | 261.4 | 2.1 |
| Sitc 0 to 9 | 9695.7 | 100.0 | 9714.4 | 100.0 | 10859.3 | 100.0 | 11125.1 | 100.0 | 12435.9 | 100.0 |

1. The EEC includes under the heading Latin America, the following countries: Argentina, Bolivia, Brazil, Chile, Colombia, Costa Rica, Cuba, Dominican Republic, Ecuador, El Salvador, Guatemala, Haiti, Honduras, Mexico, Nicaragua, Panama, Paraguay, Peru, Uruguay, Venezuela.
2. European Currency Units (ECU). Current value IECU = US$0.99.
3. Standard International Trade Classification; categories refer to the following products:
   SITC 0: food products and livestock. 1: Drinks and Tobacco. 2: Inedible raw materials, fuels excluded. 3: Mineral combustibles, lubricants and related products. 4: Oils, fats, and animal or vegetable waxes. 5: Chemical and related products. 6: Manufactured articles, classified mainly according to raw material. 7: Machinery and transport equipment. 8: Various manufactured articles. 9: Articles and

## EEC (9 countries) trade with Argentina
### Value: ECU million[1]

| | 1975 | % | 1976 | % | 1977 | % | 1978 | % | 1979 | % |
|---|---|---|---|---|---|---|---|---|---|---|
| *Imports* | | | | | | | | | | |
| Sitc 0[2] | 666.4 | 76.4 | 970.0 | 72.1 | 1165.5 | 64.5 | 1047.9 | 53.2 | 1106.8 | 52.3 |
| Sitc 1 | 10.6 | 1.2 | 16.1 | 1.2 | 18.4 | 1.0 | 23.6 | 1.2 | 26.2 | 1.2 |
| Sitc 2 | 76.3 | 8.7 | 159.8 | 11.9 | 295.8 | 16.4 | 509.2 | 25.9 | 592.0 | 28.0 |
| Sitc 3 | 0.0 | 0.0 | 7.6 | .6 | 7.8 | .4 | 4.1 | .2 | 14.8 | .7 |
| Sitc 4 | 29.9 | 3.4 | 46.7 | 3.5 | 112.5 | 6.2 | 101.1 | 5.1 | 96.8 | 4.6 |
| Sitc 5 | 32.3 | 3.7 | 31.5 | 2.3 | 45.6 | 2.5 | 54.6 | 2.8 | 58.6 | 2.8 |
| Sitc 6 | 30.6 | 3.5 | 80.5 | 6.0 | 117.0 | 6.5 | 148.4 | 7.5 | 162.4 | 7.7 |
| Sitc 7 | 12.2 | 1.4 | 18.6 | 1.4 | 20.7 | 1.1 | 49.1 | 2.5 | 31.5 | 1.5 |
| Sitc 8 | 12.4 | 1.4 | 12.6 | .9 | 21.6 | 1.2 | 26.4 | 1.3 | 21.6 | 1.0 |
| Sitc 9 | 2.0 | .2 | 1.7 | .1 | 2.7 | .1 | 3.5 | .2 | 6.9 | .3 |
| Sitc 0 to 9 | 872.7 | 100.0 | 1344.9 | 100.0 | 1807.7 | 100.0 | 1967.9 | 100.0 | 2117.5 | 100.0 |
| *Exports* | | | | | | | | | | |
| Sitc 0 | 3.3 | .4 | 3.5 | .5 | 10.4 | 1.0 | 12.1 | 1.1 | 28.9 | 1.7 |
| Sitc 1 | 8.4 | 1.0 | 4.3 | .6 | 6.4 | .6 | 9.5 | .9 | 15.6 | .9 |
| Sitc 2 | 11.6 | 1.4 | 10.8 | 1.5 | 15.7 | 1.6 | 13.3 | 1.2 | 22.2 | 1.3 |
| Sitc 3 | 6.2 | .8 | 3.7 | .5 | 5.9 | .6 | 9.9 | .9 | 41.1 | 2.4 |
| Sitc 4 | .3 | 0.0 | .1 | 0.0 | .5 | .1 | .7 | .1 | 1.6 | .1 |
| Sitc 5 | 179.1 | 22.4 | 165.5 | 22.9 | 192.0 | 19.1 | 163.5 | 14.9 | 306.5 | 17.6 |
| Sitc 6 | 191.1 | 23.9 | 89.7 | 12.4 | 113.7 | 11.3 | 129.7 | 11.8 | 234.1 | 13.4 |
| Sitc 7 | 368.3 | 46.1 | 405.1 | 56.0 | 589.8 | 58.8 | 640.4 | 58.5 | 901.2 | 51.8 |
| Sitc 8 | 21.4 | 2.7 | 16.7 | 2.3 | 41.5 | 4.1 | 64.0 | 5.8 | 111.2 | 6.4 |
| Sitc 9 | 9.1 | 1.1 | 23.3 | 3.2 | 27.8 | 2.8 | 51.7 | 4.7 | 79.1 | 4.5 |
| Sitc 0 to 9 | 798.5 | 100.0 | 722.7 | 100.0 | 1003.7 | 100.0 | 1094.9 | 100.0 | 1741.4 | 100.0 |

1 and 2. See notes on Table 2.

*Source:* European Commission, Directorate-General for External Relations, Statistics Office.

# TABLE 4

## EEC (9 countries) trade with Brazil
### Value: ECU million[1]

| | 1975 | % | 1976 | % | 1977 | % | 1978 | % | 1979 | % |
|---|---|---|---|---|---|---|---|---|---|---|
| *Imports* | | | | | | | | | | |
| Sitc 0[2] | 865.9 | 39.1 | 1119.5 | 40.7 | 1826.7 | 53.2 | 1516.8 | 49.9 | 1678.2 | 46.6 |
| Sitc 1 | 65.3 | 3.0 | 83.2 | 3.0 | 102.6 | 3.0 | 104.7 | 3.4 | 136.0 | 3.8 |
| Sitc 2 | 913.8 | 41.3 | 990.1 | 36.0 | 840.9 | 24.5 | 686.9 | 22.6 | 843.5 | 23.4 |
| Sitc 3 | 1.0 | 0.0 | .6 | 0.0 | .6 | 0.0 | 2.0 | .1 | 1.8 | .1 |
| Sitc 4 | 33.4 | 1.5 | 57.4 | 2.1 | 51.9 | 1.5 | 74.2 | 2.4 | 95.7 | 2.7 |
| Sitc 5 | 33.8 | 1.5 | 31.9 | 1.2 | 37.7 | 1.1 | 37.8 | 1.2 | 56.2 | 1.6 |
| Sitc 6 | 189.9 | 8.6 | 297.8 | 10.8 | 336.1 | 9.8 | 310.1 | 10.2 | 420.9 | 11.7 |
| Sitc 7 | 57.7 | 2.6 | 81.8 | 3.0 | 144.3 | 4.2 | 208.9 | 6.9 | 233.4 | 6.5 |
| Sitc 8 | 49.0 | 2.2 | 83.9 | 3.0 | 88.4 | 2.6 | 91.9 | 3.0 | 125.1 | 3.5 |
| Sitc 9 | 3.1 | .1 | 6.3 | .2 | 4.1 | .1 | 7.1 | .2 | 7.9 | .2 |
| Sitc 0 to 9 | 2213.0 | 100.0 | 2752.6 | 100.0 | 3433.3 | 100.0 | 3040.5 | 100.0 | 3598.8 | 100.0 |
| *Exports* | | | | | | | | | | |
| Sitc 0 | 42.8 | 1.9 | 53.1 | 2.4 | 73.0 | 3.3 | 61.0 | 2.9 | 60.5 | 2.5 |
| Sitc 1 | 10.3 | .4 | 9.5 | .4 | 6.3 | .3 | 11.0 | .5 | 10.3 | .4 |
| Sitc 2 | 20.8 | .9 | 22.1 | 1.0 | 26.1 | 1.2 | 26.3 | 1.2 | 27.0 | 1.1 |
| Sitc 3 | 18.8 | .8 | 18.6 | .8 | 28.5 | 1.3 | 56.8 | 2.7 | 29.4 | 1.2 |
| Sitc 4 | .5 | 0.0 | 1.0 | 0.0 | .8 | 0.0 | .8 | 0.0 | 7.1 | .3 |
| Sitc 5 | 377.6 | 16.4 | 504.1 | 22.8 | 463.5 | 21.1 | 496.7 | 23.5 | 538.0 | 22.7 |
| Sitc 6 | 477.0 | 20.7 | 288.5 | 13.1 | 275.5 | 12.6 | 281.6 | 13.3 | 318.0 | 13.4 |
| Sitc 7 | 1245.9 | 54.0 | 1202.7 | 54.4 | 1181.7 | 53.9 | 1016.9 | 48.1 | 1213.0 | 51.1 |
| Sitc 8 | 77.2 | 3.3 | 80.1 | 3.6 | 76.7 | 3.5 | 112.5 | 5.3 | 121.0 | 5.1 |
| Sitc 9 | 38.2 | 1.7 | 31.1 | 1.4 | 60.7 | 2.8 | 52.3 | 2.5 | 48.9 | 2.1 |
| Sitc 0 to 9 | 2309.1 | 100.0 | 2210.9 | 100.0 | 2192.9 | 100.0 | 2115.9 | 100.0 | 2373.3 | 100.0 |

1 and 2. See notes on Table 2.

## TABLE 3

### EEC (9 countries) trade with Chile
#### Value: ECU million[1]

| | 1975 | % | 1976 | % | 1977 | % | 1978 | % | 1979 | % |
|---|---|---|---|---|---|---|---|---|---|---|
| *Imports* | | | | | | | | | | |
| Sitc 0[2] | 44.8 | 8.8 | 85.3 | 12.3 | 90.9 | 13.9 | 129.4 | 18.0 | 134.3 | 12.5 |
| Sitc 1 | .1 | 0.0 | .3 | 0.0 | .2 | 0.0 | .3 | 0.0 | .3 | 0.0 |
| Sitc 2 | 80.7 | 15.8 | 134.2 | 19.3 | 135.6 | 20.7 | 132.4 | 18.4 | 243.6 | 22.8 |
| Sitc 3 | 0.0 | 0.0 | 0.0 | 0.0 | 0.0 | 0.0 | 0.0 | 0.0 | 7.0 | .7 |
| Sitc 4 | 3.2 | .6 | 1.4 | .2 | 7.4 | 1.1 | 13.4 | 1.9 | 14.5 | 1.4 |
| Sitc 5 | 3.7 | .7 | 3.5 | .5 | 4.4 | .7 | 6.7 | .9 | 7.8 | .7 |
| Sitc 6 | 376.2 | 73.6 | 463.6 | 66.6 | 413.4 | 63.2 | 432.2 | 60.0 | 657.6 | 61.5 |
| Sitc 7 | .2 | 0.0 | .3 | 0.0 | .6 | .1 | .5 | .1 | .8 | .1 |
| Sitc 8 | .5 | .1 | 3.6 | .5 | .8 | .1 | .6 | .1 | .8 | .1 |
| Sitc 9 | 1.6 | .3 | 3.9 | .6 | 1.3 | .2 | 4.8 | .7 | 3.3 | .3 |
| Sitc 0 to 9 | 511.0 | 100.0 | 696.1 | 100.0 | 654.4 | 100.0 | 720.4 | 100.0 | 1070.1 | 100.0 |
| *Exports* | | | | | | | | | | |
| Sitc 0 | 7.7 | 3.3 | 2.5 | 1.1 | 21.8 | 7.2 | 38.6 | 11.2 | 48.5 | 9.7 |
| Sitc 1 | .4 | .2 | 1.8 | .8 | 4.1 | 1.4 | 5.6 | 1.6 | 10.0 | 2.0 |
| Sitc 2 | 2.7 | 1.2 | 2.9 | 1.3 | 6.7 | 2.2 | 5.5 | 1.6 | 9.9 | 2.0 |
| Sitc 3 | .3 | .1 | 1.2 | .5 | 2.6 | .9 | 2.3 | .7 | 2.4 | .5 |
| Sitc 4 | 4.5 | 1.9 | 1.4 | .6 | .7 | .2 | 1.0 | .3 | 1.2 | .2 |
| Sitc 5 | 28.1 | 11.9 | 35.7 | 15.6 | 51.7 | 17.1 | 56.3 | 16.3 | 71.5 | 14.4 |
| Sitc 6 | 33.4 | 14.2 | 20.6 | 9.0 | 33.5 | 11.1 | 40.8 | 11.8 | 53.4 | 10.7 |
| Sitc 7 | 145.1 | 61.5 | 143.7 | 62.5 | 155.0 | 51.3 | 164.5 | 47.5 | 261.0 | 52.4 |
| Sitc 8 | 10.7 | 4.6 | 16.1 | 7.0 | 23.8 | 7.9 | 25.5 | 7.4 | 34.2 | 6.9 |
| Sitc 9 | 2.8 | 1.2 | 3.8 | 1.7 | 2.1 | .7 | 6.3 | 1.8 | 5.6 | 1.1 |
| Sitc 0 to 9 | 235.7 | 100.0 | 229.8 | 100.0 | 302.0 | 100.0 | 346.4 | 100.0 | 497.8 | 100.0 |

1 and 2. See notes on Table 2.

*Source:* European Commission, Directorate-General for External Relations, Statistics Office.

## TABLE 6

### EEC (9 countries) trade with Colombia
### Value: ECU million[1]

| | 1975 | % | 1976 | % | 1977 | % | 1978 | % | 1979 | % |
|---|---|---|---|---|---|---|---|---|---|---|
| *Imports* | | | | | | | | | | |
| Sitc 0[2] | 276.6 | 66.5 | 425.2 | 75.1 | 578.6 | 81.2 | 682.2 | 83.9 | 696.0 | 81.2 |
| Sitc 1 | 5.1 | 1.2 | 7.9 | 1.4 | 6.3 | .9 | 7.3 | .9 | 6.1 | .7 |
| Sitc 2 | 62.8 | 15.1 | 66.7 | 11.8 | 67.3 | 9.4 | 58.3 | 7.2 | 43.8 | 5.1 |
| Sitc 3 | 13.9 | 3.3 | 1.0 | .2 | 1.0 | .1 | 16.4 | 2.0 | 51.2 | 6.0 |
| Sitc 4 | 0.0 | 0.0 | 0.0 | 0.0 | 0.0 | 0.0 | 0.0 | 0.0 | 0.0 | 0.0 |
| Sitc 5 | 1.3 | .3 | 2.1 | .4 | .5 | .1 | 1.7 | .2 | 2.5 | .3 |
| Sitc 6 | 47.2 | 11.4 | 52.1 | 9.2 | 46.9 | 6.6 | 35.5 | 4.4 | 48.2 | 5.6 |
| Sitc 7 | 3.1 | .8 | 2.6 | .5 | 3.5 | .5 | 5.6 | .7 | 2.3 | .3 |
| Sitc 8 | 5.1 | 1.2 | 6.4 | 1.1 | 6.9 | 1.0 | 5.2 | .6 | 5.3 | .6 |
| Sitc 9 | .8 | .2 | 1.9 | .3 | 1.5 | .2 | 1.1 | .1 | 2.1 | .2 |
| Sitc 0 to 9 | 416.0 | 100.0 | 566.0 | 100.0 | 712.7 | 100.0 | 813.1 | 100.0 | 857.4 | 100.0 |
| *Exports* | | | | | | | | | | |
| Sitc 0 | 3.4 | 1.1 | 5.6 | 1.8 | 20.1 | 4.6 | 6.8 | 1.6 | 18.5 | 3.5 |
| Sitc 1 | 3.5 | 1.1 | 4.1 | 1.3 | 5.0 | 1.1 | 7.9 | 1.8 | 9.0 | 1.7 |
| Sitc 2 | 2.8 | .9 | 4.3 | 1.4 | 6.9 | 1.6 | 6.4 | 1.5 | 7.0 | 1.3 |
| Sitc 3 | .4 | .1 | .6 | .2 | .8 | .2 | .6 | .1 | 6.8 | 1.3 |
| Sitc 4 | .1 | 0.0 | .3 | .1 | .3 | .1 | .9 | .2 | .4 | .1 |
| Sitc 5 | 63.9 | 20.6 | 78.4 | 25.3 | 97.5 | 22.4 | 99.1 | 22.7 | 89.4 | 16.7 |
| Sitc 6 | 34.9 | 11.2 | 27.3 | 8.8 | 40.3 | 9.3 | 46.4 | 10.6 | 65.4 | 12.3 |
| Sitc 7 | 138.5 | 44.5 | 171.5 | 55.4 | 240.2 | 55.2 | 239.7 | 54.9 | 303.2 | 56.8 |
| Sitc 8 | 13.1 | 4.2 | 14.1 | 4.6 | 20.3 | 4.7 | 23.8 | 5.4 | 27.4 | 5.1 |
| Sitc 9 | 50.3 | 16.2 | 3.5 | 1.1 | 3.6 | .8 | 5.5 | 1.3 | 6.7 | 1.3 |
| Sitc 0 to 9 | 311.0 | 100.0 | 309.7 | 100.0 | 435.0 | 100.0 | 437.1 | 100.0 | 533.8 | 100.0 |

1 and 2. See notes on Table 2.

EEC (9 countries) trade with Peru
Value: ECU million[1]

| | 1975 | % | 1976 | % | 1977 | % | 1978 | % | 1979 | % |
|---|---|---|---|---|---|---|---|---|---|---|
| *Imports* | | | | | | | | | | |
| Sitc 0[2] | 52.6 | 20.2 | 53.6 | 18.1 | 53.7 | 17.9 | 52.9 | 20.2 | 64.3 | 15.2 |
| Sitc 1 | .3 | .1 | .8 | .3 | .7 | .2 | 1.6 | .6 | 1.0 | .2 |
| Sitc 2 | 120.9 | 46.5 | 141.1 | 47.6 | 115.5 | 38.4 | 104.2 | 39.9 | 153.0 | 36.2 |
| Sitc 3 | 0.0 | 0.0 | 0.0 | 0.0 | 0.0 | 0.0 | 0.0 | 0.0 | 0.0 | 0.0 |
| Sitc 4 | 32.3 | 12.4 | 2.9 | 1.0 | 1.4 | .4 | 1.6 | .6 | 12.2 | 2.9 |
| Sitc 5 | .3 | .1 | .5 | .2 | .5 | .2 | .5 | .2 | 1.3 | .3 |
| Sitc 6 | 49.7 | 19.1 | 93.1 | 31.4 | 123.8 | 41.2 | 93.7 | 35.8 | 184.9 | 43.8 |
| Sitc 7 | 1.6 | .6 | .6 | .2 | 1.4 | .5 | .7 | .3 | .4 | .1 |
| Sitc 8 | 1.6 | .6 | 3.3 | 1.1 | 2.8 | .9 | 2.1 | .8 | 4.1 | 1.0 |
| Sitc 9 | .6 | .2 | .5 | .2 | .8 | .3 | 4.1 | 1.6 | 1.3 | .3 |
| Sitc 0 to 9 | 259.9 | 100.0 | 296.4 | 100.0 | 300.5 | 100.0 | 261.3 | 100.0 | 422.5 | 100.0 |
| *Exports* | | | | | | | | | | |
| Sitc 0 | 15.9 | 3.1 | 18.6 | 5.4 | 17.7 | 6.0 | 12.7 | 5.0 | 6.6 | 1.4 |
| Sitc 1 | 1.3 | .2 | .5 | .1 | .6 | .2 | .9 | .4 | 1.0 | .2 |
| Sitc 2 | 3.7 | .7 | 1.6 | .5 | 1.4 | .5 | 1.2 | .5 | 1.6 | .3 |
| Sitc 3 | 2.2 | .4 | 2.0 | .6 | .8 | .3 | 4.0 | 1.6 | 1.1 | .2 |
| Sitc 4 | 4.6 | .9 | .3 | .1 | .9 | .3 | .4 | .2 | .3 | .1 |
| Sitc 5 | 96.7 | 19.1 | 76.5 | 22.2 | 58.2 | 19.9 | 52.9 | 20.7 | 64.2 | 13.3 |
| Sitc 6 | 100.7 | 19.9 | 44.9 | 13.0 | 43.9 | 15.0 | 28.3 | 11.1 | 33.4 | 6.9 |
| Sitc 7 | 230.7 | 45.6 | 175.7 | 50.9 | 144.3 | 49.2 | 139.6 | 54.7 | 352.2 | 73.2 |
| Sitc 8 | 17.9 | 3.5 | 14.8 | 4.3 | 14.2 | 4.8 | 9.4 | 3.7 | 8.6 | 1.8 |
| Sitc 9 | 32.5 | 6.4 | 10.4 | 3.0 | 11.3 | 3.9 | 5.9 | 2.3 | 12.3 | 2.6 |
| Sitc 0 to 9 | 506.2 | 100.0 | 345.1 | 100.0 | 293.3 | 100.0 | 255.3 | 100.0 | 481.4 | 100.0 |

1 and 2. See notes on Table 2.

*Source:* European Commission, Directorate-General for External Relations, Statistics Office.

# TABLE 8

## EEC (9 countries) trade with Mexico
## Value: ECU million[1]

| | 1975 | % | 1976 | % | 1977 | % | 1978 | % | 1979 | % |
|---|---|---|---|---|---|---|---|---|---|---|
| *Imports* | | | | | | | | | | |
| Sitc 0[2] | 77.2 | 24.7 | 121.2 | 32.4 | 133.2 | 31.0 | 95.6 | 24.7 | 125.8 | 27.9 |
| Sitc 1 | 8.6 | 2.7 | 12.9 | 3.4 | 13.5 | 3.1 | 13.3 | 3.4 | 6.4 | 1.4 |
| Sitc 2 | 64.1 | 20.5 | 61.7 | 16.5 | 78.0 | 18.2 | 58.9 | 15.2 | 67.9 | 15.0 |
| Sitc 3 | 7.7 | 2.5 | 2.5 | .7 | .3 | .1 | 6.3 | 1.6 | 1.6 | .4 |
| Sitc 4 | .3 | .1 | .5 | .1 | 1.3 | .3 | 1.2 | .3 | .8 | .2 |
| Sitc 5 | 36.0 | 11.5 | 41.4 | 11.0 | 44.9 | 10.5 | 43.7 | 11.3 | 39.1 | 8.7 |
| Sitc 6 | 77.1 | 24.7 | 77.6 | 20.7 | 98.8 | 23.0 | 73.8 | 19.1 | 92.9 | 20.6 |
| Sitc 7 | 28.9 | 9.2 | 32.9 | 8.8 | 35.6 | 8.3 | 74.9 | 19.4 | 92.1 | 20.4 |
| Sitc 8 | 10.8 | 3.4 | 12.4 | 3.3 | 18.4 | 4.3 | 14.5 | 3.8 | 17.9 | 4.0 |
| Sitc 9 | 2.1 | .7 | 11.5 | 3.1 | 5.5 | 1.3 | 4.3 | 1.1 | 6.6 | 1.5 |
| Sitc 0 to 9 | 312.7 | 100.0 | 374.6 | 100.0 | 429.5 | 100.0 | 386.6 | 100.0 | 451.1 | 100.0 |
| *Exports* | | | | | | | | | | |
| Sitc 0 | 6.2 | .6 | 14.2 | 1.5 | 24.4 | 3.1 | 26.7 | 2.1 | 32.1 | 2.1 |
| Sitc 1 | 15.0 | 1.5 | 16.1 | 1.7 | 13.8 | 1.7 | 14.4 | 1.1 | 26.1 | 1.7 |
| Sitc 2 | 6.4 | .7 | 6.1 | .6 | 5.8 | .7 | 10.3 | .8 | 13.0 | .8 |
| Sitc 3 | 1.5 | .2 | 3.7 | .4 | 4.5 | .6 | 3.9 | .3 | 6.2 | .4 |
| Sitc 4 | .7 | .1 | .9 | .1 | .7 | .1 | .7 | .1 | .7 | 0.0 |
| Sitc 5 | 120.1 | 12.4 | 125.5 | 13.0 | 130.3 | 16.3 | 147.9 | 11.6 | 184.3 | 11.9 |
| Sitc 6 | 150.9 | 15.6 | 85.4 | 8.8 | 109.0 | 13.6 | 373.9 | 29.2 | 268.5 | 17.4 |
| Sitc 7 | 614.4 | 63.4 | 657.5 | 67.9 | 468.4 | 58.5 | 642.1 | 50.1 | 919.2 | 59.5 |
| Sitc 8 | 44.2 | 4.6 | 51.8 | 5.3 | 35.4 | 4.4 | 48.7 | 3.8 | 70.1 | 4.5 |
| Sitc 9 | 9.2 | .9 | 7.4 | .8 | 8.3 | 1.0 | 12.1 | .9 | 23.4 | 1.5 |
| Sitc 0 to 9 | 968.6 | 100.0 | 968.6 | 100.0 | 800.6 | 100.0 | 1280.9 | 100.0 | 1543.7 | 100.0 |

1 and 2. See notes on Table 2.

## EEC (9 countries) trade with Venezuela
### Value: ECU million[1]

| | 1975 | % | 1976 | % | 1977 | % | 1978 | % | 1979 | % |
|---|---|---|---|---|---|---|---|---|---|---|
| *Imports* | | | | | | | | | | |
| Sitc 0[2] | 10.9 | 1.4 | 14.6 | 1.8 | 26.9 | 5.3 | 22.1 | 3.8 | 22.3 | 2.4 |
| Sitc 1 | .4 | .1 | .2 | 0.0 | .1 | 0.0 | .1 | 0.0 | .1 | 0.0 |
| Sitc 2 | 117.6 | 15.6 | 122.8 | 15.2 | 84.2 | 16.5 | 67.9 | 11.8 | 91.5 | 9.6 |
| Sitc 3 | 619.7 | 82.1 | 654.9 | 80.9 | 373.1 | 73.1 | 434.1 | 75.3 | 756.6 | 79.6 |
| Sitc 4 | 0.0 | 0.0 | 0.0 | 0.0 | 0.0 | 0.0 | 0.0 | 0.0 | 0.0 | 0.0 |
| Sitc 5 | 0.0 | 0.0 | 6.2 | .8 | 5.9 | 1.2 | 4.0 | .7 | 10.7 | 1.1 |
| Sitc 6 | 3.2 | .4 | 7.7 | 1.0 | 7.7 | 1.5 | 29.6 | 5.1 | 59.5 | 6.3 |
| Sitc 7 | .9 | .1 | 1.9 | .2 | 10.8 | 2.1 | 13.8 | 2.4 | 4.0 | .4 |
| Sitc 8 | .3 | 0.0 | .3 | 0.0 | .5 | .1 | 1.1 | .2 | 2.9 | .3 |
| Sitc 9 | 2.1 | .3 | 1.1 | .1 | 1.2 | .2 | 3.8 | .7 | 2.9 | .3 |
| Sitc 0 to 9 | 755.0 | 100.0 | 809.6 | 100.0 | 510.4 | 100.0 | 576.5 | 100.0 | 950.6 | 100.0 |
| | | | | | | | | | | |
| *Exports* | | | | | | | | | | |
| Sitc 0 | 65.6 | 6.1 | 66.3 | 4.9 | 117.4 | 5.6 | 96.5 | 5.2 | 81.4 | 5.9 |
| Sitc 1 | 40.2 | 3.7 | 40.9 | 3.0 | 61.6 | 2.9 | 82.6 | 4.4 | 65.7 | 4.7 |
| Sitc 2 | 10.5 | 1.0 | 12.9 | .9 | 17.8 | .8 | 13.9 | .7 | 16.4 | 1.2 |
| Sitc 3 | 5.7 | .5 | 2.6 | .2 | 22.5 | 1.1 | 4.4 | .2 | 13.9 | 1.0 |
| Sitc 4 | 9.4 | .9 | 5.2 | .4 | 2.4 | .1 | 3.4 | .2 | 2.1 | .1 |
| Sitc 5 | 140.8 | 13.0 | 157.8 | 11.6 | 207.6 | 9.9 | 202.4 | 10.8 | 187.4 | 13.5 |
| Sitc 6 | 236.1 | 21.8 | 284.6 | 20.9 | 396.0 | 18.9 | 380.9 | 20.4 | 268.4 | 19.3 |
| Sitc 7 | 490.3 | 45.3 | 668.0 | 49.0 | 1110.1 | 52.8 | 942.6 | 50.5 | 624.3 | 45.0 |
| Sitc 8 | 64.9 | 6.0 | 80.1 | 5.9 | 109.0 | 5.2 | 113.6 | 6.1 | 99.4 | 7.2 |
| Sitc 9 | 18.1 | 1.7 | 46.1 | 3.4 | 56.4 | 2.7 | 27.3 | 1.5 | 29.9 | 2.2 |
| Sitc 0 to 9 | 1081.6 | 100.0 | 1364.5 | 100.0 | 2100.7 | 100.0 | 1867.6 | 100.0 | 1388.8 | 100.0 |

1 and 2. See notes on Table 2.

*Source*: European Commission, Directorate-General for External Relations, Statistics Office.

# TABLE 10

## Origin of Latin American Imports, 1961-63 and 1976-78
### In Per Cent

| Country | Average 1961-63 | | | | | | | Average 1976-78 | | | | | | |
|---|---|---|---|---|---|---|---|---|---|---|---|---|---|---|
| | United States | European Economic Community[1] | Japan | Canada | Middle East | Latin America[2] | Other countries | United States | European Economic Community[1] | Japan | Canada | Middle East | Latin America[2] | Other countries |
| Argentina | 26.8 | 39.5 | 3.9 | 2.6 | — | 12.7 | 14.5 | 18.4 | 27.9 | 8.0 | 2.0 | 2.0 | 24.6 | 17.1 |
| Bahamas | 56.4 | 22.1 | 0.2 | 6.1 | — | 9.0 | — | 17.6 | 12.8 | 0.3 | 1.0 | 37.0 | 3.1 | 28.2 |
| Barbados | 14.7 | 44.5 | 1.8 | 10.5 | — | 10.4 | 18.1 | 26.3 | 26.3 | 3.3 | 7.7 | 0.1 | 24.3 | 12.0 |
| Bolivia | 43.6 | 27.6 | 7.3 | 0.3 | — | 15.1 | 6.1 | 26.4 | 15.0 | 12.8 | 0.7 | — | 30.3 | 14.8 |
| Brazil | 32.3 | 24.5 | 4.6 | 1.7 | 4.8 | 15.0 | 17.1 | 21.1 | 19.4 | 7.7 | 2.5 | 26.4 | 10.7 | 12.2 |
| Chile | 37.9 | 30.1 | 2.8 | 0.1 | 1.1 | 19.3 | 8.7 | 24.0 | 14.9 | 10.0 | 1.6 | 5.4 | 31.8 | 12.3 |
| Colombia | 51.8 | 26.2 | 3.2 | 2.0 | — | 5.6 | 11.2 | 39.4 | 21.7 | 9.9 | 3.0 | 0.1 | 15.3 | 10.6 |
| Costa Rica | 47.3 | 26.4 | 7.0 | 3.3 | 0.1 | 9.0 | 6.9 | 35.0 | 14.6 | 13.4 | 1.8 | 0.1 | 28.2 | 6.9 |
| Dominican Republic | 47.4 | 28.0 | 6.8 | 6.0 | 0.1 | 2.7 | 9.0 | 46.0 | 11.0 | 7.4 | 2.3 | — | 19.3 | 14.0 |
| Ecuador | 43.8 | 33.5 | 3.5 | 3.5 | 0.1 | 7.4 | 8.2 | 37.8 | 19.1 | 15.8 | 2.0 | 0.1 | 12.7 | 12.5 |
| El Salvador | 36.5 | 29.9 | 6.9 | 2.1 | — | 21.4 | 3.2 | 29.7 | 14.9 | 10.9 | 1.3 | — | 37.2 | 6.0 |
| Guatemala | 47.8 | 24.9 | 5.2 | 2.0 | 0.1 | 11.2 | 8.8 | 33.9 | 16.2 | 11.1 | 1.7 | 0.1 | 27.4 | 9.6 |
| Guyana | 21.2 | 45.9 | 2.2 | 7.6 | — | 13.0 | 10.1 | 26.6 | 29.9 | 3.7 | 4.1 | — | 26.2 | 9.5 |
| Haiti | 57.9 | 23.2 | 0.2 | 2.6 | — | 2.5 | 13.6 | 50.6 | 14.7 | 7.2 | 6.9 | — | 4.8 | 15.8 |
| Honduras | 50.1 | 15.2 | 7.7 | 1.3 | — | 14.8 | 10.9 | 45.3 | 11.5 | 9.8 | 2.3 | — | 26.6 | 4.5 |
| Jamaica | 27.7 | 43.0 | 3.4 | 10.6 | — | 7.4 | 7.9 | 36.2 | 16.1 | 2.7 | 5.5 | — | 22.7 | 16.8 |
| Mexico | 69.1 | 18.1 | 1.8 | 3.2 | — | 1.3 | 6.5 | 62.2 | 16.5 | 6.2 | 2.3 | — | 4.8 | 8.0 |
| Nicaragua | 49.4 | 21.2 | 5.9 | 2.3 | — | 13.2 | 8.0 | 30.5 | 12.4 | 8.4 | 1.0 | — | 40.2 | 7.5 |
| Panama | 47.7 | 14.8 | 3.2 | 1.3 | 0.2 | 12.4 | 20.4 | 35.1 | 8.9 | 5.5 | 1.4 | 5.5 | 36.3 | 7.3 |
| Paraguay | 25.2 | 24.5 | 8.3 | — | — | 22.4 | 19.6 | 11.3 | 20.2 | 7.2 | 0.1 | — | 43.5 | 17.7 |
| Peru | 40.3 | 30.9 | 5.3 | 2.3 | 0.1 | 13.4 | 7.7 | 34.4 | 22.9 | 7.7 | 2.9 | 0.4 | 20.8 | 10.9 |
| Trinidad and Tobago | 13.3 | 27.0 | 1.1 | 4.8 | 20.4 | 26.6 | 6.8 | 20.5 | 15.0 | 4.3 | 3.3 | 31.2 | 5.7 | 20.0 |
| Uruguay | 19.0 | 37.8 | 1.5 | 1.5 | 5.3 | 21.6 | 13.3 | 10.4 | 20.5 | 2.9 | 1.2 | 13.4 | 37.1 | 14.5 |
| Venezuela | 53.5 | 28.1 | 4.1 | 4.4 | 0.1 | 2.6 | 7.2 | 41.9 | 25.9 | 9.5 | 4.1 | — | 8.6 | 10.0 |
| Latin America | 41.8 | 28.1 | 3.7 | 3.0 | 1.8 | 10.7 | 10.9 | 32.2 | 19.2 | 7.9 | 2.6 | 10.8 | 14.7 | 12.6 |

1. Belgium, Denmark, Federal Republic of Germany, France, Ireland, Italy, Netherlands, United Kingdom.
2. Member countries of the IDB.

*Source:* Inter-American Development Bank, Annual Report 1981.

# TABLE 11

## Destination of Latin American Exports, 1961-63 and 1976-78
### In Per Cent

| | Average 1961-63 | | | | | | | Average 1976-78 | | | | | | |
|---|---|---|---|---|---|---|---|---|---|---|---|---|---|---|
| Country | United States | European Economic Community[1] | Japan | Canada | Middle East | Latin America[2] | Other countries | United States | European Economic Community[1] | Japan | Canada | Middle East | Latin America[2] | Other countries |
| Argentina | 9.1 | 60.1 | 3.5 | 0.4 | 0.4 | 13.1 | 13.4 | 7.7 | 32.7 | 5.6 | 0.5 | 2.6 | 25.8 | 25.1 |
| Bahamas | 91.7 | 5.5 | — | 1.8 | — | 1.0 | — | 83.1 | 12.4 | 0.7 | 0.6 | 0.1 | 1.4 | 1.7 |
| Barbados | 6.7 | 53.5 | — | 13.8 | — | 1.2 | 24.8 | 29.7 | 19.2 | 0.1 | 5.7 | — | 17.2 | 28.1 |
| Bolivia | 31.7 | 58.9 | 2.4 | — | — | 5.4 | 1.6 | 33.6 | 21.7 | 2.7 | — | — | 28.8 | 13.2 |
| Brazil | 39.3 | 31.0 | 2.6 | 1.6 | 0.7 | 6.4 | 18.4 | 19.6 | 30.7 | 5.6 | 1.2 | 2.7 | 13.4 | 26.8 |
| Chile | 35.7 | 42.1 | 6.3 | 0.1 | 0.1 | 8.9 | 6.8 | 12.2 | 34.4 | 11.6 | 1.1 | 1.2 | 26.9 | 13.7 |
| Colombia | 56.7 | 24.8 | 0.8 | 1.7 | — | 6.5 | 9.5 | 32.7 | 32.8 | 3.4 | 1.7 | 0.1 | 13.2 | 16.1 |
| Costa Rica | 57.4 | 32.1 | 0.6 | 0.6 | — | 5.4 | 3.9 | 34.4 | 24.3 | 1.0 | 0.3 | 0.8 | 28.3 | 10.9 |
| Dominican Republic | 74.1 | 14.5 | 1.9 | 0.8 | 0.3 | 1.4 | 7.0 | 67.7 | 10.6 | 0.9 | 1.2 | — | 4.1 | 15.5 |
| Ecuador | 61.0 | 24.2 | 4.8 | 0.6 | — | 6.8 | 2.6 | 39.7 | 12.5 | 1.3 | 2.5 | — | 34.1 | 9.9 |
| El Salvador | 30.7 | 31.5 | 20.0 | 0.5 | — | 15.4 | 1.9 | 29.9 | 30.4 | 7.0 | 0.4 | — | 26.9 | 5.4 |
| Guatemala | 49.6 | 27.8 | 9.4 | 0.5 | 0.1 | 7.5 | 5.1 | 32.9 | 23.8 | 5.2 | 0.5 | 1.8 | 25.2 | 10.6 |
| Guyana | 18.7 | 27.5 | 0.5 | 28.8 | — | 13.6 | 10.9 | 19.8 | 39.8 | 3.0 | 4.9 | 0.1 | 18.2 | 14.2 |
| Haiti | 52.4 | 36.8 | 4.8 | 0.2 | — | 1.8 | 4.0 | 61.2 | 31.8 | 0.3 | 1.2 | 0.3 | 2.7 | 2.5 |
| Honduras | 60.7 | 13.1 | 0.8 | 2.9 | — | 19.2 | 3.3 | 54.5 | 23.9 | 3.8 | 0.3 | 0.1 | 13.0 | 4.4 |
| Jamaica | 36.0 | 29.7 | 0.2 | 21.3 | — | 1.7 | 11.1 | 40.0 | 21.8 | 0.7 | 7.5 | — | 10.1 | 19.9 |
| Mexico | 60.6 | 6.6 | 6.9 | 0.8 | 0.1 | 4.3 | 20.7 | 64.9 | 6.9 | 3.9 | 1.2 | 2.0 | 11.5 | 9.6 |
| Nicaragua | 42.6 | 25.1 | 20.3 | 3.3 | — | 5.3 | 3.4 | 27.5 | 26.2 | 11.2 | 0.7 | 0.1 | 24.9 | 9.4 |
| Panama | 75.1 | 6.0 | 0.5 | 5.1 | — | 5.0 | 8.3 | 46.7 | 19.2 | 0.3 | 1.2 | 1.1 | 14.5 | 17.0 |
| Paraguay | 22.5 | 26.0 | 0.1 | — | — | 30.3 | 21.1 | 11.7 | 39.2 | 6.1 | 0.3 | — | 26.5 | 16.2 |
| Peru | 35.4 | 40.1 | 7.3 | 0.5 | 0.3 | 9.3 | 7.1 | 30.9 | 21.2 | 12.6 | 0.5 | 0.6 | 13.6 | 20.6 |
| Trinidad and Tobago | 25.7 | 38.1 | 0.1 | 4.8 | 0.1 | 5.1 | 26.1 | 70.3 | 6.7 | — | 0.9 | — | 8.3 | 13.8 |
| Uruguay | 13.9 | 56.3 | 2.0 | 0.6 | 0.4 | 6.1 | 20.7 | 14.4 | 33.0 | 1.5 | 0.6 | 6.4 | 27.0 | 17.1 |
| Venezuela | 35.7 | 16.4 | 0.6 | 7.1 | — | 10.1 | 30.1 | 44.3 | 8.3 | 0.5 | 14.2 | — | 13.1 | 19.6 |
| **Latin America** | **37.2** | **29.4** | **3.3** | **3.2** | **0.2** | **8.4** | **18.3** | **37.0** | **21.3** | **4.1** | **3.5** | **1.3** | **15.8** | **17.0** |

1. Belgium, Denmark, Federal Republic of Germany, France, Ireland, Italy, Netherlands, United Kingdom.
2. Member countries of the IDB.

*Source:* Inter-American Development Bank, Annual Report 1981.

## TABLE 12

### EEC agreements with Latin American countries

| Country[1] | Entry into force | Duration | Official Journal No.[2] | Notes |
|---|---|---|---|---|
| Argentina | 1.1.1972 | 3 years renewable | L249 1971 | Non-preferential trade agreement — annual renewal by exchange of letters.[3] |
| | *signed 18.9.79 de facto 1.1.1978. | 31.12.1982 | L298 1979 | Agreement on trade in textiles. |
| | 6.11.1963 | 20 years | 186 1963 | Agreement for co-operation on the peaceful uses of nuclear energy. |
| Bolivia | 1.1.1976 | Unlimited | L313 1979 | Agreement on trade in hand-made products. |
| Brazil | 1.8.1974 | 3 years renewable | L102 1974 | Non-preferential trade agreement. |
| | *signed 23.1.80 de facto 1.1.1978 | 31.12.1982 | L 70 1980 | Agreement on trade in textiles. |
| | 24.6.1965 | 20 years | L 79 1969 | Agreement for co-operation on the peaceful uses of nuclear energy. |
| | 18.9.1980 | 5 years renewable | | Framework agreement for commercial and economic co-operation. |
| Chile | 1.1.1978 | Unlimited | L313 1979 | Agreement on trade in hand-made products. |
| Colombia | *de facto 1.1.1978 | 5 years | L357 1977 | Agreement on trade in textiles. |
| El Salvador | 1.1.1978 | Unlimited | L313 1979 | Agreement on trade in silk fabrics and hand-woven cotton fabrics |

| Country | Date | Duration | Reference | Description |
|---|---|---|---|---|
| Haiti | *signed 15.1.1980 de facto 1.1.1978 | 31.12.1982 | L 70 1980 | Agreement on trade in textiles. |
| Ecuador | 1.1.1976 | Unlimited | L313 1979 | Agreement on trade in hand-made products. |
| Guatemala | *signed 7.11.1979 de facto 1.1.1978 | 31.12.1982 | L350 1979 | Agreement on trade in textile products. |
| Honduras | 1.1.1977 | Unlimited | L313 1979 | Agreement on trade in silk fabrics and hand-woven cotton fabrics. |
| | 1.1.1977 | Unlimited | L313 1979 | Agreement on trade in hand-made products. |
| Mexico | 1.11.1975 | 5 years renewable | L247 1975 L262 1975 | Non-preferential agreement on commercial and economic co-operation. |
| | *de facto 1.1.1978 | 31.12.1982 | L357 1977 | Agreement on trade in textiles. |
| Panama | 1.1.1976 | Unlimited | L313 1979 | Agreement on trade in hand-made products. |
| Paraguay | 1.1.1976 | Unlimited | L313 1979 | Agreement on trade in hand-made products. |
| Peru | *signed 1.9.1980 de facto 1.1.1978 | 31.12.1982 | L350 1979 L234 1980 | Agreement on trade in textile products. |
| | 1.1.1977 | Unlimited | L313 1979 | Agreement on trade in hand-made products. |
| Uruguay | 1.8.1974 | 3 years renewable | L333 1973 L209 1974 | Non-preferential trade agreement. |
| | *signed 28.1.1980 de facto 1.1.1978 | 31.12.1982 | L70 1980 | Agreement on trade in textile products. |
| | 1,1,1975 | Unlimited | L313 1979 | Agreement on trade in hand-made products. |

1. Textile agreements concluded under the Arrangement regarding International Trade in Textiles are indicated by an asterik.
2. Main references to the Official Journal of the European Communities.
3. Argentina renounced the agreement in November 1979.

# Appendix 2 — Investment

## TABLE 13

Direct Private Investment (net) by Development Assistance Committee (DAC)[1] countries in Latin America[2]

Value: US$ millions

| | 1969 | 1970 | 1971 | 1972 | 1973 | 1974 | 1975 | 1976 | 1977 | 1978 |
|---|---|---|---|---|---|---|---|---|---|---|
| Total Latin America | 126.26 | 105.01 | 167.46 | 166.36 | 306.33 | 332.25 | 500.08 | 428.81 | 426.30 | 450.10 |
| % | 100.0 | 100.0 | 100.0 | 100.0 | 100.0 | 100.0 | 100.0 | 100.0 | 100.0 | 100.0 |
| Argentina | 19.27 | 19.11 | 58.34 | 30.62 | 85.39 | 25.27 | 34.14 | 2.68 | 20.97 | 114.27 |
| % | 15.3 | 18.2 | 34.8 | 18.1 | 27.9 | 7.7 | 6.8 | 0.6 | 4.9 | 25.4 |
| Brazil | 61.35 | 58.80 | 64.39 | 116.32 | 188.80 | 252.40 | 344.20 | 337.57 | 245.00 | 265.69 |
| % | 48.5 | 56.0 | 38.5 | 68.6 | 61.5 | 76.0 | 68.8 | 78.7 | 57.5 | 59.0 |
| Mexico | 24.40 | 4.40 | 34.54 | 13.80 | 14.57 | 16.62 | 28.23 | 32.22 | 113.81 | 17.30 |
| % | 19.3 | 4.2 | 20.7 | 8.1 | 4.8 | 5.0 | 5.6 | 7,5 | 26.7 | 3.8 |
| Andean Group[3] | 8.68 | 3.17 | 3.42 | - 3.25 | 8.54 | 20.68 | 31.43 | 10.10 | 35.88 | 40.09 |
| % | 6.9 | 3.0 | 2.0 | — | 2.8 | 6.2 | 6.3 | 2.4 | 8.4 | 8.9 |
| CACM | 1.20 | 1.05 | 0.68 | 0.41 | 0.82 | 1.13 | 0.99 | 1.13 | 2.25 | 3.78 |
| % | 1.0 | 1.0 | 0.4 | 0.2 | 0.3 | 0.3 | 0.2 | 0.3 | 0.5 | 0.8 |
| Other LA countries[4] | 11.36 | 18.48 | 6.09 | 8.46 | 8.21 | 15.85 | 61.09 | 45.11 | 8.39 | 8.97 |
| % | 9.0 | 17.6 | 3.6 | 5.0 | 2.7 | 4.8 | 12.3 | 10.5 | 2.0 | 2.1 |

1.  DAC members: Australia, Austria, Belgium, Canada, Denmark, Finland, France, Germany, Italy, Japan, Netherlands, New Zealand, Norway, Sweden, Switzerland, UK, USA (no data available for Denmark).
2.  See Table 2 Note 1.
3.  Excluding Chile after 1977.
4.  Six countries plus Chile after 1977.

Source: Commission of the European Communities, Directorate-General for External Relations, Statistics Office.

## TABLE 14

### Direct Private Investment (net) by EEC and other DAC[1] countries in Argentina

Value: US$ millions

| | 1969 | 1970 | 1971 | 1972 | 1973 | 1974 | 1975 | 1976 | 1977 | 1978 |
|---|---|---|---|---|---|---|---|---|---|---|
| *Investing countries* | | | | | | | | | | |
| West Germany | 8.37 | 7.82 | 10.00 | 9.69 | 19.33 | 1.54 | 10.63 | -1.65 | 8.81 | 33.65 |
| Belgium | -0.90 | 0.60 | 1.29 | 0.25 | 4.40 | 13.34 | 1.23 | 0.90 | 0.33 | -1.46 |
| France | 0.00 | 0.00 | 0.00 | 0.00 | 52.09 | 1.25 | 4.92 | 9.00 | 10.89 | 93.30 |
| Italy | -0.90 | 11.49 | 52.21 | 1.25 | 3.12 | -4.11 | -2.73 | -4.87 | 0.94 | -8.92 |
| Netherlands | — | — | — | — | — | — | 1.40 | -0.70 | 0.00 | -2.30 |
| United Kingdom | 12.70 | -0.80 | -5.16 | 19.43 | 6.45 | 13.55 | 18.69 | — | — | — |
| Total for six EEC countries | 19.27 | 19.11 | 58.34 | 30.62 | 85.39 | 25.57 | 34.14 | 2.68 | 20.97 | 114.27 |
| USA | 93.00 | 62.00 | 64.00 | 38.00 | 3.00 | 9.00 | -2.00 | 26.00 | 139.00 | 146.00 |
| Japan | 1.66 | 2.33 | 0.12 | 0.99 | 1.79 | 0.32 | -10.87 | -2.30 | -0.36 | 1.29 |
| Other DAC countries | 0.00 | 0.32 | 0.19 | 0.09 | 2.04 | 0.00 | 0.00 | — | — | 0.49 |
| Total DAC countries (bilateral) | 113.93 | 83.76 | 122.65 | 69.70 | 92.22 | 34.89 | 21.27 | 26.38 | 159.61 | 262.05 |
| % EEC in total DAC | 16.9 | 22.8 | 47.6 | 43.9 | 92.6 | 73.3 | 100.0 | 9.3 | 13.1 | 43.6 |
| % USA .. .. .. | 81.6 | 74.0 | 52.2 | 54.5 | 3.3 | 25.8 | — | — | — | 55.7 |
| % Japan .. .. .. | 1.5 | 2.8 | 0.1 | 1.4 | 1.9 | 0.9 | — | 90.7 | 86.9 | 0.5 |

1. See Table 13, Note 1.
*Source:* Commission of the European Communities, Directorate-General for External Relations, Statistics Office.

233

## TABLE 15

### Direct Private Investment (net) by EEC and other DAC[1] countries in Brazil
#### Value: US$ millions

| | 1969 | 1970 | 1971 | 1972 | 1973 | 1974 | 1975 | 1976 | 1977 | 1978 |
|---|---|---|---|---|---|---|---|---|---|---|
| *Investing countries* | | | | | | | | | | |
| West Germany | 28.72 | 25.66 | 34.20 | 48.95 | 72.17 | 133.35 | 155.62 | 211.69 | 166.27 | 192.60 |
| Belgium | 1.50 | 0.30 | 0.00 | 5.02 | 4.19 | 3.75 | 6.40 | 13.12 | −4.22 | 2.53 |
| France | 0.00 | 0.00 | 0.00 | 0.00 | 29.89 | 29.46 | 45.33 | 47.00 | 59.36 | 21.90 |
| Italy | 8.84 | 3.55 | 2.32 | 9.71 | −0.97 | 13.95 | −9.54 | 39.87 | −4.80 | 0.56 |
| Netherlands | — | — | — | — | — | — | 12.00 | 25.89 | 28.39 | 48.10 |
| United Kingdom | 22.29 | 29.29 | 27.87 | 52.64 | 83.52 | 72.89 | 134.39 | — | — | — |
| Total for six EEC countries | 61.35 | 58.80 | 64.39 | 116.32 | 188.80 | 252.40 | 344.20 | 337.57 | 245.00 | 265.69 |
| USA | 149.00 | 204.00 | 195.00 | 416.00 | 697.00 | 766.00 | 821.00 | 329.00 | 422.00 | 999.00 |
| Japan | 11.55 | 22.43 | 104.22 | 96.20 | 370.83 | 285.89 | 275.44 | 201.00 | 214.32 | 194.57 |
| Other DAC countries | 2.59 | 8.24 | 7.61 | 0.20 | 0.00 | 2.53 | 0.58 | 1.54 | 4.43 | 5.45 |
| Total DAC countries (bilateral) | 224.49 | 293.47 | 371.22 | 628.72 | 1256.63 | 1306.82 | 1441.22 | 869.11 | 885.75 | 1464.71 |
| % EEC in total DAC | 27.3 | 20.0 | 17.4 | 18.5 | 15.0 | 19.3 | 23.9 | 38.8 | 27.7 | 18.1 |
| % USA .. .. .. | 66.4 | 69.5 | 52.5 | 66.2 | 55.5 | 58.6 | 57.0 | 37.9 | 47.6 | 68.2 |
| % Japan .. .. .. | 5.1 | 7.6 | 28.1 | 15.3 | 29.5 | 21.9 | 19.1 | 23.1 | 24.2 | 13.3 |

1. See Table 13, Note 1.
*Source:* Commission of the European Communities, Directorate-General for External Relations, Statistics Office.

## TABLE 16

### Direct Private Investment (net) by EEC and other DAC[1] countries in Mexico

Value: US$ millions

| | 1969 | 1970 | 1971 | 1972 | 1973 | 1974 | 1975 | 1976 | 1977 | 1978 |
|---|---|---|---|---|---|---|---|---|---|---|
| *Investing countries* | | | | | | | | | | |
| West Germany | 16.63 | 4.79 | 9.69 | 3.42 | 29.63 | 10.73 | 8.80 | 17.96 | 99.44 | 11.85 |
| Belgium | 0.00 | 0.40 | 0.00 | 0.31 | 0.23 | 0.08 | 2.69 | 0.02 | 0.29 | 0.04 |
| France | 0.00 | 0.00 | 0.00 | 0.00 | −0.70 | 1.36 | 2.86 | 14.29 | 6.44 | 3.30 |
| Italy | 1.27 | 2.41 | 0.53 | 1.86 | −0.30 | −2.83 | −1.12 | −0.55 | −0.55 | 0.21 |
| Netherlands | — | — | — | — | — | — | 0.30 | 0.50 | 8.19 | 1.90 |
| United Kingdom | 6.50 | −3.20 | 24.32 | 8.21 | −14.29 | 7.28 | 14.70 | — | — | — |
| Total for six EEC countries | 24.40 | 4.40 | 34.54 | 13.80 | 14.57 | 16.62 | 28.23 | 32.22 | 113.81 | 17.30 |
| USA | 170.00 | 131.00 | 44.00 | 151.00 | 213.00 | 445.00 | 323.00 | −73.00 | 188.00 | 449.00 |
| Japan | 1.07 | 0.50 | 0.56 | 15.91 | 26.67 | 18.72 | 19.21 | 17.16 | 23.46 | 32.38 |
| Other DAC countries | 0.85 | 1.54 | 0.00 | 0.01 | −1.79 | 0.00 | 0.00 | — | — | — |
| Total DAC countries (bilateral) | 196.32 | 137.44 | 79.10 | 180.72 | 252.45 | 480.34 | 370.44 | −23.62 | 325.27 | 498.68 |
| % EEC in total DAC | 12.4 | 3.2 | 43.7 | 7.6 | 5.7 | 3.5 | 7.6 | 65.2 | 35.0 | 3.5 |
| % USA .. .. .. | 86.6 | 95.3 | 55.6 | 83.6 | 83.8 | 92.6 | 87.2 | — | 57.8 | 90.0 |
| % Japan .. .. .. | 0.5 | 0.4 | 0.7 | 8.8 | 10.5 | 3.9 | 5.2 | 34.8 | 7.2 | 6.5 |

1. See Table 13, Note 1.
*Source*: Commission of the European Communities, Directorate-General for External Relations, Statistics Office.

235

# TABLE 17

### Direct Private Investment (net) by EEC and other DAC[1] countries in the Andean Group[2]

#### Value: US$ millions

| Investing countries | 1969 | 1970 | 1971 | 1972 | 1973 | 1974 | 1975 | 1976 | 1977 | 1978 |
|---|---|---|---|---|---|---|---|---|---|---|
| West Germany | 4.48 | 2.13 | 0.85 | -2.18 | 1.96 | 9.21 | 9.86 | 7.27 | 11.37 | 16.14 |
| Belgium | 0.40 | 0.30 | 0.00 | 0.35 | 0.03 | 0.92 | 2.28 | -0.07 | 0.00 | 0.40 |
| France | 0.00 | 0.00 | 0.00 | 0.00 | 8.26 | 9.43 | 8.19 | 3.61 | 21.61 | 20.60 |
| Italy | 2.41 | 0.34 | 0.18 | 1.58 | -1.33 | -0.70 | 1.11 | 3.22 | 2.90 | 3.35 |
| Netherlands (Peru) | — | — | — | — | — | — | — | 3.29 | 0.00 | -0.40 |
| United Kingdom | 1.39 | 0.40 | 2.39 | -3.00 | -0.38 | 1.82 | 9.99 | | | — |
| Total for six EEC countries | 8.68 | 3.17 | 3.42 | -3.25 | 8.54 | 20.68 | 31.43 | 10.10 | 35.88 | 40.09 |
| USA | 24.00 | -22.00 | 43.00 | -65.00 | -28.00 | -189.00 | 662.00 | -365.00 | 354.00 | 264.00 |
| Japan | 18.47 | 38.11 | 1.24 | 2.79 | 9.86 | 384.32 | -40.93 | 7.34 | 7.56 | 20.79 |
| Other DAC countries | 0.49 | 0.04 | 0.13 | 0.09 | 0.28 | 1.19 | 1.66 | 0.55 | 0.00 | 0.84 |
| Total DAC countries (bilateral) | 51.64 | 19.32 | 47.79 | -65.37 | -9.32 | 217.19 | 654.16 | -346.51 | 397.44 | 325.72 |
| % EEC in total DAC | 16.8 | 7.7 | 7.2 | — | 45.7 | 5.1 | 4.5 | 54.6 | 9.0 | 12.3 |
| % USA .. .. .. | 46.5 | — | 90.0 | — | — | — | 95.2 | — | 89.1 | 81.1 |
| % Japan .. .. .. | 35.8 | 99.2 | 2.6 | 96.9 | 52.8 | 94.6 | — | 42.4 | 1.9 | 6.4 |

1. See Table 13, Note 1.
2. Bolivia, Chile, Colombia, Ecuador, Peru, Venezuela (excluding Chile after 1977).
Source: Commission of the European Communities, Directorate-General for External Relations, Statistics Office.

## TABLE 18

### Direct Private Investment (net) by EEC and other DAC[1] countries in the CACM[2]

Value: US$ millions

| | 1969 | 1970 | 1971 | 1972 | 1973 | 1974 | 1975 | 1976 | 1977 | 1978 |
|---|---|---|---|---|---|---|---|---|---|---|
| *Investing countries* | | | | | | | | | | |
| West Germany | 0.50 | 0.20 | 0.68 | 0.28 | 0.34 | 0.72 | 1.17 | 0.96 | 2.29 | 2.53 |
| Belgium | 0.70 | 1.00 | 0.00 | 0.13 | 0.23 | 0.15 | 0.11 | 0.11 | -0.04 | 0.49 |
| France | 0.00 | 0.00 | 0.00 | 0.00 | 0.25 | 0.25 | -0.28 | 0.10 | 0.00 | 0.20 |
| Italy | 0.00 | -0.15 | 0.00 | 0.00 | 0.00 | 0.01 | -0.01 | -0.04 | 0.00 | 0.96 |
| Netherlands | — | — | — | — | — | — | — | — | — | — |
| United Kingdom | — | — | — | — | — | — | — | — | — | — |
| Total for six EEC countries | 1.20 | 1.05 | 0.68 | 0.41 | 0.82 | 1.13 | 0.99 | 1.13 | 2.25 | 3.78 |
| USA | — | — | — | — | — | — | — | — | — | — |
| Japan | 1.00 | 1.50 | 3.36 | 2.84 | 2.04 | 7.18 | 1.02 | 10.06 | 3.12 | 7.27 |
| Other DAC countries | 0.00 | 0.00 | 0.00 | 0.00 | 1.27 | 3.50 | 7.74 | 1.30 | 0.04 | 0.06 |
| Total DAC countries (bilateral) | 2.20 | 2.55 | 4.04 | 3.25 | 4.13 | 11.81 | 9.75 | 12.49 | 5.41 | 11.11 |
| % EEC in total DAC | 54.5 | 41.2 | 16.8 | 12.6 | 19.9 | 9.6 | 10.2 | 9.0 | 41.6 | 34.0 |
| % USA .. .. .. | — | — | — | — | — | — | — | — | — | — |
| % Japan .. .. .. | 45.50 | 58.8 | 83.2 | 87.4 | -49.4 | 60.8 | 10.5 | 80.5 | 57.7 | 65.4 |

1. See Table 13, Note 1.
2. Central American Common Market: Costa Rica, Guatemala, Honduras, Nicaragua, El Salvador.
*Source*: Commission of the European Communities, Directorate-General for External Relations, Statistics Office.

237

## TABLE 19

### Direct Private Investment (net) by EEC and other DAC[1] countries in other Latin American countries[2]

#### Value: US$ millions

| | 1969 | 1970 | 1971 | 1972 | 1973 | 1974 | 1975 | 1976 | 1977 | 1978 |
|---|---|---|---|---|---|---|---|---|---|---|
| *Investing countries* | | | | | | | | | | |
| West Germany | 11.99 | 14.49 | 2.43 | 0.11 | 1.35 | 7.35 | 12.94 | 3.41 | 4.98 | −6.97 |
| Belgium | −1.90 | 2.20 | 3.09 | 6.09 | 1.84 | −1.83 | −2.64 | 16.67 | 13.31 | −1.87 |
| France | 0.00 | 0.00 | 0.00 | 0.00 | 2.28 | 0.71 | 1.89 | 6.19 | 9.70 | 9.04 |
| Italy | 0.37 | 0.69 | 0.23 | 0.63 | −0.86 | −0.85 | 19.41 | 17.55 | −19.60 | −0.43 |
| Netherlands[3] | — | — | — | — | — | — | 26.59 | 1.29 | 0.00 | 9.20 |
| United Kingdom | 0.90 | 1.10 | 0.34 | 1.63 | 3.60 | 8.77 | 2.90 | — | — | — |
| Total for six EEC countries | 11.36 | 18.48 | 6.09 | 8.46 | 8.21 | 15.85 | 61.09 | 45.11 | 8.39 | 8.97 |
| USA[3] | 139.00 | 166.00 | 215.00 | −4.00 | 204.00 | 0.00 | 221.00 | −71.00 | 211.00 | 145.00 |
| Japan | 5.69 | 13.81 | 0.87 | 10.56 | 13.54 | 2.38 | 2.67 | 21.63 | 41.53 | 80.95 |
| Other DAC countries | 0.04 | 0.00 | 0.00 | 0.00 | 0.00 | 0.00 | 0.00 | 25.44 | 0.12 | — |
| Total DAC countries (bilateral) | 156.09 | 198.29 | 221.96 | 15.02 | 225.75 | 18.23 | 284.76 | 21.18 | 261.04 | 234.92 |
| % EEC in total DAC | 7.3 | 9.3 | 2.7 | 44.5 | 3.6 | 86.9 | 21.5 | 48.9 | 3.2 | 3.8 |
| % USA .. .. .. | 89.1 | 83.7 | 96.9 | — | 90.4 | — | 77.6 | — | 80.8 | 61.7 |
| % Japan .. .. .. | 3.6 | 7.0 | 0.4 | 55.5 | 6.0 | 13.1 | 0.9 | 23.5 | 15.9 | 34.5 |

1. See Table 13, Note 1.
2. Chile (from 1977), Cuba, Dominican Republic, Haiti, Panama, Paraguay, Uruguay.
3. Direct Private Investment (net) in Panama.
*Source:* Commission of the European Communities, Directorate-General for External Relations, Statistics Office.

238

# Appendix 3 — Debt and Sources of Capital

## TABLE 20

### Latin America: Balance of Payments Summary[1], 1977-79
#### In Millions of Dollars

| Country | 1977 Balance on | | | | 1978 Balance on | | | | 1979 Balance on | | | |
|---|---|---|---|---|---|---|---|---|---|---|---|---|
| | Merchandise Trade[2] | Current Account | Capital Account | Reserves and Related Items[3] | Merchandise Trade[2] | Current Account | Capital Account | Reserves and Related Items[3] | Merchandise Trade[2] | Current Account | Capital Account | Reserves and Related Items[3] |
| Argentina | 1,861.0 | 1,294.8 | 507.9 | 1,836.5 | 2,923.4 | 1,868.0 | 306.7 | -2,192.3 | 1,803.6 | -426.4 | 4,412.2 | -4,232.6 |
| Bahamas | -234.3 | 108.9 | 59.1 | -19.6 | -290.1 | 96.5 | -21.2 | 7.1 | -385.9 | 81.3 | -25.7 | -15.6 |
| Barbados | -159.4 | -30.7 | 37.5 | -4.8 | -176.5 | -3.5 | 34.1 | -21.7 | -247.5 | -19.0 | 34.8 | -12.9 |
| Bolivia | 6.7 | -165.7 | 264.3 | -133.9 | -150.6 | -384.6 | 329.8 | 163.8 | -154.1 | -465.6 | 472.7 | -31.8 |
| Brazil | -98.1 | -5,107.8 | 6,223.9 | -495.0 | -1,156.8 | -7,035 | 11,291.8 | -4,559.8 | -2,706.7 | -10,465.2 | 6,324.3 | 2,907.0 |
| Chile | 141.3 | -547.6 | 615.3 | -141.3 | -77.6 | -877.7 | 1,646.4 | -719.9 | -80.1 | -896.6 | 1,980.6 | -1,055.6 |
| Colombia | 734.4 | 440.1 | -26.9 | -572.1 | 434.4 | 132.7 | 224.1 | -494.5 | 814.0 | 528.4 | 741.6 | -1,449.6 |
| Costa Rica | -97.4 | -225.3 | 341.5 | -96.6 | -207.6 | -371.5 | 323.1 | 25.4 | -341.7 | -578.3 | 530.3 | 99.7 |
| Dominican Republic | -67.4 | -262.3 | 224.6 | -8.8 | -184.3 | -320.0 | 371.5 | 10.5 | -225.3 | -341.0 | 506.5 | -101.0 |
| Ecuador | 40.3 | -341.4 | 503.4 | -112.0 | -174.9 | -701.2 | 662.3 | -5.4 | 199.0 | -584.9 | 659.0 | -23.5 |
| El Salvador | 112.5 | 26.2 | 23.6 | -43.4 | -105.9 | -243.0 | 334.9 | -34.2 | 170.6 | 10.6 | -118.7 | 108.1 |
| Guatemala | 76.5 | -31.9 | 239.1 | -179.6 | -184.9 | -264.5 | 395.6 | -72.7 | -181.4 | -206.8 | 213.3 | 22.2 |
| Guyana | -27.3 | -95.6 | 94.9 | 6.2 | 41.9 | -28.9 | 33.6 | -18.7 | -18.8 | -74.1 | 18.7 | 55.4 |
| Haiti | -62.6 | -37.6 | 70.4 | -13.1 | -55.5 | -42.2 | 56.6 | -6.3 | -91.9 | -59.7 | 61.9 | -9.4 |
| Honduras | -20.3 | -129.0 | 201.4 | -66.3 | -28.4 | -157.4 | 154.4 | -9.5 | -28.9 | -198.7 | 153.0 | -22.5 |
| Jamaica | 93.5 | -68.1 | 56.9 | 4.0 | 22.2 | -138.0 | 62.9 | 86.4 | -67.9 | -142.5 | 2.0 | 167.1 |
| Mexico | -1,016.9 | -1,849.3 | 2,171.5 | -375.5 | -1,343.4 | -2,594.1 | 3,474.3 | -429.4 | -2,215.8 | -4,545.3 | 4,882.5 | -315.2 |
| Nicaragua | -67.5 | -181.4 | 190.3 | -5.0 | 92.8 | -25.0 | -53.0 | 87.4 | 227.0 | 160.6 | -219.1 | -68.5 |
| Panama | -505.3 | -157.3 | 217.4 | 7.4 | -567.4 | -210.5 | 263.5 | -86.4 | -770.8 | -315.0 | 288.0[a] | 26.2 |
| Paraguay | -36.0 | -61.6 | 190.0 | -105.1 | -81.8 | -124.3 | 295.7 | -178.7 | -125.6 | -141.9 | 300.0 | -156.3 |
| Peru | -439.0 | -925.8 | 1,099.8 | -65.4 | 333.0 | -197.8 | 162.8 | -18.8 | 1,381.1 | 617.6 | 487.1 | -1,042.6 |
| Trinidad and Tobago | 704.5 | 231.3 | 273.7 | -444.4 | 474.8 | 0.5 | 240.6 | -320.5 | 478.8 | 288.1 | 330.1 | -333.0 |
| Uruguay | -68.2 | -160.1 | 303.9 | -179.3 | -23.7 | -126.6 | 98.0 | -126.7 | -337.8 | -316.8 | 395.2 | -66.5 |
| Venezuela | -678.3 | -3,100.9 | 274.4 | 214.8 | -1,849.2 | -5,367.3 | 1,685.2 | 1,894.3 | 3,361.8 | -288.1 | 1,037.5 | -1,019.4 |
| Latin America | 192.8 | -11,378.1 | 14,157.8 | -4,665.6 | -2,336.1 | -17,115.5 | 22,373.7 | -7,020.5 | 455.7 | -18,379.3 | 23,467.8 | -6,570.3 |

1. Excluding errors and omissions.
2. Exports and imports valued at f.o.b. prices.
3. According to conventional usage, the sign (-) means an increase.
a. Provisional.

Source: Inter-American Development Bank, Annual Report 1981.

239

# TABLE 21

## Structure of Latin America's External Public Debt[1] by Type of Creditors, 1960-79

### In Per Cent Based on Total Outstanding at Year End

| Country | Office Multilateral | | | Official Bilateral | | | Suppliers | | | Private Banks[2] | | | Other Credits[3] | | |
|---|---|---|---|---|---|---|---|---|---|---|---|---|---|---|---|
| | 1960 | 1970 | 1979 | 1960 | 1970 | 1979 | 1960 | 1970 | 1979 | 1960 | 1970 | 1979 | 1960 | 1970 | 1979 |
| Argentina | — | 21.7 | 22.0 | 51.7 | 17.7 | 8.8 | 40.9 | 34.9 | 20.1 | 5.6 | 7.2 | 40.8 | 1.8 | 18.5 | 8.3 |
| Bahamas | n.a. | — | ·40.4 | n.a. | 38.0 | 21.0 | n.a. | 18.0 | 3.5 | n.a. | 44.0 | 35.1 | n.a. | — | — |
| Barbados | n.a. | — | 58.2 | n.a. | 18.8 | 24.6 | n.a. | — | | — | — | 17.2 | n.a. | 81.2 | 2.3 |
| Bolivia | — | 9.8 | 27.9 | 49.7 | 50.1 | 32.9 | — | 10.2 | 5.8 | — | 3.3 | 31.1 | 50.3 | 26.6 | 6.5 |
| Brazil | 9.3 | 18.4 | 11.8 | 43.2 | 41.8 | 10.4 | 28.9 | 23.4 | 10.4 | 15.6 | 11.7 | 60.9 | 3.0 | 4.7 | 6.5 |
| Chile | 16.9 | 9.9 | 9.1 | 24.2 | 46.5 | 27.0 | 14.4 | 20.5 | 10.3 | 19.8 | 17.3 | 49.4 | 24.7 | 5.8 | 4.2 |
| Colombia | 36.3 | 38.7 | 46.8 | 28.7 | 42.3 | 23.1 | 10.3 | 11.3 | 5.0 | 10.9 | 5.3 | 24.3 | 13.8 | 2.4 | 0.8 |
| Costa Rica | 12.7 | 46.7 | 37.4 | 36.4 | 35.7 | 19.1 | 9.1 | 4.4 | 2.9 | 21.8 | 8.8 | 39.3 | 20.0 | 4.4 | 1.3 |
| Dominican Republic | — | 9.7 | 36.7 | — | 72.3 | 34.3 | 100.0 | 7.0 | 0.1 | — | 11.0 | 28.9 | — | — | — |
| Ecuador | 44.2 | 29.8 | 23.0 | 27.4 | 29.6 | 10.6 | 14.7 | 31.8 | 7.9 | 7.4 | 7.7 | 56.3 | 6.3 | 1.1 | 2.2 |
| El Salvador | 93.9 | 51.6 | 64.1 | — | 34.9 | 32.5 | — | — | | — | 11.1 | 3.4 | 6.1 | 2.4 | — |
| Guatemala | 31.4 | 30.7 | 67.0 | 47.0 | 34.1 | 32.2 | — | 1.7 | 0.1 | 21.6 | 25.6 | 0.7 | — | -7.9 | — |
| Guyana | | 9.9 | 27.5 | | | | | | | | | | n.a. | 12.2 | 11.6 |

| | | | | | | | | | | | | | | | |
|---|---|---|---|---|---|---|---|---|---|---|---|---|---|---|---|
| Haiti | 7.9 | 2.2 | 70.8 | 71.1 | 64.5 | 27.7 | 10.5 | 24.4 | 0.3 | — | — | 1.2 | 10.0 | 8.9 | — |
| Honduras | 78.3 | 70.8 | 58.9 | 13.1 | 26.4 | 23.3 | 4.3 | 2.8 | 1.5 | 4.3 | — | 16.3 | — | — | — |
| Jamaica | n.a. | 24.0 | 27.2 | n.a. | 24.0 | 40.1 | n.a. | — | 1.7 | n.a. | 8.8 | 24.3 | n.a. | 43.2 | 6.7 |
| Mexico | 16.2 | 29.7 | 12.3 | 33.9 | 12.9 | 3.9 | 15.2 | 10.1 | 1.2 | 25.8 | 36.6 | 75.9 | 8.9 | 10.7 | 6.7 |
| Nicaragua | 65.8 | 40.5 | 37.5 | 29.3 | 33.6 | 36.0 | — | 4.5 | 1.6 | 4.9 | 21.4 | 24.2 | — | — | 0.7 |
| Panama | 11.8 | 32.4 | 21.2 | 44.1 | 31.0 | 14.1 | — | 24.5 | 1.6 | — | 2.1 | 49.0 | 44.1 | 10.0 | 14.1 |
| Paraguay | 9.1 | 32.6 | 44.0 | 77.3 | 44.5 | 31.1 | 9.1 | 22.2 | 10.7 | 4.5 | 0.7 | 14.2 | — | — | — |
| Peru | 26.8 | 20.1 | 10.9 | 16.6 | 28.7 | 37.9 | 26.8 | 36.5 | 14.0 | 6.8 | 12.7 | 37.2 | 23.0 | 2.0 | — |
| Trinidad and Tobago | — | 34.4 | 15.4 | — | 20.5 | 26.4 | 14.3 | 3.3 | — | 38.1 | 12.3 | 49.8 | 47.6 | 29.5 | 8.4 |
| Uruguay | 45.5 | 29.6 | 25.9 | 9.1 | 31.9 | 11.5 | — | 5.1 | 2.8 | — | 19.7 | 39.5 | 45.4 | 13.7 | 20.3 |
| Venezuela | — | 35.1 | 2.5 | 14.3 | 13.8 | 2.3 | 25.1 | 15.0 | 3.7 | 60.6 | 32.0 | 74.7 | — | 4.1 | 16.8 |
| **Latin America** | **12.9** | **23.9** | **16.5** | **37.5** | **32.2** | **12.9** | **23.9** | **19.2** | **7.3** | **16.4** | **16.4** | **56.8** | **9.3** | **8.3** | **6.5** |

1. Debt repayable in foreign currency at more than one-year terms, contracted directly by public agencies or by private entities with government guarantee. Includes the undisbursed balance.
2. Includes also financial institutions other than banks.
3. Includes nationalization and bond issues.
— Zero or not significant.
n.a. Not available.

*Source:* Inter-American Development Bank (Annual Report 1981) based on official statistics from the member countries and the World Bank.

## TABLE 22

**Ratio of Latin America's External Public Debt Service[1] to Value of Exports of Goods and Services[2], 1960-79**

In Per Cent

| Country | Average 1960-61 | Average 1970-71 | 1974 | 1975 | 1976 | 1977 | 1978 | 1979 |
|---|---|---|---|---|---|---|---|---|
| Argentina | 21.4 | 21.1 | 17.1 | 22.2 | 19.0 | 15.7 | 27.9 | 18.0 |
| Bahamas | n.a. | n.a. | 2.6 | 2.7 | 2.1 | 2.0 | 1.5 | 1.1 |
| Barbados | n.a. | 1.0 | 1.8 | 1.8 | 1.8 | 3.2 | 2.0 | 2.7 |
| Bolivia | 25.6 | 11.6 | 11.1 | 14.6 | 16.2 | 21.3 | 48.7 | 29.6 |
| Brazil | 34.0 | 15.3 | 14.0 | 17.4 | 19.1 | 21.2 | 31.2 | 37.6 |
| Chile | 18.4 | 20.3 | 11.7 | 28.7 | 31.7 | 33.6 | 38.7 | 26.4 |
| Colombia | 13.5 | 13.0 | 15.9 | 11.3 | 9.7 | 9.1 | 10.0 | 13.4 |
| Costa Rica | 4.8 | 10.1 | 9.6 | 10.6 | 9.5 | 9.0 | 23.4 | 23.4 |
| Dominican Republic | 0.7 | 6.6 | 4.9 | 5.0 | 6.2 | 6.3 | 9.5 | 14.1 |
| Ecuador | 7.8 | 10.9 | 7.2 | 4.5 | 5.8 | 7.3 | 12.4 | 29.5 |
| El Salvador | 2.4 | 4.8 | 4.7 | 9.1 | 4.0 | 6.0 | 2.6 | 3.2 |
| Guatemala | 2.3 | 7.7 | 3.8 | 1.7 | 1.4 | 1.2 | 1.8 | 2.2 |
| Guyana | n.a. | 3.2 | 4.4 | 4.3 | 11.3 | 12.0 | 16.1 | 29.7 |
| Haiti | 5.2 | 4.1 | 6.5 | 7.5 | 7.1 | 6.9 | 5.9 | 4.1 |
| Honduras | 3.3 | 3.1 | 3.6 | 4.6 | 6.4 | 7.2 | 8.6 | 13.0 |
| Jamaica | n.a. | 3.6 | 2.9 | 2.7 | 5.9 | 8.7 | 11.1 | 9.0 |
| Mexico | 14.9 | 23.7 | 19.2 | 25.5 | 31.6 | 44.3 | 54.6 | 65.5 |
| Nicaragua | 4.9 | 12.0 | 10.8 | 12.1 | 12.0 | 13.7 | 12.6 | 28.4 |
| Panama | 1.5 | 8.6 | 18.2 | 8.5 | 12.3 | 18.3 | 61.2 | 35.5 |
| Paraguay | 6.4 | 12.4 | 8.2 | 10.5 | 8.1 | 6.7 | 7.8 | 8.9 |
| Peru | 8.6 | 14.0 | 17.3 | 14.8 | 14.6 | 19.0 | 18.0 | 21.9 |
| Trinidad & Tobago | n.a. | 3.1 | 2.2 | 1.2 | 2.9 | 0.6 | 1.2 | 2.3 |
| Uruguay | 5.4 | 22.2 | 31.0 | 41.4 | 29.6 | 30.3 | 46.7 | 10.3 |
| Venezuela | 4.6 | 3.4 | 4.4 | 5.8 | 4.1 | 8.0 | 7.5 | 9.9 |
| **Latin America** | **14.4** | **13.7** | **11.1** | **13.9** | **15.0** | **18.0** | **26.2** | **28.4** |

1. Total of interest and principal payments.
2. Excludes payments on investment income.
n.a. Not available.

*Source:* Inter-American Development Bank (Annual Report 1981) based on official statistics from the member countries, the World Bank
and the International Monetary Fund

# TABLE 23

## Publicized Euro-Currency Credits[1] and Foreign and International Bond Issues[2], 1975-79
### In Millions of Dollars or Equivalent

| Borrowing Country | 1975 Credits | 1975 Bonds[3] | 1976 Credits | 1976 Bonds[3] | 1977 Credits | 1977 Bonds[3] | 1978 Credits | 1978 Bonds[3] | 1979 Credits | 1979 Bonds[3] |
|---|---|---|---|---|---|---|---|---|---|---|
| Argentina | 34.4 | 16.0 | 895.5 | — | 828.1 | 43.0 | 1,273.0 | 266.4 | 2,122.8 | 416.6 |
| Bahamas | — | — | — | — | 10.0 | — | 10.0 | — | — | — |
| Barbados | — | — | — | — | — | — | — | — | — | — |
| Bolivia | 90.1 | 35.0 | 161.0 | — | 100.0 | 15.0 | 227.0 | — | 47.0 | — |
| Brazil | 2,119.8 | 53.4 | 3,288.3 | 193.3 | 2,341.1 | 855.8 | 5,110.7 | 936.1 | 5,713.8 | 735.6 |
| Chile | 116.5 | — | 125.0 | — | 226.5 | — | 1,145.0 | 50.0 | 685.0 | 83.5 |
| Colombia | 46.0 | — | 135.0 | — | 43.0 | — | 85.0 | — | 888.5 | — |
| Costa Rica | — | — | 40.0 | — | 54.0 | — | 220.8 | 20.0 | 152.0 | — |
| Dominican Republic | — | — | — | — | — | — | 60.0 | — | 195.0 | — |
| Ecuador | 55.0 | — | 87.0 | — | 428.0 | 7.9 | 252.1 | 62.0 | 935.5 | — |
| El Salvador | 45.0 | — | 7.2 | — | — | — | — | 25.0 | — | — |
| Guatemala | — | — | 15.0 | — | — | — | — | — | — | — |
| Guyana | 24.0 | — | 4.0 | — | — | — | — | — | — | 8.0 |
| Haiti | — | — | — | — | — | — | — | — | 93.0 | — |
| Honduras | — | — | 10.0 | — | 16.0 | — | — | — | 126.0 | — |
| Jamaica | 103.0 | — | 15.0 | — | 32.0 | — | — | — | — | — |
| Mexico | 2,150.9 | 270.3 | 2,139.5 | 427.9 | 2,895.4 | 1,347.8 | 6,553.6 | 687.5 | 7,654.5 | 363.0 |
| Nicaragua | 55.0 | — | — | — | 40.0 | — | 15.0 | — | 155.0 | — |
| Panama | 130.0 | — | 151.9 | 13.9 | 147.0 | 27.0 | 553.5 | 215.1 | — | 110.7 |
| Paraguay | — | — | — | — | — | — | — | — | 7.0 | — |
| Peru | 434.0 | — | 350.0 | — | 144.4 | — | — | — | 525.4 | — |
| Trinidad and Tobago | 5.1 | — | — | — | 150.0 | — | — | 150.0 | 39.0 | — |
| Uruguay | 130.0 | — | 81.5 | — | 60.0 | — | 230.0 | — | 40.0 | — |
| Venezuela | 200.0 | — | 1,129.0 | — | 1,650.1 | 437.6 | 2,079.6 | 689.6 | 3,225.9 | 153.6 |
| **Latin America** | **5,739.1** | **374.4** | **8,634.9** | **635.1** | **9,165.6** | **2,734.1** | **17,815.3** | **3,101.7** | **22,605.4** | **1,871.0** |

1.  The amounts shown are publicized gross commitments and do not necessarily reflect the extent to which these loans have actually been drawn down.
2.  Foreign bonds are those issued in a single national market. 'International Bonds' are those which are sold in two or more markets simultaneously.
3.  Includes both public offerings and private placements.
n.a.  Not available.

*Source:* Inter-American Development Bank (Annual Report 1981) based on official statistics from member countries and the World Bank.

LAS 7